Praise for *Cats and People*

"The Lockridges have produced what is far and away the best and most comprehensive general book on cats since Carl Van Vechten wrote *The Tiger in the House*."

—*Chicago Sunday Tribune*

"Informal but informative, this may be used as a manual, yet will be relished by the nonailurophile as extra-specially good nonfiction."

—*Library Journal*

"*Cats and People* has the most [information] and holds it together with a human interest so strong that people with any interest in cats or in other people will . . . in the course of being continuously entertained, find out a good deal."

—*New York Herald Tribune*

Cats and People

Cats and People

FRANCES *and* RICHARD LOCKRIDGE
With a New Introduction by Otto Penzler

DRAWINGS BY HELEN STONE

KODANSHA INTERNATIONAL
New York • Tokyo • London

Kodansha America, Inc.
114 Fifth Avenue, New York, New York 10011, U.S.A.

Kodansha International Ltd.
17-14 Otowa 1-chome, Bunkyo-ku, Tokyo 112, Japan

Published in 1996 by Kodansha America, Inc.
by arrangement with the Lockridge Estate.

First published in 1950 by J. B. Lippincott Company.

This is a Kodansha Globe book.

Library of Congress Cataloging-in-Publication Data
Lockridge, Frances Louise Davis.
    Cats and people / Frances and Richard Lockridge ; with drawings by Helen Stone.
        p.   cm.—(Kodansha globe)
    Originally published: Philadelphia : Lippincott, 1950.
    Includes bibliographical references and index.
    ISBN 1-56836-115-7 (pb)
    1. Cats. I. Lockridge, Richard, 1898–   . II. Title.
III. Series.
SF442.L58   1996
599.74'428—dc20   95-53872

Printed in the United States of America

96 97 98 99 00 Q/FF 10 9 8 7 6 5 4 3 2 1

To Pammy and Martini

Contents

THE AUTHORS ARE indebted to many people and to several cats for much of the material upon which this book is based, although none, human or feline, is responsible for errors we may have made or inferences we may ill-advisedly have drawn. The identity of the cats is revealed in subsequent pages. Among the men and women who have been generous in helping us, making suggestions which had not occurred to us, supplying information which we might not otherwise have found, are: Ken McCormick, editor-in-chief of Doubleday and Company; Lee Weber; Dr. Edwin H. Colbert, Curator of Fossil Amphibians and Reptiles, American Museum of Natural History; William Bridges, Curator of Publications, New York Zoological Society; Richard Pough, Curator of Conservation, American Museum of Natural History; Sydney H. Coleman, executive vice president of the American Society for the Prevention of Cruelty to Animals; John Kieran; Dr. Louis J. Camuti, protector of many cats, including ours, and most delightful of raconteurs; Miss Hettie Gray Baker, distinguished friend of cats; George and Arlene Bye; Mrs. James S. Carpenter, recorder of the Cat Fanciers' Association, Inc.; Miss Elsa Wunderlich; Dr. Ernest Brennecke, Jr., of Columbia University; Dr. C. J. Warden, of the same university; Charles A. Kenny, editor and publisher of *Cats Magazine;* Mrs. Sumner Smith, co-owner of the lamented Deuces Wild, and J. Davidson Stephen, architect, who stood ready to re-design a house to provide it with a cat door.

THE ARTIST would like to express her appreciation to several amiable cats, who served as models—

Mickey Malloy   Lilah-Moni
Melissa and her kittens   Kramir

Introduction

by Otto Penzler

LET'S FACE IT: cats aren't all that intelligent. They certainly *look* smart, and in their patience and surface calm they *act* smart, but they're not. No cat has ever written a symphony, played chess, or known where Bulgaria is. A cat's culinary preference is for a *mouse,* for heaven's sake! How smart is that?

They are, however, gorgeous creatures and carry themselves with a quiet dignity that engenders respect. And they often do things that we humans find so endearing it is impossible not to take them into our hearts.

This is a book about cats and the people who love them. Frances and Richard Lockridge, detective-story writers by trade and cat lovers by avocation, knew that to live with the small creature taxonomically designated *Felis catus* is to engage in nonstop speculation about its essence. Writers (best known as the creators of the Mr. and Mrs. North mystery series) and not ethologists, they approached this rather delightful problem ex-laboratory, as it were, with their magnifying glasses fixed on their surroundings and on the furry beings twining themselves around their ankles.

Employing inductive reasoning—the path not taken in the bulk of mystery fiction, where the description of a single culprit rather than an entire species is the goal—the authors bolster their spirited arguments about the True Nature of cats with tidbits from the sort of wide-ranging research that obviously was a great deal of fun to pursue. If you don't think the Lockridges had a swell time compiling this volume, just glance at the index, which runs from Abyssinian to Wyatt, Sir Henry, with Bandages and Bloodlines, Israelites and Itching, Lap-

Sitting and Lent, and Weasels and Witches all sandwiched intriguingly in-between.

Browsing among observations and conclusions of previous cat scholars and cat fanciers, the Lockridges happily dig back into long-forgotten musty annals, putting together material at exactly the half-way mark of this century. The level of ailurophobia and basic cat misinformation they discovered sent them into a fine fever of indignation. Among the unreliable theorists they exhumed is one Dr. Nathaniel Southgate Thaler, a Harvard dean and author of an 1895 volume with the deceptively objective-sounding title *Domesticated Animals*. His unconcealed anticat bias elicits their deepest scorn. "I have been unable to find any authenticated instances which go to show the existence in cats of any real love for their masters," Thaler claimed. Still worse is his certainty that dogs dote on their masters in ways that their languidly purring opposites are incapable of. This is no minor matter, for if any message is central to *Cats and People* it is that implied by the conjunction in the title—that not only are cats *and* people a natural joining, mutually respectful and affectionate, but that the origins of the human-feline relationship reaches back into the farthest corners of antiquity.

Many pampered pusses are regarded today as the supreme entities of their households, and the Lockridges remind the reader that the same animals' sleek ancestors were deified in the Egypt of several thousand years B.C. Even earlier, in the shadowy dawn of history and possibly prehistory, the cat may have been regarded as a totem by primitive tribes. "He would have been then at once a familiar and a little of god—not yet wholly a god, a god in the making, a creature edging toward divinity."

How do the authors explain this shift to a more extreme level of veneration? The cat, they write, was "a helpful little god; by protecting the grain of those [farmers] who protected him, he may have helped them to be better fed than the men of other tribes, and so stronger." In a world where the struggle to survive was everything, gods in the making needed to display some definite utilitarian value. Eventually cat worship reached the point where entire Egyptian noble families would mourn the death of a family cat. Still, the moment was fast approaching when the pedestal would be toppled and the small whiskered beast, unaware of all the fuss, would simply trot off into the future, well on the road to becoming what is known in modern civilization as a pet.

For all their gracefully wielded erudition aimed at establishing a historic lineage, it is this familiar sense of the role cats play in the lives of *Homo sapiens* to which the Lockridges repeatedly return. Certainly a commonly held belief is that the world may be divided neatly into "dog people" and "cat people." It is also true that a particular conceit of the latter camp is that cats, unlike their often eager-to-please rivals, can never be owned. The Lockridges, however, dismiss this notion as well-meaning but nonetheless misguided "cat sentimentality," devoting some of the book's most memorable passages to anecdotal observations of the six cats—Pam, Jerry, Martini (known as Teeney), Gin, Sherry, and Pete—who have, they feel, most unambiguously belonged to them.

As they watch their cats pounce and frolic and as they delineate for the reader the subtleties of each feline personality, the Lockridges show themselves to be the best sort of amateur naturalists. Maintaining a steady, sympathetic gaze, they strive to record both ritual (cats at courtship, the hunting cat, and so on) and anomaly (for example, the momentarily embarrassed cat). They are also aware that the articulateness of cats manifests its own vocabulary; though it lacks a dictionary, feline communication can be intuitively understood by those who try. A true living language, it contains perhaps the most expressive, as well as the most mysterious, sound that any animal, including man, is capable of—the purr. What does it mean? No one knows for sure, but what is certain is that these audible vibrations convey a great deal while specifying nothing at all.

The Lockridges' own verbal style is plain but eloquent. Content to leave every bit of the showing off to their four-footed subjects, they occasionally approach the realm of poetry, as when they describe the Siamese cat, the breed they find themselves most drawn to: "There is a clarity about them, both in the shape of their bodies and the pattern in their fur, which is a delight in a blurring world, where so few things are any longer as clear as things should be."

The Lockridges believe not only in the supremacy of cats but also in the superiority of those who love them. (Mark Twain is known to have said, "If man could be crossed with the cat, it would improve man, but it would deteriorate the cat.") Cats accommodate and are companions to people who, in turn, provide services; thus the cat fulfills a role it neither intends nor was intended to fulfill, and the now-ancient and ongoing partnership continues, through every generation, to be freshly rewarding. Furthermore, by Frances and Richard Lockridge's highly readable account, mankind not only gains immediate benefit from its relationship with the cat but is lent a special, immutable grace in the process.

The Lockridges are not the only mystery writers to have taken a break from mayhem to turn their talents to cat watching. John D. MacDonald, creator of the suspense-adventure series featuring Travis McGee, revealed his softer side in an affectionate memoir, *The House Guests* (1965). And in the 1970s, Englishwoman Patricia Moyes, author of the genteel Henry and Emmy Tibbett books, wrote two charming works of feline nonfiction: *After All, They're Only Cats* and *How to Talk to Your Cat* (concurring with the Lockridges, she favors the Siamese breed).

Cat "characters" have also turned up as sleuths demonstrating the ability to sniff out villains, for example, in the best-selling books of Lilian Jackson Braun (*The Cat Who Could Read Backwards, The Cat Who Knew Shakespeare,* and others) and in the Gordons' Undercover Cat series (the first of which was filmed successfully in 1965 as *That Darn Cat*). It should be remembered that there were Siamese Sherlocks hissing at bad guys and making their masters look clever long before Braun's Koko and Yum Yum first scratched around the scene of a crime in the mid-1960s. Many mystery fans remain devoted to the memory of the noisily assertive cats who first strolled across the pages of Frances and Richard Lockridge's *The Norths Meet Murder* back in 1940.

Martini and her daughters, Gin and Sherry, lived with amateur detectives Jerry North, a Manhattan publishing executive, and Pam, his classic screwball heroine of a wife. In its heyday of the 1940s and postwar 1950s, this part-human, part-feline household living in the heart of Greenwich Village was an immensely popular team, perhaps because their humorous entanglements with crooks and killers stood in welcome contrast to that era's grimmer real-life headlines. Introduced in 1936 as a series of lighthearted *New Yorker* sketches, the Norths went on to appear in twenty-six mystery novels and had the distinction of seeing themselves become characters on stage, radio, television, and the big screen.

According to Richard Lockridge, the Norths, taking their name from the bridge column position, began as rather closely autobiographical figures (Bright Young Married Couple Cutely Copes in the Big City). They evolved, however, into incorrigible part-time sleuths after Lockridge's own reporting job at the *New York Sun* brought him into professional contact with a series of sensational murder trials. The fact that Frances Lockridge thought that producing a mystery novel —a genre they both enjoyed reading—might help out the household budget played a major role in her initial decision to try one. She began the book without the familiar Norths, who were added when Richard decided to collaborate. (Pam and Jerry, it should be noted, were also the names the Lockridges gave to a pair of cats who lived with them in the 1940s; a part-Siamese sister and brother, they appear frequently as exemplars in *Cats and People*.)

The Lockridge marriage and writing partnership lasted forty-one years. Together they wrote, in addition to the North tales, a series featuring Inspector Merton Heimrich of the New York State Police, as well as a couple of other less well-known series characters: Nathan Shapiro of the NYPD and New York City D.A. Bernie Simmons. The Lockridges also published four children's books: *The Proud Cat* (1951), *The Lucky Cat* (1953), *The Nameless Cat* (1954), and *The Cat Who Rode Cows* (1955). Richard alone wrote *One Lady, Two Cats* for children in 1967. In 1960 they served as co-presidents of the Mystery Writers of America.

Frances Lockridge died in 1963. In 1965 Richard remarried, and in 1982 he died, surviving his second wife, the writer Hildegarde Dolson, by only a year.

As writers who understood and valued words, Frances and Richard

Lockridge paid tribute to their cats—indeed, to all cats—in the way they knew best. This delightful book is a token of their personal and professional esteem for the gorgeous little critters who so greatly enhanced their lives.

I started by saying that cats aren't all that intelligent. No cat has ever written a symphony, played chess, or known where Bulgaria is. To be fair, however, it's only appropriate to ask: How many humans qualify?

Cats and People

One Cat, One Person

SHE SITS ON the floor, front paws together in unexampled neatness, tail curved to body, and regards with round eyes one of the two humans toward whom she feels in a special way. Her eyes are now completely round and formed of concentric circles with the pupil, which can become a slit when she chooses, a black depth not to be fathomed. Otherwise, her eyes are blue. She appears expectant, but it is impossible to guess what she expects.

She has eaten after, as always, waiting until her children have finished, since she will take part in no unseemly scramble for food. Her toilet pan does not need changing; she would mention the fact if it did. She is feeling well, because her eyes are clear and her coat is smooth. If she wished to sit upon the lap which is offered, she would enquire—perhaps it is more accurate to say that she would warn. She does not, it may therefore be assumed, seek at this moment any outward expression of affection from this human, nor to express her own. She wishes merely to look; although her kind have lived with man for upward of four thousand years, racial memories do not satisfy personal curiosity.

Under that intent gaze, many humans grow ill at ease and some grow resentful. There are some, indeed, who grow afraid, and they may—but this is debatable—carry a gene of memory which reminds them that, a million years or so ago, much larger animals sat as she sits, or crouched as she can crouch, and looked at something like a human which was in a tree and not a chair, and had every cause to be afraid.

The human at whom she looks does not share that fear, nor grow particularly ill at ease. Yet one cannot be entirely impervious to her quiet, unblinking gaze. That goes without saying. One becomes conscious of it in spite of almost any preoccupation. And in the end one returns the look; realizes that it is time to speak first. "Yes, Teeney?" one says. "What is it, Teeney?" She will slowly, and partly, close her eyes, then. The tip of her tail will move. Her eyes, narrowed, become slanting eyes, Oriental. This movement of her tail is response, without comment. She has heard; she has been polite; she has acknowledged the relationship between herself and this larger animal of a newer breed. And she continues to look, expecting something. Does she want a crumpled cigarette package thrown for her, so that she can bring it back as she used to do when she was the only cat? Does she want fingers to move behind her pointed ears, to stroke under the delicate, but dangerously powerful, jaw? Or does she merely want to sit and think? To ponder, as T. S. Eliot is sure she does at such moments, her "deep and inscrutable singular Name?"

But whether she can think at all, much less ponder, has been for years a matter of considerable, sometimes acrimonious, debate. The debate has been complicated, made sometimes almost incomprehensible, by one often forgotten consideration: We apply to her words which may not be applicable to her; words which reveal, more than they reveal anything about the cat, our own helpless confinement within a pattern of values applicable only to a certain genus of primates. In other words, we anthropomorphize her. We say she is "cruel" or "sly" or "proud"; that she is "intelligent" or "playful" or "affectionate" or "mysterious." When she hunts, she "poaches," and when she takes advantage of an unclosed refrigerator door to extract half a roast chicken, she is "thieving"—a "bad" cat.

None of these words, one supposes, are words a cat would use, since one would suppose that a cat has no great interest in abstractions. She has words of her own—once, not too seriously, a vocabulary of some six hundred words was attributed to her. Certainly she is able to express herself, understandably, to another cat, to her own kittens, to a dog or a squirrel and, most completely of all, to a human who will listen. But she has never told anyone whether she can "think," although many have tried to wring a statement out of her.

She is beautiful, certainly, and she seems to know it or, at any rate, to know when she is admired. She is marvelously constructed for her purpose in life, which is to spring upon and kill animals which she finds good to eat. Her grace is phenomenal—and if, by any accident, she does an awkward thing, or a foolish one, she shows every sign of embarrassment. She behaves as if she were easily made jealous—another human word, of course. She forms what appear to be strong preferences as between one human and another; the individual who sits there on the floor, still looking up, sometimes hisses at a person she meets daily and who has always been kind to her. And when we both had to leave her once, she did not eat at all for ten days, although at the time she was nursing kittens. When we returned, she would not speak to us for hours, but she ate as if she were starving.

It is difficult to be objective about her, and mankind has seldom been able to. She has been worshipped as a god, and hated and destroyed as a devil; she has been the familiar of witches and of prophets. It is said of her, with that romantic exaggeration which seems to enter into almost all discussions of her kind, that one either hates or loves her, and it is widely felt that one must like her kind or her cousin, the dog, and may not be fond of both. (But she, herself, can get along happily enough with both dogs and people and often does.) She is a great victim of the human inclination to generalize: "All cats are thus and so, do this and that." But in no group is individuality more marked or are individual differences more numerous. And she is one of the most sentimentalized of animals, both by her admirers and those who detest her.

The cat on the floor does not move. Her eyes do not falter. "Teeney?" she hears again, and again her eyes partially close and the tip of her tail twitches. "What is it, Teeney? What do you want?" She opens her mouth and yawns, displaying four of the sharpest canines known to the animal world. She finds an ear needs scratching. But then she is motionless again, again unwavering in her regard.

She weighs about six pounds, which is small even for the smallest of her tribe. Her face is sootily masked; her ears are so deep a brown as to be almost black, and her tail and legs are similarly dark. She is one of our cats; she is the "main cat," the "cat major." She knows this, whatever else she knows, nor does she permit us to forget it.

She is one of our cats because we own her and because we can do things which concern her vitally whether she permits or not. This is because we are, individually, larger than she and, collectively, equipped with certain instruments which she lacks. We can, for example, use the telephone—she does not like us to use the telephone, and may make an angry chattering sound—and summon a doctor for her, and hold her while the doctor injects into her writhing body certain liquids which will, in the end, be good for her. And because it seemed to her best interest, and was certainly to ours, we have seen that never again will she cry her dark, discordant passion to the world, saying, "Here I am! Come to me!" although that has meant that she will not again, either, wake us time after time through a long night, leading us to a box so that we might know that surely now, now miraculously, she had given birth. She, and her two daughters, eat what we feed them, although not without expressing their preferences; they live where we take them, in town or in country. At night they are shut up, although no cat stays in by night of choice. Now and then we give them pills, which no cat likes.

So it is absurd to say, as people are constantly saying, that we do not own them, that "nobody owns a cat." That is one of the prevalent forms of the cat sentimentality. We own them, we can do what we like with them; if, as happens to be true, we do, willingly, nothing to harm them, that is their good fortune. They live with people who like cats and, in return, we have cats who appear to like humans, on a selective basis. But then, we do not like all cats. Of course, we do not own their spirits, do not seek to make them slavish. We never could, even if we respected them and ourselves so little as to try. They will not——

But now the cat on the floor speaks. The remark is short, inflected —the human has learned by experience—as a question. "Why yes," the human says. "Come on."

The cat comes to lap, landing softly, claws retracted. She stands a moment, examining at closer range this familiar human face. Then she arranges herself not on lap, but on chest, so that her head just touches a human jawbone. She extends a paw, touching gently a human neck. Then she begins to purr. She does not purr loudly, as her children do, but there is contentment in the sound. So that was what she wanted, after all. Felis domestica, of the subfamily Felinae and the family Felidae, the superfamily Feloidea, the suborder Fissipedia, and the order Carnivora of the cohort Ferungulata and the class Mammalia, is in one of the places Felis domestica likes to be, when not catching mice.

Felis and all the rest is her show name in the aeon-old animal fair, where her kind has won the blue ribbon for survival. But we call her Martini and, most often, Teeney, because she is our main cat, and we called her that when she was only so long, could trot and had not yet learned to walk, and cocked her tail straight up.

2

The Cats Begin

To Martini and her kind, people are upstarts, lately come to the earth, still an experimental breed. It may be that, looking at us with round eyes, she is wondering only how long we will last; in their many million years of life, the cats have seen many apparently promising animals arise, flourish and finally disappear; their ancestral memories may encourage scepticism as to the durability of anything but cats. A few civets have, to be sure, had longer life but civets are poor relations of the cat.

There was a time when there were no cats. Forty million years ago, give or take a few million years, the cat was merely inherent in a small and primitive mammal which palaeozoologists have now agreed to call Miacis. Miacis had a long body and a long tail; his legs were short; in general he had the appearance of a weasel. Among the mammals then taking over the earth from the giant reptiles, Miacis probably was inconspicuous and did not promise much; promised no more, indeed, than the little monkeys chattering in the forests. But from Miacis came all the land-living carnivores—the dogs and bears, the raccoons and the hyenas and the cats. Some of these came soon and others late; the cats were among the earliest. Evolution was to continue for millions of years before the cat had a true dog to worry about.

Miacis lived in the late Eocene epoch. He lived surrounded by horses about the size of sheep, rhinoceroses which were like horses and camels which resembled gazelles. He produced civets, at first not too much unlike himself, and the civets suddenly became cats. The rapidity of this transformation still a little surprises palaeontologists. "Looking back at the change from a perspective of forty million years it seems as if the cats suddenly appeared at the very beginning of Oligocene times, with very little developmental fanfare to make their entrance onto the stage of fierce competition in a world of enemies," writes Dr. Edwin H. Colbert of the American Museum of Natural History. "One might say that certain civets jumped into the role of the cats with all the evolutionary rapidity of a quick-change actor in a hard-pressed double part."

Having become cats, these new animals were content and, except for one famous variant, made few alterations in the aeons which followed. It is true, of course, that some grew big and others small, some acquired spots and others took on stripes, the fur of a few grew thick and one species lost its fur almost entirely before nature, disturbed by behavior so uncatlike, extinguished the aberrant. Cats have yellow eyes and green and blue; in strong light the pupils of some narrow to slits and those of others to pin points. The cheetah, somewhere along the line, lost most or all of the ability to retract his claws and was modified for speed on the straight-away. But the changes were insignificant; the essential cat has been immemorially so basic that Mivart wrote of six-pound Martini and of the greatest lion when he termed cats among the most perfectly specialized of the Carnivora and continued:

"Feeding upon other animals, which it must pursue with noiseless stealth and capture by an exertion of supreme activity, the cat has padded feet which make no sound in movement; muscles of enormous power and bulk in proportion to its size and attached to bones adjusted to each other at such angles as to form the most complete system of springs and levers for propelling the body known in the whole group; the claws are sharper and curved into strong hooks more than in any other mammal, and by action of special muscles are withdrawn under sheathlike pads, that they may escape wear and injury when not in use. No teeth are better fitted for their work, the great canines for tearing, and the scissor-like premolars for shearing off lumps of flesh small enough to swallow. In the eye, the fibres of the iris, opening to the widest extent, expand the pupil to full circle, admitting the darkness of night and by rapid and spontaneous contraction shut off all excess of blinding light at midday and permit minute exactness of vision under either extreme."

Through such eyes, during millions of years, cats have watched others change while remaining themselves intact. They have seen the monkeys leave the trees, cautiously and with wary eyes for the predators. They have seen their dog cousins slowly achieve dogdom, a point reached perhaps two million years ago; they saw, also, that some of the doglike descendants of Miacis chose another course, became "bear dogs" (Daphaenus) and, in the end, bears. They were present, leaping, hungry, dangerous, when some animals wore forked horns on their noses, others twined useless great tusks and one turned its face into a shovel. Most of these animals, the great cats of the time found very good to eat.

Of those prehistoric great cats there were two kinds, one of which might have come if one called "Here, Hoplophoneus"—might have come very fast and with great ferocity. The other, early in the Oligocene epoch not very different in appearance, would have answered to the name Dinictis, or, in the manner of all cats, not have answered if it was not to his convenience. Both of these cats had the shape of cats, the muscles and eyes and claws of cats, and both had rather long canine teeth. But Hoplophoneus made, quite clearly, what was in the end to prove a mistake, although it gave him a great name among the animals of all time; made him, for many millions of years, the most terrifying animal alive. During man's own prehistoric times, the descendants of Hoplophoneus were very much around and very horrible to see. It may be now that some of those who cringe from the little cats of the household, shrink uncontrollably even from a creature so small as Martini, remember the great fanged animal which for so long roved the world, carrying in its mouth terrible swift swords.

Hoplophoneus had somewhat longer canines than Dinictis, the "true cat." And, while always remaining cats, the strains of which the two were prototypes diverged. The canines of one grew longer and longer, projected farther and farther below the under jaw, became stabbing knives. With this specialization there came others as corollaries. The skull was elongated to provide anchorage for the great neck muscles; the whole of the cat grew more massive as its striking power increased, equipping it to prey upon the most ponderous of the now extinct creatures which populated so much of the earth. By the late Pleistocene, this cat had culminated in Smilodon, the saber-tooth. He was still alive a mere twenty thousand years ago.

It has been suggested that the fangs which were Smilodon's greatest distinction and major weapon were in themselves the cause of his final downfall—that, at the very end, his sabers had grown so long that he could no longer get his lower jaw past them, and thus perished of a kind of lockjaw in the midst of plenty, having become so ideally equipped to prey that he could no longer eat. It is a pleasant theory, ironically satisfying and not without precedent, at least by analogy. The giant reptiles may have died out because they became, in the end immobilized by their defensive armour, as in later days the steel-encompassed knight succumbed to swifter weapons. Modern man has, in perfecting his armaments been forced to frequent compromise—armour plate as against speed in battleships, for example.

But probably it was not because he got himself in this plight that the saber-tooth vanished from the earth, to the relief of the herbivores. Modern study has convinced palaeontologists that Smilodon could, in spite of his canines, open his lower jaw, which seems to have been specially hinged for the purpose. It is now believed he died out for the simplest of reasons: His food died out first. He lived on giant sloths and other such beasts; he was equipped to overpower the mighty, but the slow. Sloths and the like died out; perhaps Smilodon had his part in this, although it probably was not a major part. Thus in the end, Smilodon starved, in the midst of game which he could not catch, and so we may never see him in a zoo, where the descendants of Dinictis—the quick leapers, in all but a few cases the climbers, the feline cats—may with safety be observed. And we do not invite diminished saber-tooths to sit upon our laps.

The descendants of Dinictis, some of which were a third larger than the largest of present-day cats, were quite as deadly to other animals as was Smilodon, and probably rather more so to man, since they moved more rapidly and probably were more intelligent. Presumably they preyed, as their wild descendants do today, primarily on grazing, quick-running things; when the saber-tooth was tearing at a thick-skinned sloth, his contemporaries among the true cats were eating of the little camels and the horses which ran on three toes. They were leaping where Smilodon lunged; sharpening their wits as they stalked animals which, it must often have been, were to be caught on the first leap or not at all. And all but the largest of the true cats were climbers; no doubt they climbed for monkeys. Like monkeys, as they climbed they could look out over the earth.

Both the saber-tooths and the true cats went everywhere in those days, known to us now by the bones of the ancient dead. Cats prefer warmth and now, in their wild state, live chiefly in areas where the sun is hot. But at one time or another, it was warm enough for cats almost everywhere on earth and they left their bones everywhere except in the polar reaches and in Australia and a few islands. North America was a favorite haunt of the cats, as it was of the mammoths, the early camels and the ground sloths. The big cats snarled over their kill where Los Angeles is now, and some of them fell into tar pits and were preserved. When ice came down from the North, the big cats went with their dinners into the peninsula of Florida, predators and victims both seeking warmth, as has been true more recently.

The two kinds of cats seem, for all anyone can tell today, to have got along reasonably well together. At any rate, their rivalry appears to have been personal, not racial. The true cats killed what the saber-tooths could not catch; the saber-tooths lived on what the true cats found too tough. Now and then, as individuals, they must have clashed, and engaged in cat fights of a magnitude difficult to imagine, making the air quiver with their screams, lacerating the earth with their raging struggle. But there is no indication that saber-tooths fought true cats as such; combat must as often have been intra-mural, for it is the nature of a cat, meeting another cat, to prepare for battle.

It is also the nature of the cat to eat meat and, in the wild state, to kill its own. The cat is a great believer in fresh food; many things which the dog finds delectable obviously nauseate the cat and no animal, if given half a chance, is more fussily particular. Meat hung just long enough for human consumption may well be rejected by the house cat with one annoyed sniff and, if human ways are not mended, the cat—if conditions allow—may seek his own supplies in the field. (But most cats prefer fresh beef even to the freshest mouse and not many of them will go to the trouble of eating birds if any substitute can be found.) Driven to it, the house cat will eat vegetables, not taking literally—as the great cats do—its membership in the order of the Carnivora. This, of course, is true of many other members of the order, as everyone knows who has met bears.

Other things—matters of structure, of dentition, of descent—are associated with food habits to place Martini, along with a small black dog named Smoky, who visits her and would like to make friends, and receives no friendly response to his overtures, among the carnivores. Along with her, and the lion in the zoo, there are many other, and widely assorted, creatures in this order of the class Mammalia, to which man also belongs. (Man himself is not a carnivore, although he eats meat. He is a primate.) This is the language of the taxonomist, whose business is the classification of animals, living and dead—the sorting out of nature, the arrangement of life. Taxonomy is a world into which the layman must enter gingerly, as into a labyrinth, and preferably unrolling a ball of twine as he progresses so that he may be guided back. Yet, glimpsed even dimly, it is a fascinating world, filled with unexpected discoveries. The cat, for example, has many relatives one would not expect and this without stretching the point necessary to include, say, the seal and the sea lion, which are also Carnivora, but of the suborder Pinnipedia, aquatic animals. The cat, along with the dog—and the skunk, the bear and the hyena—is a member of the suborder Fissipedia.

Below suborders come superfamilies and of these there are two: the Canoidea, sometimes called the Arctoidea, and the Feloidea, which was long called, and is still much called, the Aeluroidea. These are the superfamilies of the dog and the cat; of the Canidae, which includes dogs and jackals too, the wolf and all the little foxes and of the Felidae, in which come all the cats, living and dead, true cat and saber-tooth, which is, if one is a taxonomist, to say Felinae and Maichairodontinae—if one is a taxonomist and adept at Latin pronunciation. That is simple enough.

But among the Canoidea are also included a family called Ursidae, which is the family of bears; a family called Procyonidae, one of whose members is the panda, and a Family Mustelidae, which includes such varying animals as the mink, the otter and the skunk, so almost universally considered a rather regrettable form of cat. The cat has also rather unexpected near relatives. These include, as one would expect, the civets (Viverridae), one of which is so catlike that it may be a missing link in the feline family, and the mongooses. The occurrence in the group of the hyena (Hyaenidae) including, presumably, the one who laughs, is less to be anticipated —and, one supposes, this is a cousin to which no cat would point with pride.

The classification of the Felidae themselves has, through the years, involved the taxonomists in discussions which, in an atmosphere less scholarly, might easily have degenerated into squabbles. Dr. George Gaylord Simpson, approaching the subject in his *Classification of Mammals,* remarks that there "are irreconcilable differences of opinion regarding the phylogeny, and hence the major taxonomy, of the felids, in addition to the usual many disagreements as to details" and, a little later, dismisses the contentions of one fellow scholar with the remark that "this argument is almost as disingenuous as it is ingenious," harsh words indeed from a curator of Fossil Mammals and Birds. This dissension, apparent in relation to a prehistoric creature which may be either hyena or cat, grows more marked as the taxonomists approach the living cats, where differences of opinion grow so detailed as to become, to the lay mind, barely comprehensible.

Thus among the true cats (subfamily Felinae) most of whom are alive, almost any two authorities encountered give different general classifications for the cats we see about us. To some, almost all cats —except Acinonyx, the cheetah—are of the genus Felis, so that our

Martini becomes an individual known scientifically as belonging to the species Felis domestica and the lion in the zoo is Felis leo. But to others, even so characteristic a cat as the ocelot is a member of a genus of his own, Leopardus.

Dr. Simpson himself allows only three genera: Felis, into which he tosses all the small cats, including the lynx; Panthera, the big cats—lion, leopard, tiger, jaguar—and Acinonyx in which the long-legged, fixed-claw cheetah is alone. When we think of Martini and her daughters, of the late Jerry and our greatly loved Pammy, of black and white Pete of many years ago, of the cats who rub against our legs in grocery stores, of the feral black who for long haunted a garbage pit in a summer camp, holding her own against dogs and crows, we think of them, in so far as we can, in Dr. Simpson's terms. They are Felis domestica, however their breeds vary. They are the cats who sit and look at people; they are the cats who have been tamed by man.

Why it should have been this way about, and not the other, is only partially clear. Forty million years ago, an impartial observer might well have considered the future something of a toss-up, with the odds a little favoring cat. The early cats were probably as intelligent as the little monkeys; there is now little to choose in this respect between the monkey who has remained one and the cat, and this even though most tests rigged up by man clearly, and for obvious reasons, favor the simian. Physically, the cat, from the first, was the stronger and the more agile; it was not he who had to rely on cunning, not he who needed to be sly. Against even the modern cats, who, at their most ferocious and their largest, are not the cats of prehistory, the simians, weight for weight, monkey for cat, are hopelessly outmatched. Not long ago in California a gorilla was mortally hurt by a black panther about a third its size when the gorilla, busy with his meddling hands, managed to unlock a door separating their cages. Man himself, unarmed, not protected by clothing, not wearing the toughened skin of another animal on his feet, would have trouble enough with a water-front tom and probably would be fortunate to escape alive from the attack of an ocelot, who is not greatly larger than the house cat.

It might have been that the cats changed, not the monkeys; that from the ancient cats there evolved a race of beings super-feline as man is super-simian. Many have speculated on this and none with more grace and wisdom than the late Clarence Day, so widely—but too exclusively—known as the man who had a Father. Super-cats would have made good people—swift and solitary, violent but full of grace. They would have been dangerous, certainly, but to one another as individuals. They would never, as Mr. Day points out, have fought in armies, for that is not the way of cats; they would have chattered less, speaking only about matters of moment. And they would, surely, have been beautiful, as no monkey, however improved, can hope to be. Being armed in their own bodies, they would have had no need to invent weapons.

Perhaps it is this last, this cat sufficiency as animal, which kept him where he is, the tamed of man, not the tamer. If the ancient tree monkey was to go anywhere, if he was to keep alive, he needed all his wits about him, and the use of wits is supposed to sharpen them. In the end, he needed more than that since, even when he reached ape stature—he was not, one supposes, ever a gorilla for strength during his way to manhood—he was physically a match only for the smaller, unwarlike, animals and those he must have had trouble catching. He needed weapons which would amplify his feeble strength; a sadly large part of history is the story of how he got those weapons and what he did with them. In satisfying this need, which still continues, he may very well tear the earth apart under himself, and under cats too.

One may assume that the monkey was, even forty million years ago, ordained to triumph, in spite of the odds against him. The hand is quicker than the paw, and from very early times monkeys used their hands. From grasping a tree limb to swing from, it is not far—only a few millions years—to breaking off the tree limb and swinging it. And then, watch out animals, here comes Man! Your claws are better, your teeth sharply violent, your bodies lithe and quick. If you are a cat, man's broadest jump is no more for you than a lazy pounce. But you cannot get near man, or not always, not often enough. His arm is longer by club-length, and now he is throwing the club at you, now he is using stones; now, evolution help us all, he has thonged a sharpened stone to the end of his club and made himself a terrible claw. And as he does these things, in part *because* he does these things, he grows more intelligent and crafty. He digs pits for you to fall in, saber-tooth. In time he will learn to tether a goat in your path, lion, and wait in ambush until you come for it and then kill you with steel and fire. By that time, Martini, he will have a language in which to call you and all your kind "sly," call you "treacherous."

The cat needed none of this paraphernalia, or did not know he did—and could not have used it, in any case. You can pull at things with a paw, as you can kick at them with a hoof; if your paw is clawed, you can even pick things up. But you cannot grasp them, cannot in any real sense use them. From the first the monkey could, and by the time he had a thumb it was all over. By that time he was man.

And monkeys had, moreover, something which the cat has never had—something the scientist calls genetic plasticity, the inherent ability to vary, to change. It is true that other animals have this also. The dog has, for example, so that one kind of dog became a bear and, when man took over the dog's breeding, a creature which had begun as a wolf took on such varying forms as the great Dane and the Chihuahua; the English bulldog and the whippet. Nothing comparable happened to the cat, and nothing that man has done to promote artificial change has had any appreciable result. By selective breeding, man can change color in cats—change it a very little. He may sometimes modify the thickness and length of fur. But he always comes up with cats—pretty much the same size and shape within a species, with the cat skull and jaw. The first true cats had about the same skull; a scientist can tell from two photographs that one is of a fossilized feline skull which had a brain in it some millions of years ago and the other of a cat skull which was a cat six months ago. A layman cannot, without instruction. Man can breed lion and tiger together—cats interbreed with great freedom, knowing other cats when they meet them—and get another big cat, rather oddly marked, not quite lion and not quite tiger but not essentially different from either.

Cats are, that is, genetically fixed, and they have been, for all practical purposes, since they quit being viverrids. Some are bigger than others, most have tails and a few do not, they come in coats of many colors. But nowhere along the line did an aberrant strain result in super-cat. So, at some time or other, the little cats made up with man.

When this happened, and how it happened, no one knows or will ever know. Most probably, it happened independently in a good many places where men and small cats met. Cats may well have taken the first step, finding that where men lived, outside men's caves, there might be fresh meat to be had—bones man had only partly cleaned, so that they still held nutriment for a cat; parts of animals which man did not choose to eat, although they were fresh enough. (There could not have been many of these last; with its own kill, a cat is about as choosy as man.) And man, finding these small cats not dangerous, may have approved them as primitive garbage incinerators. And some man, more sensitive than his brothers, more gentle, may have picked up a kitten. Many men may have picked up many kittens, in many parts of the earth.

To almost everyone, kittens are charming and delightful. Many people who cannot abide grown cats succumb to kittens. (And too many, who would call the cat cruel, turn kittens out to die when they begin to grow into cats. Every autumn the country fills with young cats abandoned by summer countrymen; cities swarm with cats who have outgrown human affection.) Cavemen and cave-children may well have found wild kittens engaging, and some such kittens must have been reciprocally entertained. So the cavecat may have come into being; may have blinked into the fire when men found fire and learned to purr when touched. The fire alone may have brought cats, since cats love fire, love all warm places.

When man became a husbandman, and began to store his grain, the small cat found another reason to approve of man. Where men store grain, they end by storing rats and mice. Where rats and mice are numerous, there are almost certain to be cats. By the time he was storing grain, man was able to recognize cause and effect—to the degree, at any rate, he has ever found this possible. The more rodents, the less grain; the more cats, the fewer rodents. Then the cat had found his life's work; he has been engaged in it ever since. He has been a pet, of course, as to man he has been so many other things. But at bottom he has been, and is today, a working animal. It has not seemed like work to him; it is not in a cat's nature to be a drudge. Certainly he would never dream of pulling things around and only in mythology has anyone ever ridden on a cat. But if his sport seems to man like useful work, the cat does not mind. Cats are quite tolerant of human idiosyncrasies which do not discommode cats.

It is highly probable that the cat was not the first animal to tolerate man's idiosyncrasies. In the cat's long existence, his association with people is merely an incident; it is as if, after a long lifetime, he had only just now dropped in to tea. During by far the greater part of the cat's time on earth he had no alternative, since there were around no men worthy, in the eyes of cat or man, of the name. And then the association was by no means immediate. Man's association with another offspring of Miacis came first—almost certainly it came first. By the time man came along, so did the dog.

Roughly, which is to say within a few aeons one way or another, these two more recent animals have a birthday in common. For the dog it is somewhere in the late Pliocene, possibly a couple of million years ago. For man it may have come at about the same time, or a little later—in the early days of the Pleistocene, which followed the Pliocene. These timings depend to a considerable degree on what one calls man, and also on what one calls dog. We can call Eoanthropus a man, and Tomarctus a dog, since one looked rather like a man and the other not unlike a dog. It is, however, improbable that they ever met. A much later man, by then unmistakable, encountered the wolf, and after a longer time, they got together. There is evidence that they had joined forces almost ten thousand years ago, and the period may be even longer. It is assumed, although it cannot be proved, that at that time the cat still went his solitary way.

The dog's way was not then solitary, if it ever had been. Gregarious and intelligent, not so well equipped as the cat for single combat, the wolf which was to become the dog early learned that there is strength in union. Many wolves, hunting in relays, are better than one wolf; in time they can run down the fleetest creature. A family of wolves might kill a bear and a pack of wolves could; the pack might have a chance even against the big cat. As the dog was learning this, so also was the man. One may assume, although no one can ever know, that it was man who first perceived, as a faint glimmer in his dark mind, the advantage of combining these unions into one.

And one may assume also that it was as an assistant in the hunt that the dog first proved his use. The dog could outrun man, if it came to the chase; he could smell things that man could not smell, and so give warning—a warning which must often have been that a great cat was dangerously on the prowl. So in the end the wolf changed into the dog and, as time went on and man's habits changed, became in many other ways useful. There are many things a dog can do, and a dog is not proud. A dog will pull a sled or a wagon; a dog will fight for man and help in his police work; a dog will lead a man to game and bring game to man's feet. A dog will herd man's sheep and cattle and in other respects make himself useful about the house.

In the early days, man and dog together probably found that they were a match for the cat. Their youth as animals gave them kinship, although it can hardly be supposed that either realized this. Their comparative physical weakness as individuals, their common gregariousness, brought them together naturally. It may have been several thousand years before the cat joined them to make that triumvirate of the fireside, that uneasy triangle of man and cat and dog, none of which is always sure of the others, in all of which—but in the cat most—wildness is not quite tamed.

The cat is first definitely known as a member of this group in ancient Egypt, from which we derive our surest knowledge of most things in early civilization. The cat begins to be represented in carvings about forty-five hundred years ago, but by then he was evidently well tamed—he was not, that is, an animal on toleration, sitting at the edge of the circle. He was sitting under his master's chair; sometimes he was tethered to it by a ribbon. He sat straight, his tail curled around him, which is the way of cats who have nothing immediately to fear. He was at home, and appeared for a long time to have been so.

It is possible—it is even rather probable—that he was elsewhere at that time a domesticated animal. (Extremists about cats make heavy-handedly a distinction here: the cat is never "domesticated," he is merely "tamed." This is an example of the sentimentalization of cats, which modifies so much of our thinking about them. It is semantic-splitting of minor importance; the dog is a tamed wolf.) The cat is thought, for example, to have been a domestic animal in both North and South America before the coming of the white man. He was almost certainly tamed in various parts of the East. He has, in other words, a multiple origin—Pallas' cat, Felis manul, was not native to Egypt; he probably was tamed; he may have been the ancestor of the modern long-hair. Some other cat of early civilization may have given rise to the present-day Siamese.

The first Egyptian cat probably was a small, native animal, still existent in its wild state, known as the Caffre—the word is variously spelled. He had pale fur and black-soled feet. He may have been the first cat to eat at man's table. He was the first cat to become a god.

3

The Cat Becomes a God

THERE IS A twilight zone between prehistoric and historic times and in this zone the cat is a shadow; he may be postulated but he cannot be proved. Before the Egyptians began to tell their story in carvings and in images, there may have been in North Africa tribes of men far more primitive in culture than those who built an intricate civilization on the Nile and gave men who lived later their surest glimpses of the distant past. These tribes may have had totems, as most primitive peoples had; of one of these tribes, the totem may have been the cat. They may have formed a cat clan, as many centuries later some Scots were united in a clan under the sign of the cat; as in Sumatra, certain tribesmen considered themselves descended from a cat.

Totem animals, if of an agreeable kind—small enough, harmless enough, controllable enough—are often kept available by members of their tribe, and so in those distant days in Egypt the cat may have been. He would have been then at once a familiar and a little of a god—not yet wholly a god, a god in the making, a creature edging toward divinity. He was, if this early tribe was one of farmers, a helpful little god; by protecting the grain of those who protected him, he may have helped them to be better fed than the men of other tribes, and so stronger. Perhaps, as the centuries went on, as the cats and the cat men multiplied, this tribe became dominant in Egypt. Bubastis may have been their city, for long afterward it was the city of the cat. About these matters no one knows with any precision. It is true, of course, that now and then men have spoken with assurance, as if they had been present at the time. "In very early times, that is to say anywhere from four thousand to ten thousand years before Christ, the Egyptian cat was the straight-forward totem animal we have described." That is Professor William Martin Conway, speaking in England in 1891, somewhat after the fact. One can say of the theory only that it is persuasive. N. and B. Langton, who studied the subject for some thirty years, are less certain. "No Egyptian myth or legend about the first contact between cat and man seems to be known," they write, regretfully, and fall to speculating whether man captured cat or was adopted by him—and to speculating, too, what manner of cat that first one was.

Most probably, he was the Caffre, but even that is not certain. By the time he was so well established in Egypt that he was constantly having his picture made, he was almost certainly to some degree a blend, basically Caffre but with tabby markings more pronounced. By then he had pointed ears (generally) and sat almost straight-backed, rather as modern Siamese often do, although the Siamese is not, so far as anyone knows, a lineal descendant of the Egyptian cat. But in his first representation, he may not have been a cat at all—not, that is, Felis domestica, although almost certainly he was feline.

That first representation of what may have been a cat is, as the Langtons describe it, a carving of "two feline animals climbing up standards or ritual instruments on two fragments from Abydos which bear the name of King Den of the First Dynasty." Den—Den Semti or Den-setui—may have lived between 5383 and 5363 B.C. or may have been a couple of thousand years closer to our time. And one of the animals climbing the standard may have been meant to represent a lion, since he had a tufted tail. (But the lion does not climb standards; the lion, uncharacteristically, does not climb like a cat.) It has been suggested that these animals were not cats of any kind, great or small, but mongooses. But they have not got noses or tails like mongooses. Let us think of them as cats; it provides a starting point.

But if cats, these "feline animals," were still a considerable time from being gods, it is only possible that they were, in a sense, vestigial totem animals. It is not until much later that the first hint of worship begins to creep in; not until comparatively late days—the

days of the New Empire, a mere thirty-five hundred years or so ago
—did the cat become sacred and associated with the goddess Pasht,
who had many names—Bast, Bastet, to the Greeks Bubastis. Or
they may have been sacred only in the sense that they were inviolate,
as Eastern peoples have held so many animals. And it must always

be remembered that, even after the god association was well established, cats remained also what they have always been—pets and
catchers of rodents. Special honors may have been paid to individuals from time to time; little, furry Pashts may have reposed on
cushions and received homage. But for the most part they went as
a cat insists on going, on their own four feet. No cat, god or com-
moner, is happy with his feet not under him; the cat never knows
when he may have to start going somewhere.

Certainly by the time of the XVIIth Dynasty, cats were everywhere, and were pictured in all possible catlike activities. They
were pictured on tombs; images were made of them in all available
materials from gold to mud. Carvings show them sitting under
chairs, in one or two instances tied by ribbons to chair legs; they
show them gnawing at bones, eating fish, with mice under paws;
they show cat families of mother and children—never more than
four kittens—the children sometimes nursing. Some of these repre-
sentations are so real that they might almost purr; others are stylized; the images vary in size, widely; some evidently were worn as
charms. According to the Langtons, all Egyptian cats carried their
tails curled to the right although, as they gravely note, "in life the
cat is impartial."

The Langtons' collection appears to show two kinds of cats, the
short-eared and blunt-nosed; the long-eared and sharp-nosed. The
most usual colors represented, in so far as these colors can now be
deciphered, were ginger body with black markings. Most of the
cats were, to some degree at least, striped. In some instances, colored
stones were used to show the markings. And one Egyptian picture
shows a cat clearly engaged in helping its master hunt, an activity of
which Jules Fleury-Husson, who wrote under the name Champfleury one of the earliest books about cats, was inclined to look on
with grave doubts. Such an activity, he commented, would be
"miraculous" and he seemed inclined to believe that some ancient
artist had made it up.

The representation, which is in fair condition, certainly shows a
cat retrieving wild fowl from a marsh and it would appear that he
is doing it at human behest, or at least in human association. And

there is nothing miraculous about this at all; at the most it would be a little unusual. Cats do not, generally, go into water unless they have to, but they have no trouble swimming and a few of them apparently like it. There are many instances of cats fishing for themselves, and not always with the paw-from-bank technic. Many cats have been observed diving for fish, and appearing to enjoy it very much. And the cat is by instinct a retriever. He will bring his own game home to the family cave, as all cat owners constantly discover; he will lay a new-caught rabbit at a human's feet, although almost always merely as a display, and with the full intention of picking it up again himself. With no effort at all—in one evening— a cat can be taught to play a retrieving game with anything small enough for a cat's mouth, preferably a catnip mouse.

Martini would do that indefinitely before there were other cats, which involved new rules and brought about new games. She would do it until both of us were exhausted and herself show no signs of weariness. The plaything would be laid at the selected human feet, and Martini would speak. She would, politely, give time for an answer. She would speak again, still with reasonable politeness—a Siamese cat is not equipped for gentle speech, but she was not peremptory. Only after several remarks had failed to gain attention would she put paw to knee, with only enough claw showing to prove, if we had doubted it, that claw was there. It was then high time to throw the mouse for her—to throw it down the long hall of a city apartment, with Martini after it in a mad scramble, to wait for it to be returned.

She liked it best if two humans would participate, and we used to sit in chairs ten feet or so apart. Then the trick was more intricate, more complicated. One of us would throw the mouse; Martini would return it, not to the one who had thrown but to the other. The other would throw; back the mouse would go to the first. This alternation continued, on occasion, for an hour or so and without mistake. Now and then, to be sure, she would begin to forget, would approach the one to whom tribute was not due, and on whom obligation was not imposed. But she always caught herself in time— in time, usually, to look sidewise at the person whose turn it was not, make a small disapproving sound (as if the near mistake were human, not feline) and to deny any thought of uncertainty by a wider than usual detour. Cats do not like to make mistakes; it embarrasses them.

If cats will do things like this, and almost all of them will, it is hard to see any reason why they would not enjoy hunting for small game and we have no doubt that in Egypt they did. They were well treated then; a well-treated cat is a cooperative animal. That a cat would sit under a chair, even a king's chair, with a ribbon around its neck—and sit there long enough to serve as a model for a sculptor—is rather harder to believe. "In the name of Rē, sit still!" the harassed sculptor must often have said. "Don't eat the ribbon, chaou!" Or he may have said "mau" or "mai" or "meau," since there appear to have been several words for "cat." Or we may, down through the centuries, merely not understand him very well.

And we do not, although many have written learnedly on the subject, understand the Egyptian religion very well. "To obtain a clear and connected view of Egyptian religion seems to be an impossibility, for the plain reason that the Egyptians never had such a view themselves," James Baikie remarks in a tone of resignation at one point in his *History of Egypt.* So when the cat was identified with Pasht, who had so many other names—who was, Herodotus suggests, identical with Diana—he became, in some respects, more mysterious than ever.

Pasht was, depending as one looked at her, goddess of the sun and the moon, of love and of the chase; she was at once good and evil; she was related to, and sometimes thought of as the same as, Sekhmet and Ashtoreth. And she was not always represented in the same form, and by no means always as a cat, although the cat form became more common as the centuries passed. She was not even cat-headed in the Vth Dynasty; it is conceivable that she became so when the postulated cat clan became powerful, since through history man has adopted the older gods and changed them to suit himself. And Pasht was lion-headed before she was cat-headed. She is shown, in all, in four forms: cat-headed, cat-headed and cat-limbed, lion-headed and as a cat. Nobody knows why. She was a mutable goddess.

Through the labyrinthine way of religion and the cat, M. Oldfield Howey charts as clear a course as one is likely to find anywhere. Of the cat and Pasht (or Bast) he writes:

"As the cat sees in the darkness, so the sun, which journeyed into the underworld at night, saw through its gloom. Bast was the representative of the moon, because that planet was considered as the sun god's eye during the hours of darkness. For as the moon reflects the light of the solar system, so the cat's phosphorescent eyes were held to mirror the sun's rays when it was otherwise invisible to man. Bast as the cat-moon held the sun in her eyes during the night, keeping watch with the light he bestowed upon her, whilst her paws gripped and bruised and pierced the head of his deadly enemy, the serpent of darkness. Thus she justified her title of tearer and render and proved it was not incompatible with love."

This proof was necessary; it must be remembered that Pasht was also goddess of love. She needed to be great in all things, and most of all as "tearer and render" in time of solar eclipse. For then, Howey writes, "a terrific battle would take place—a titanic combat between darkness and light, evil and good. Fearful of the issue, mankind breathlessly watched the peril of the sun god, shouting, shaking the sistrum to terrify the serpent foe. Suddenly the celestial cat would leap upon the deadly reptile with fiery eyes and bristling coat and Apap [the serpent] would fly bleeding and torn to the depths of darkness. After the eclipse was thus ended, the veneration of the Egyptian people for the sacred animal was always intensified."

Intensified it must have been, and one hopes in human ways—the way of a human with a cat. Did small and furry "mau" or "chaou" get extra tidbits in Egyptian houses after he had thus saved the world from darkness? Was he perhaps allowed, on this special occasion, to sit where he had always wanted to sit and did not—his owners thought, and he did not tell them otherwise—ever really sit? Was he stroked, and were his ears scratched? Or was he, for a few days, too terrible in his majesty for these attentions and so more venerated than loved?

The sistrum the Egyptians shook to abash the serpent, urge on the goddess cat, was always associated with the cat; the cat's image was atop this odd device, which was part musical instrument and symbolically phallic in design. In this representation, the cat presumably—and appropriately enough—represented fecundity. Because the cat was, again to quote Howey, "the emblem of the time-honored ideal of virgin-motherhood, the Egyptian great mother-goddess who might be any one of a number of goddesses in feline form." This association of the cat with virginity is, certainly, one of the most curious of human conceits; virginity is a concept obviously inconceivable to the cat. In a land which was full of cats, the Egyptians could hardly have failed to notice this. Presumably, when the cat was cat she was merely little "maou" who rubbed against ankles and caught mice; only on more formal occasions was she divine.

But these two views of the cat did, of course, have a meeting place, and it was all to the good for the cat. Even when merely cat, she was inviolate, to some degree sacred. A Roman soldier who killed a cat—so behaving, one would think, very like a Roman—was almost torn apart by an Egyptian mob. It was unhealthy to be first to come upon a dead cat, lest it be thought that you had contributed to its death. One devious ancient captain, assailing an Egyptian city, threw cats over its walls and sent his men after them while the Egyptians were seeking to solve the dilemma presented by this sudden rain of gods.

Since cats were never voluntarily destroyed, and are as fecund as any goddess of love could desire, they became very numerous in Egypt—so numerous that one Greek, a tourist of Egypt's later days, reported that it was in that land more common to encounter a god than a man. Lest, in this over-population of feline gods some should know want, one ruler—El-Daher-Beydars—left funds to provide a "Cats' Orchard" for, as M. Champfleury's translator has it, "necessitous and masterless cats." Since all cats regard themselves as necessitous come mealtime, since it is inconceivable that any cat believes he has a master, however the human may define the relationship, the garden must have been often crowded and the commissary taxed. But the thought was a kindly one, and many Egyptians must have provided in their last testaments for the continued care of some favorite cat, as cat lovers—and dog lovers too, of course—have so often done down through history.

Yet the best cared for, the most carefully protected, cat does not live forever, although he lives proportionately to his life expectancy —which, without accident, is ten years—longer than man. So cats died in Egypt, and when the family cat died the family went into mourning, its members shaving off their eyebrows. The cat was mummified, just as a person was, and if he had been a well-to-do cat he might have a tomb of his own, with his picture carved upon its walls. "He was a very special cat," some member of Egypt's aristocracy may have informed his artisan. "He had a habit of sitting thus, his head a little on one side, looking up at me. Carve him so." And afterward, until it was time for his own portrait to be carved on the wall of his own tomb, such a man must now and then have visited the place where the cat lay and looked at the pictured cat—although by then he had other cats, and fine cats too—and sighed, and remembered the warmth of living cat against the leg, the purr of living cat, the certain ways one cat had which other cats had not.

If you were an Egyptian during the great days of the cat and of Egypt too for that matter, you placed little pots of milk in the tomb, lest the cat grow hungry in the nether world and find himself forgotten. But, of course, if you were an Egyptian then, the chances were against your being able to provide a tomb, the perfect means of distributing wealth having not then been discovered. So your cat, although mummified, did not have the very best funeral, and did not have a tomb at all. Perhaps then you waited until a feast of the cat goddess and carried the small mummy with you to the temple, and buried it there in the place provided. Perhaps you took it to one of the cat cemeteries, of which one of the greatest was on the east bank of the Nile at Beni-Hasan. There hundreds of thousands of cat mummies were buried and, as time went on and Egypt became no longer Egypt, dug up again. They were dug up in recent years—and sold off by the ton and used as fertilizer. Many of the mummies were shipped to England, which was catless at the time those cats lived, and to which they could not have been exported.

For Egypt was jealous of its cats and it was a crime to smuggle a tamed Felis caffre beyond the confines of the empire. Perhaps the virtue which dwelt in the cat god was considered a secret weapon, upon which Egypt's greatness somewhat depended. Perhaps it was merely that the Egyptians doubted whether there were enough cats to go around the world, and had a sufficient rodent problem of their own. But if the cat was a national secret, or merely a national resource, the secret leaked, as secrets inevitably do, however vociferous national spokesmen grow about them.

Cats do not seem, in the earliest days, to have been very widely distributed. Probably they were known, and may have been separately domesticated, in various parts of the East. But the Israelites appear not to have known the cat; at least he is not mentioned in Jewish writings, except in one sentence in the Apocrypha—and there it is doubted whether the reference was actually to a cat. In early Greece and even in early Rome there seem to have been no cats. In China, it has been guessed—but only guessed—cats were not known until about the beginning of the Christian Era.

When the domestic cat left Egypt and entered Europe he went— as gods have so often gone—with commerce. Presumably Phoenician traders, taking their lives in their hands when they passed Egyptian customs, sailed the first of Egypt's purring gods across the Mediterranean—as pets, as mousers, as curiosities. Once in Europe, the cat made himself at home. He found a multitude of cousins.

For when we speak of England, for example, as "catless" it is not true in the larger sense. So far as is known there were no tamed cats there before the Romans invaded. But the woods were filled, as the woods of all Europe were, with the common wildcat, Felis catus—a cat who has persisted in some parts of Europe, and notably in Scotland, until modern times. This cat was about the size of the Egyptian cat, although more definitely tabby—very sharply striped or blotched. (This marking would appear to be basic in almost all cats; it may even appear faintly in the Siamese, where it is entirely unwelcome to breeders. The Egyptian cat seems to have had, from very early, a tendency to tabby.)

Some of these new cats brought to Europe from Egypt got out at night, as cats have a tendency to do. Then there was a new cat cry heard in the European forests, and if it was a cry with an Egyptian accent it was none the less distinguishable for what it was. The cat has a universal language, and is never in doubt as to what is and what is not a cat. She cats from Europe cried in the darkness, and in the light, too—modesty is a recessive in the feline—her immemorial invitation and no cat on the loose cries long in vain. Somewhere, there is always another cat, and he comes if he is able.

So out of trees the European cats came, and into trees the newcomers from Egypt went after them, and many kittens were had by all. Felis catus met Felis caffre and they came to equal, to produce, most of our present-day Felis domestica. That is, at any rate, the prevailing theory. Long-hairs, Siamese and some others may have had a different, or partly different, ancestry. But the cat sleeping in the window of the grocery story on Sunday, the cat on his hind legs at the city garbage can, the cat in the country barn and the sleek short-hair who knows always where his next meal is coming from and how to get it, who may let a child pull his tail—all of these can look back through centuries and see the forests of Europe, and a wildcat who was a dangerous customer; can listen back and hear the jungle cries of this new mating. And, unless steps have been taken, today's cat will leave the store window, rise from his cushion, seek out the best available approximation of a forest and make those cries himself.

It may be assumed that the progeny of the native wildcat and of the domesticated caffre (who may himself have already become of mixed breed) were less difficult to tame than the wildcat had been. The female Egyptian, if she had found a home in this new world, undoubtedly had her kittens in it, and they were tame cats from the first, because their mother explained things to them. And some of the kittens of the wild females may have had a longing in them for the sight and sounds of men, and for man's fire—and man's abundant mice—and warily approached and in the end let themselves be fed and petted. By that time, the European was ready for the cat.

He may not always have been, and not only because of his lower stage of civilization. He may not have had mice, which also are an importation from the East. He did not have a good many things, including some of our modern diseases. But the mice came, and then it was essential that the cat come too; the Greeks apparently experimented with martens for a time as mousetraps, but found them unsatisfactory; for the mouse, there is nothing to equal the cat. So the cat found welcome in Europe, and gradually spread throughout it, as now he has spread throughout the world.

But for this new enlargement of his sphere, he paid a penalty. He ceased to be a god, but without ceasing to have about him the attributes of magic. He entered upon an uneasy association with the nether world and from that association he has only recently, not everywhere yet, freed himself. He is still waiting, as for so long he has patiently waited, for man to grow up. Now and then he must doubt whether this is ever likely to occur.

4

The Supernatural Cat

HISTORICALLY, THE CAT was a god and afterward became a devil. This progression is by no means unusual; it is the common lot of gods to descend into the darkness. But it is not the common lot of animals to establish and for thousands of years maintain a supernatural association. Snakes and toads, to be sure, have had much traffic with non-human beings; the bull has been sacred and the innocent hare a companion, or even a second self, of witches. Man has had doubts from time to time about the owl. But only the cat has so consistently stalked the strangely lit corridors of the human mind, where good and evil fight in awesome forms.

There have been many conjectures as to why this should be true, as it has been true from early Egypt until yesterday—perhaps until today. Looked at rationally, there is little awesome about the domestic cat: he is small and unlikely to hurt us; he is an ornament who is also useful, and the demons he sometimes seems to observe are, one may be almost certain, not his but ours. He will lie on his back, appearing to smile, and present to friends an unprotected belly to be tickled; if he is good-humored he may even allow a child to pull his tail. He is playful beyond most animals, and not only as a kitten, and if he has other habits seemingly less innocent he is in this by no means unique. Yet even now there are many who, seeing him, act as if they had encountered Satan under circumstances more than customarily unpropitious.

That these victims of the cat fear are, in a day when most of our devils are human ones and we witch-hunt not for witches, still peculiarly sensitive to the supernatural in the cat may be guessed, although it cannot be proved. If so, they are left a little stranded, having no acceptable forms into which they may rationalize their instinctive terror. They cannot explain to themselves their awe of cat on the simple ground that the cat is Pasht, who was not altogether a comfortable goddess. Nor can they reasonably contend that the animal from which they shrink is a wizard in transformation, waiting to lay a spell upon them. Such beliefs are no longer in the mode. The human instinct which prompted them remains powerful, but has lost a supporting framework.

It is possible that the identification of the cat with the supernatural has been, at least to a considerable degree, always such a framework of rationalization, subconsciously intended to provide a reasonable extenuation of an innate terror. A man may be in awe of a god without loss of dignity; there is no shame in fear of the Devil. This self-justification may have begun, in a dim fashion, when man was only beginning to become man, that is, shortly after he came down out of the trees. For then, the cats he knew were terrible.

Chattering in his tree, the early simian saw many horrible things which were associated with this powerful and gliding enemy, who moved with a grace so unsimian. There went beauty and death together, coupled with an unfair ability to climb trees. Fear of cat burned into the small animal on his branch and he chattered his terror to his friends. The little monkey may have been the first ailurophobe. The first man may have inherited a fear which was deep in nerves and muscles, was a spectre in the growing simian mind.

And early man himself had ample reason to share the monkey's terror, for he lived amid difficulties in the day of the biggest cats. It is probable, indeed, that the big cats—Smilodon and the descendants of Dinictis—were man's greatest peril, and that they did much to slow the increase of human population when man was still seeking to inherit the earth. Looking at them, early man must have felt great awe along with his great terror, and must also have felt some envy. Here was an animal infinitely stronger than he, and at the same time incomparably quicker. Here was a creature which could jump without effort to places men could hardly reach by climbing;

here an adversary so armed that a single lazy sweep of a paw could dash a man into bloody nothingness. This animal was wily, too— almost, in the areas of their meeting, as ingenious as man himself.

Now the simian is a proud animal and probably has always been. If any other animal seems greater than the simian—more graceful, more beautiful, stronger—justice has manifestly miscarried. When justice miscarries in this respect, devious forces are evidently at work; the powers of evil have given the adversary a helping hand. A creature so powerful to work harm must be inspired by the spirit of evil or, more generally, by any supernatural force. (Most of man's primitive gods were at once, or alternately, evil and good.) The Devil is in the cat; he is an awesome god on four legs, with eyes like fire. It is possible that if we throw him a child or two, in the spirit of sacrifice, he may relent. It is likely that if we adopt him as our totem animal, we may inherit his great fierceness and strength. (Thousands of years later, the cat was often an heraldic symbol—a symbol of savage pride and great deadliness.)

In some such atmosphere of human, and even prehuman, terror the cat may first have found his place in man's web of magic and religion—the web which is to protect man from peril, in which the sun is caught so that it will rise again each day and not leave the world forever in darkness; the netting under which the corn god is caught and slain, so that he may be resurrected in the spring and bring vegetation to life with him. The cat may have started to be a god because man was in such awed fear of him.

And closer inspection, made possible when the cat became a companion of man, probably did much to support the belief that there was something uncanny about the cat. For one thing, the cat, if allowed his own way, is considerably nocturnal—much more so than man's other familiars in the animal world which, if less rigid about it than man, generally prefer to sleep at night. The cat has no such preference, and this is very peculiar—very suspicious—in the cat. Man is afraid of the dark and may always have been. (When the big nocturnal cats were about, he had every reason to be.) Man has always supposed that night is a time for evil spirits to abound. And here is the cat, by preference going out at night, when man and dog know it is time to sleep beside the fire. Walking at night, seeing at night, is for creatures which are obsessed—the cat is one of them; the owl also is nocturnal.

Both cat and owl have eyes which are fixed or, in the case of the cat, nearly so. Owls are supposed to stare at people and certainly cats do. A misguided cat hater, who apparently had met few cats, once accused the tribe of being unable to meet the human eye and said of them, as men say of other men so inhibited, that they were "shifty." Early cat keepers, more observant, undoubtedly noticed what everyone who has had any contact with cats has noticed: that meeting the human eye is one of the things a cat does best and most often. And about this unrelenting stare there is, certainly, a quality a little uncanny. The cat's eyes seem shallow, for one thing; one is conscious on looking into them that one cannot really see into them, and becomes in time uneasily persuaded that the cat is having no such difficulty with human eyes. The cat not only looks at the human; the cat very obviously looks through the human, possibly at something behind him. It is most disconcerting to be stared at by a cat and an imaginative person is apt to begin to feel that more than cat is looking at him through the cat's eyes. This feeling must have been both more frequent and more acute among the men and women of a few thousand years ago; they used their imaginations more, since so much more was left to the imagination. (We no longer imagine a sun god in a dazzling golden chariot; we postulate an immensely distant ball of flaming gases.)

The uneasiness engendered by the cat's habit of staring may have reinforced man's belief that there was more to the cat than met the eye. And the cat's eyes, in themselves, behave oddly, which is to say they do not behave as eyes should, which is the way man's do. In addition to not being almost blind at night, the cat's eyes widen and narrow with the waning and waxing of the light, and this may be interpreted—has been interpreted—as evidence of the cat's kinship with sun and moon. Pasht was, it will be recalled, the moon god- dess, among other things. Mystically, this identification with the moon is reinforced by the cat's inclination to sleep curled in a moon- like circle.

The cat's sinuous movements may have seemed further indication that he was linked with the supernatural, and this is probably again because of man's fears. Man fears the snake, which is also sinuous. Man resents, no doubt because he fears, things which he considers "slinky." One is almost forced, reluctantly, to the conclusion that man is inherently antagonistic to, and suspicious of, grace, possibly because, by comparison to so many animals, and most of all to the cat, man himself has so little. The enchantress is always graceful in the stories mankind tells itself; hearts of gold notoriously beat only under the roughest and most ungainly of exteriors.

Now most of these experiences and observations which may have led mankind to consider the cat a creature of magic are of attributes basic to the cat as an animal, and hence concern nothing which is the fault of, or a virtue in, the cat. The big cat killed man thousands of years ago because he was hungry, and man was a suitable size for a dinner, and easy to catch. The cat moves gracefully because he is for his purposes almost perfectly constructed; his eyes widen and narrow with the light because that suits his convenience very well, and he hunts at night because that time is his best time for hunting. Staring at men so, and putting them on the defensive, seems, however, to be something he goes out of his way to do, and in at least one other respect the cat seems to have helped bring on himself the supernatural identification from which he has both gained and suffered.

For there can be no doubt that many cats behave as if they were in at least occasional contact with forces beyond our comprehension, and this they seem to do voluntarily, even wilfully. No one can be sure of this, since a cat's purposes are inscrutable if one is neither a cat nor inclined to the easy identification of feline with human motivation—an identification which miscolors much of what we as people think of cats. It may be that cats who see things which are not there, or had better not be, are neurotic cats.

Such a cat, walking across a floor, will stop suddenly and whirl and stare at nothing, and sometimes even bristle a little at the invisible thing he sees. He will move toward this nothingness cautiously, seeming to walk upon tiptoes; he will stop and listen—a demon, perhaps, has spoken the cat's secret name; perhaps has laid a command upon him. Then the cat may give over all this as suddenly as he began, look up at a human and speak pleasantly. He will saunter off, then, all cat and only cat, seeing no more and hearing no more than a respectable house cat should. But then, just as he nears the door, he will leap suddenly to one side, as if a pit had almost opened under his feet; as if invisible fingers, probably ending in claws much like his own, had touched his fur. This can be, to the human watching, not a little disconcerting.

Our present cats behave infrequently in this fashion but we knew a cat family once whose members seemed to see nothing except things which were to us invisible and who obviously heard the most outrageous sounds. We were living at the time in a basement apartment, not at its best too cheerful, and the cats came and went at will—came in from the garden, down the stairs, possibly through the floor. They came, it appeared, ghost-hunting, as other cats might frequent an area known to be rich in mice. There were three of them, as we remember it, but they came to seem more numerous; the whole apartment came, finally, to seem strangely crowded—very strangely crowded. When we began ourselves to think we saw what the cats saw and hear what they heard we went elsewhere.

It is true that these cats had more than usual reason for wariness, being subjects of the Boss of Morton Street, who was a cat to make anyone jumpy. He came in and out too, although not so often, but he did not see ghosts. He saw us very clearly, and so far as we could tell saw us as prey. He was large and black; scarred but, it was clear, inevitably victorious. He had an odd scuttling movement which we had never seen in a cat before and have never seen since; his features were set in a perpetual snarling frown and he seemed to be an exception to the rule that all cats have retractable claws. He never retracted his. He viewed us, we became certain, as mice and we managed never to confront him singly, which would clearly have been foolhardy. The lesser cats, the haunted cats, also ran frantically at his approach; they lived in nervous fear of him, as to a degree did we. So it may be that they had merely become neurotic, and were

constantly seeing or hearing the Boss of Morton Street even when he
was elsewhere, killing Great Danes.

It is also probable that most cats, because their hearing is so much
more acute than ours, are frequently startled by sounds which are to
us inaudible; that, if we could hear what they hear, we would perceive that the sound was not really that of a devil's voice, was
perhaps no more than the crash of a pin dropped on a carpet, of a
tiny insect stirring in the grass. It may be, also, that they are bodily
much more sensitive than we and so receive impressions through
skin and fur to which our coarser nerves are impervious. Many cats
are, unquestionably, so hyper-sensitive; there are cats who cannot
bear to have their tails touched, even with great gentleness. Martini,
although not extreme in this, is tail-sensitive beyond most cats; when
one of her kittens touched her tail in play she was beside herself, and
always bit the kitten, whereas most mother cats assent to the kitten's
belief that the maternal tail is a natural plaything.

The better one knows cats, the more understandable they become
—within, of course, limits. The cat who sees ghosts, when one
knows him well, is almost certainly thus reacting to imperceptible,
but still physical, stimuli. The human can so reassure himself; so
rationalize away eerie behavior. If we now knew the basement cats,
having known since so many cats, we would no doubt find them
more rational than they seemed many years ago. (The Boss would
still seem, certainly, the most fearsome cat of our acquaintance; he
may even have been Satan himself.) The basement cats did not
really see ghosts—we think. Martini does not listen to voices from
the underworld—we are almost sure. But if we really believed in
ghosts, or in the underworld, we would be less confident. If we
believed in ghosts and were afraid of cats we would not, admittedly,
be confident at all.

We have known few people who seemed honestly to believe in
ghosts, but a good many who were afraid of cats. Ailurophobia is
fairly widespread, in differing degrees. Anyone who harbors cats
and meets people inevitably runs into humans subject to this often
quite uncontrollable cat fear. One friend of ours became hysterical
and almost fainted when an elevator operator, having her alone in

his car, playfully mewed like a cat. All who have cats have encountered less extreme examples of the fear—in visitors who sit rigid, smiling glassily, saying politely that everything is quite all right, watching with horror the inspecting advance of a little cat. The cat, it must be noted, almost always does advance on these unfortunates; if possible, he will arrange to sit on the rigid lap.

(Ailurophobia is not to be confused with the rather common cat allergy which—presumably, at any rate—has an entirely different basis, being more physical than mystical. Cat hair, which is usually floating in the vicinity of cats, and is always on the furniture of people who have cats, and cat dander acutely affect many people subject to asthma in any of its forms. A friend of ours, who is also a business associate, can never visit us, pleasant and convenient as it would be, because where cats are or have been he cannot go—cannot go and continue to breathe. It is no good to shut up the cats in another room; the cats have been in all the rooms in which he could sit, since the cats have been everywhere in the house. It is sometimes surprising that he does not get asthma merely from meeting us, in neutral corners, so responsive is he to cats and so inevitably do we carry on our clothes some trace of cats, as all dogs instantly observe. He is also, as it happens, almost as adversely affected by dogs and horses; his cat allergy, while pronounced, is not of the pure form. He likes both dogs and horses and, so far as he knows, rather likes cats, but the possibility of social contact with any of these animals is obviously remote. But his is not cat fear, and he does not blame cats for it.)

A good deal of study has been given to true ailurophobia, with inconclusive results. Investigators have sought to discover some more tangible basis for the fear than the historic one, which obviously cannot be proved. Unfortunately, none of the other theories have turned out to be much more susceptible to proof, including the favorite one that those who fear cats have had, in extreme youth, some unfortunate, even painful, contact with a cat, so that the whole cat tribe has become warped in the human subconscious. This is one of those agreeable theories which have as their chief advantage the fact that they cannot be disproved any more than they can be proved.

You are afraid of cats but can remember no occasion, even in the dim twilight of memory, when a cat did you harm? Ah—that is the worst form of it. The very fact that you do not remember is proof that it must have happened, and hence left you with ailurophobia. But if you remember that a cat scratched you when you, also, were on all fours, and have now no fear of cats, you have not disproved the theory. You have no fear because you do remember. The vagaries of the human mind, like those of the feline mind, remain inscrutable. People, it sometimes seems, are almost as mysterious as cats.

There is, however, nothing particularly subtle about the fear itself; it can have symptoms as real as those of chicken pox. Dr. S. Weir Mitchell went rather deeply into the subject of ailurophobia, as he went into so many things. His research brought to him "indisputable evidence concerning the large number of people in whom the presence of a cat gives rise to a variety of symptoms" and he continues: "In such persons, the feeling caused by the cat is instantaneous. In the asthma victim, it is slower and cumulative and may not be felt for twenty minutes or more. Certain persons, on seeing a cat, have other symptoms with or without oppression of breathing. There may be only fear, terror, disgust. There may be added chilly sensations, horripilation, weakness, locked jaws or, as in one case, fixed open jaw, rigidity of arms, pallor, nausea, rarely vomiting, pronounced hysterical convulsions and even temporary blindness. These pass away with removal of the cat, but in a few examples leave the sufferer nervously disturbed for a day."

It is sometimes true that an extreme ailurophobe may have some, if not the most extreme, of these symptoms without even seeing a cat, or hearing one. Some people seem to be aware of the most carefully hidden cat, evidently applying extra-sensory perception to the matter. This is difficult to account for; it may be that people, like cats, are sometimes in league with supernatural powers.

People are afraid of other living creatures—many people are horrified by the sight even of the most harmless snake; a spider, businesslike in its web spinning, may arouse fear, terror and disgust, possibly even give rise to horripilation. But such fears are not difficult to understand. The snake, in addition to having done mankind a bad turn in Eden, is cold, which an animal should not be; he goes on his belly for his sins. The spider's horrible fate is to look like a spider. And both snakes and spiders may be poisonous, so it is a practical matter to give them a wide berth.

But the cat is warm and beautiful; he walks daintily on the proper number of feet; he is soft and purring on the human lap. It is strange that he should be so often feared unless the fear is in truth an inconceivably ancient one—unless one sees the Devil in the cat.

It would not be surprising if one did. The Devil was seen in the cat for a thousand years and more.

5

The Cat in Darkness

SAVE FOR HIS centuries of divinity in Egypt, the cat has been most commonly associated with the powers of darkness and with the primitive gods which were neither good nor evil, as we now differentiate, but both together. This association has been grievous for the cat, and never more so than after he came to Europe; never as acutely so as during those many generations of struggle between Christianity and the old gods which had become devils.

The gods of one religion become the demons of the next; the associates of the earlier gods share their descent into darkness, and the transformations which gods undergo in the nether world. Cat-headed Pasht was not the first god to go down with the civilization which dreamed her into being. Her temples crumbled and were not rebuilt; there came a time when no new priests were consecrated in her name. Other deities took from her the task of protecting man from the encircling darkness—from the darkness of the setting and the winter-diminished sun, from the darkness of death which night and winter symbolize. But Pasht did not finally die, as the divinities of the Druids did not die, as the primitive corn god, however often killed, was immortal. Pasht—by whatever name, Hecate or Diana or Lilith; or by new names—joined the little gods, which is to say the devils, since the word "devil" means merely "little god." She had been the "emblem of the time-honored ideal of virgin-motherhood." She became one of the mothers of all evil.

Pasht became a disinherited goddess, and joined many others—became to some degree entangled with the others, part of that intricate hierarchy of the underworld which no one can very readily sum up. Sir James G. Frazer, who came nearest, required many volumes and was now and then forced to guess. Pasht, or Diana, joined the ghosts of the dark gods the Druids had propitiated in rites often horrible; she became an associate of gods so primitive that they are nameless and all pervasive. The cat, tied to her, tied to the supernatural as he has apparently always been, went along, whether he wished or not, into this darkness. The cat became a companion of witches and wizards; that is, of those who continue to worship yesterday's gods after today's are in the ascendancy. He became an adjunct of Satan, who is a fallen god; he became an involuntary participant in the most primitive of magic rites. It was all very hard on the cat.

His martyrdom in Europe started early and it would be optimistic to say that it continues nowhere today—that there is no remote corner of that continent where it is not considered a wise thing to kill a cat at harvest time; a pious action to toss a living cat into a Lenten bonfire. (Twenty years or so ago in Pennsylvania people still believed in witchcraft; it was still sometimes thought advisable to sacrifice a cat to Satan by plunging it, living, into boiling water. A bone from the destroyed animal was afterward worn as an amulet.) The cat died magically even before the Christian Church was strong enough to begin its suppression of witchcraft, a suppression which brought death to many thousands of men and women, and to untold numbers of cats.

The ancient gods were fully in the darkness by the time the witches died at the stake, and their cats with them, or were hanged, and their cats with them. They were, at any rate, officially in the darkness, although in form and action men still worshipped them, often having forgotten the inner meaning of the rites they practiced. The ceremonies of the Druids were only dark racial memories by the time of the maximum extirpation of witches in the sixteenth and seventeenth centuries. But the Druids had found religious reasons for torturing animals, and men and women too, to death; men have seldom failed to discover the most moral justifications for cruelty. It is not in evidence that the Druids roasted cats over their bonfires, as they did snakes and other animals, including humans. There were cats around in Gaul and Britain in Druidic times—

perhaps 200 B.C. to about 200 A.D.—but they were not tame; Felis catus, the European wildcat, did not take kindly to being roasted and was not a trusting creature.

It is thought, although it is not certain, that these ancient Druidic practices had as their purpose the elimination of witches and wizards, either in their actual human form or in the bodies of the animals into which they had transformed themselves. It is possible, to be sure, that the Druids were sacrificing gods, rather than the worshippers of demons. But Frazer inclines to the belief that the tormented creatures were burned as witches, pointing out that this conjecture is confirmed "by the observation that the victims most commonly burned in modern bon-fires have been cats, and that cats are precisely the animals into which, with the possible exception of hares, witches were most usually supposed to transform themselves."

If, however, the Druids were sacrificing animals which had been altered, by magic, into representatives of the gods, they would unquestionably have utilized cats had cats been more readily available. As soon as cats did become available, they were identified as the corn god, and often killed as such, and this even in fairly recent times. Frazer lists many such sacrifices; in Amiens, until recently and perhaps even now, the "expression for finishing the harvest is 'they are going to kill the cat' and when the last corn is cut they kill a cat in the farmyard." And "at threshing, in some parts of France, a live cat is placed in the last bundle of corn [grain] to be threshed and is struck dead with the flails. Then on Sunday it is roasted and eaten as a holiday dish."

Such practices, into which the cat was incorporated as soon as he became available, were widespread throughout Europe before the final triumph of Christianity. Many of the rites involved killing the cat but at some he was an honored guest, or participant. In the fertility rites of the Daughters of Diana, the cat represented the moon and was honored both as the moon goddess and as a personification of the goddess of fertility. These rites were conditioned by the phases of the moon; they had the orgiastic character commonly associated with such rites from the most primitive times. Some segments of the Waldensian sect held dark carnival in the dark times, celebrating their belief that mankind is of Satanic origin and that the powers of darkness are no less puissant than those of light, and in their ritual the cat was prominent and strangely honored. In those days the cat was still an associate of gods of a sort—Diana was, by transmutation, the same goddess the cat had been. These gods were still suffered to exist, although only in isolated instances formally tolerated, by the new religion, chiefly because it was not yet strong enough to thrust them finally down.

Thus cats, even before the gods with which they were identified were thrust into oblivion—or as nearly into oblivion as is the lot of a god—had trying times, and were kept from their mouseholes. The things done to cats in the line of magic, even when not mortal, were usually things of which no cat could approve. No cat, or almost no cat, would elect to be thrown into a river as a central figure in a rain-making ceremony. And the Waldensian form of worship must have been an acute affront to feline dignity. There were, moreover, other reasons for torturing a cat to death than because it was a witch or a representative of the corn god. There was always sympathetic magic; there was always the chance that, since the cat was dear to the dark gods, concessions might be wrung from them by torturing the cat.

"These gods loved the cat as their chosen and sacred symbol," M. Oldfield Howey observes. "To torture it would be to oblige them to grant any request that its persecutor made a condition of its release." Thus if one wished to wring from Satan those benefits which Satan is notoriously able to provide, pressure might be exerted by roasting, slowly, over a small fire, a number of cats, preferably black. As the first cat screamed, a lesser devil—in cat form —might come and snarl rage and promises. But the aspirant for demoniac blessing would not stop, would not heed. He would put another cat on the spit, turn it slowly, and as it in turn screamed its agony a second emissary of Satan might well appear—a larger cat, more horrible, more important. This process, long continued, might be expected—was in certain parts of the world confidently expected— to bring in the end Satan himself, in the form of an enormous cat, and in a mood to give up half his kingdom, if only this torment could be stopped. Satan was, it will be seen, considered more merciful than man, more averse to hideous torture.

Thus in what was, by later standards, the practice of witchcraft, cats could be tormented and cats could be killed in those distant days in Europe, as cats have been at almost all times wherever in the world there were cats. But more cats, far more cats, during later centuries died at the hands of those who ostensibly worshipped the God of light than perished in rites dedicated to the gods of darkness. It was the godly who killed the witches and their cats.

The distinction between the gods of good and evil is, of course, one easier to make in modern times than it was in ancient times to understand. As believing Christians, or as men and women reared in a civilization where the Christian faith dominates, we find no difficulty in making a moral choice between the two forces. But God as good became a concept of the human mind rather late; the ancient gods were beyond good and evil; their caprice was as unlimited as their power. They could do neither good nor evil, except in so far as what was good for man was "good," because they were above such man-made rules. The identification of the Deity with good, with righteousness, the ascription to Him of gentleness and mercy, represent a fairly recent concept of the human mind—and represent the human at his most defensible, differentiated from all other animals by his moral sense. Even Jehovah was a god of wrath rather than of righteousness; how he grew into the God of love is poetically imagined in Marc Connelly's *Green Pastures* which so becomes, among other things, a tenderly beautiful resumé of man's religious growth.

The men and women who worshipped the moon goddess in rites which now seem to us degraded were not, it must be remembered, worshipping "evil" by intention. They were worshipping the amoral gods and, one may presume, without a sense of sin. The sense of sin came later, when as Christians they wilfully worshipped demons; when they knew they were doing "wrong"; when, as in the Black Mass, they perversely insisted upon it. The delights were enhanced, no doubt, by being forbidden; an additional fillip probably was

given by the danger in which these worshippers came to stand.
When the Church, growing slowly but inevitably during the dark
centuries, became powerful enough to move against evil the peril
became great indeed. Then those who paid obeisance to the moon
goddess and her earthly representative, the cat, were no longer innocent primitives, doing no more than their forefathers had done since
man began. Then they were witches, and they were to be rooted
out. It took a very long time to root them out; the dark gods die
hard. Even now, if the substance of those pagan beliefs has with-
ered, there remain shadows of them in the recesses of the human
mind. It is still unlucky to have the black cat, the demon cat, cross
the human path.

Witchcraft, by the time it was so called, was a subterranean survival of pagan religion; it was, in Howey's words, "survival of the
feminine principle of God—of the eternal virgin-motherhood of the
creator—and inseparably connected with it was the cat, the symbol
of this aspect of the divine.

"Hence," Howey continues, "the feline form is represented on the
apex of the sistrum that Isis carries in her hand and the cat was the
chosen transformation of Diana (or Hecate) herself in her hour of
peril when a terrible typhoon forced the gods to hide their divinity
and flee into Egypt. Having assumed feline form, Diana took
refuge in the moon and all the lunar goddesses in different coun-
tries and ages are inseparably connected with the cat. Witches, once
their priestesses, adored the moon with undiminished reverence, so
that the cat was to retain its importance in the cult of Dianism even
after the terrible degradation of mother worship. . . . To explain
the downfall of this ancient and beautiful faith, we must remember
that the cat, either by her own multiple nature or, more obviously,
when coiled in a circle, like the changing moon she represented,
showed forth the mother of nature as *all*. She was Venus the beautiful and Venus the terrible, the goddess of life and death, whose
eastern name of Al-huza or Huza stands for the Egyptian 'divine
woman' or Isis."

In the Middle Ages the Church found itself strong enough to
move against the dark gods, their priests and priestesses and, of

course, their cats. By the fifteenth century the persecution was well under way; it lasted for some three hundred years and then rather tapered off than ended. Women were put to death as witches in middle Europe in the latter part of the eighteenth century. It has been estimated that a hundred thousand witches were legally killed in Germany in the sixteenth and seventeenth centuries, that seventy-five thousand so died in France and that the righteous in Great Britain burned or hanged or drowned another thirty thousand. How many hundreds of thousands of cats died with them as their familiars, or died without human companionship for being themselves devils no one can ever guess. But it was a bad time for cats.

Christians burned cats in, or slowly roasted them over, Lenten fires everywhere in Europe. They stuffed them into wicker baskets and threw the baskets into the fire; when Elizabeth was crowned in England, such a basket of screaming cats was immolated as a warning to the underworld and an amusement for the godly. Louis XIV of France danced gayly around a fire with his nobles and their ladies in 1648, their ears filled with the horrible screams of dying cats. In Scotland they burned innumerable cats at the celebration known as Taigheirn, which lasted four days. There the cats were dedicated to the devils—which is to say the ancient gods—they served and then roasted slowly. Cats were whipped to death—"The finest pastime that is under the sun, is whipping the cat at Abrighton." If the cat were not so tenacious, not so prolific—and perhaps if he were not so useful that man's common sense in the end protects him—he might long since have been wiped out.

Cats died because they were associated with witches and people died, often people innocent even of the intent to do evil and to worship false gods, for no better reason than that they knew cats. Two old women sat at tea one evening in England in the year 1618 and they had a cat who was a friend. The cat approached, seeking food, and one of the women waved a handkerchief at him, rebuffing his advances. When she was tried, with her friend, this action was what convicted them both—they had communicated with the cat by mystic signs. They were tried for having caused, by evil spells, the illness and death of the Earl of Rutland's children and they were found guilty and hanged. It may be presumed that their cat was chased down and also killed. At the height of the witch-hunting, it was dangerous even to know a cat. He was an outcast among animals, the devil incarnate. This not all men have forgotten.

With all the Inquisition and the secular arm could do—aided by the Protestants' witch hunters—with all that could be done by their amateur helpers and their bonfires, cats were not exterminated —and neither, utterly, was belief in the cat's supernatural associations. (Neither, it may be noted, was witchcraft itself. Until very recent times, men and women in Scotland were being accused of turning themselves into cats, for evil purposes. In remote areas, as in parts of Pennsylvania, cats may still be sacrificed to Satan; they may still, in the more ancient fashion, be killed as spirits of the grain.) Cats may still presage evil, particularly if they are black; they may still, as has been widely held throughout the world, cause the death of a child by creeping upon it and sucking its breath.

This last belief, which is without factual substantiation, may well reflect fear of the vampire cat, a frightening creature which stalks the corridors of man's myth-making mind. Lilith, the dark goddess of the Hebrew mythology, changed herself into a vampire cat, El-Broosha, and in that form sucked the blood of her favorite prey, the new-born infant. The black cat is, of course, the one most likely to be Satanic and has always been. Man has been studying the supernatural cat for centuries, and throughout the world, and knows many things about him.

Thus it is widely "known" that a strange cat of any color may cause death merely by coming to a house; that if a cat of any color jumps over a coffin great evil will inevitably result unless the cat is quickly killed. In China, a cat and a dog are not allowed in a house where a dead man lies, since the presence of the animals makes it possible for the dead to arise and do great evil. Kittens born in May were held in deep distrust for centuries and even now it is believed, by certain Celtic peoples, that a May-born cat will bring snakes into the house. This probably is because May is a bad month altogether to those in whose racial memory there linger traces of Druidic magic. In May the Druids performed their spring rites, assuring the world's rebirth, and these rites involved most horrid sacrifices. After the Druid gods went underground, the witches took over, in the inevitable progression; they rode their cats, and their broomsticks, to high hills and there, with the wind howling, did all manner of unspeakable things as the month of May began.

If any kitten, May-born or not, comes to a house at night he will bring evil with him, unless he stays to fend it off. For this we can vouch; one of our most amiable cats came to us one rainy evening, crying small in the wet, and was taken in. And that night nothing at all evil beset us. The cat remained some ten years and probably throughout acted as a talisman. If, during that time, one of us had developed a stye he could have cured it by rubbing the place with the tail of the cat, since the cat was largely black. (Neither of us, to be sure, comes from Cornwall, where this belief has been widespread for generations; perhaps neither of us would have been able to say, in the proper tone, "Oh, qually way, Oh qually way," the charm which must be used as the stye is stroked. And perhaps Pete, who had his own idea of his dignity, would not willingly have permitted such usage of his tail.)

A cat is lucky or unlucky, although more often the latter, depending on circumstances. In the seventeenth century it was said, "Kiss the black cat, and that'll make ye fat; kiss ye the white one and that'll make ye lean," which indicates a nice distribution of good fortune, if selection is correctly made; kissing a white cat would, one would think, be simpler than dieting to many, although by no means to all. And there is an ancient bit of advice which goes:

"Them that ever mind the world to win
Must have a black cat, a howling dog and a crowing hen."

But if your cats leave your house, as cats sometimes will, illness will inevitably follow. (Of this we cannot be certain; one of our cats, who had shown previous evidences of mild insanity, did leave our house and never returned, but it is hard to remember whether illness resulted, although regret did and the faint lingering of sorrow.)

Cats are, naturally enough, associated with love and marriage in many superstitions, and in this connection their influence is—as one would expect—most often favorable. If a cat sneezes at a wedding, it will bring good luck to the bride. But if a maiden treads on a cat's tail she must give up, for a year, all thoughts of marriage, presumably because she has offended some dark goddess of love. A Telugu Indian wishing to marry a third wife, would first marry a cat and put a yellow string around its neck. But men should seek to make sure that the women they marry are not really cats in disguise; that has often happened. Aesop tells the regrettable story of a youth who married a beautiful maiden, not realizing that Venus, to assuage his longing, had created the maiden out of the family cat. On the wedding night, the maiden heard the scampering of a mouse, and to her cat heart all other delights paled and she scampered after it. This so annoyed Venus that she turned maiden back to cat again, and it must also have disconcerted the youth. A man whose wife has a habit of roaming at nights does well to watch her, even if there are no mice about. A Scot had a nocturnal wife once, a few generations ago, and followed when she left the house, expecting one can only guess what—not suspecting, perhaps, that he would find his wife changing to a cat and going to sea in a sieve, with seven other cats. The man called upon the Trinity, the sieve began to leak and all the cats were drowned. Such, at any rate, was the story he told abroad.

The cat has always had a great influence on the weather. Merely by washing its face it may bring on rain, and wise countrymen often killed their cats before harvest to assure dry weather. In Scotland, if a cat scratches a table she is apt to raise a wind; in Java, cats have long been utilized as rain makers. According to Frazer, this may be done merely by bathing a cat, or two cats, male and female. More intricate, and probably hence more efficacious, is the method which involves not only a cat but all the women of the village. The women enter a stream and splash one another vigorously. Then a black cat is thrown in among them and made to swim about for a time, while the women splash it. The cat is then permitted to make shore and escape. After this, the rains come.

Sailors have realized this close association of the cat with the weather since the cat first appeared on the Ark. (The rats increased too rapidly and became a plague; Noah passed his hand over the head of a lion and she sneezed forth the cat. Or, perhaps, there was a misalliance between a lioness and a monkey, which resulted in the cat. This must be considered much less probable, since there is no vestige of simian in the cat. There is an alternative origin: The sun invented the lion, and the moon, in competition, created the cat. The stars laughed at this and the moon tried again, this time producing the monkey. It is recorded that, on first seeing this new animal, the stars laughed harder than ever. Some of them, indeed, are obviously still atwinkle over the joke.) Sailors, whose life is perilous always and dependent on fortune, have been historically concerned with omens and watchful against the forces of evil. Their preoccupation, traditionally, with the cat is reflected in the reference to cats in so much nautical terminology—the cat's paw for the ripple on the ocean which presages the wind; the catboat, the cat-o'-nine-tails, the cat head and the cat-block.

Cats have, throughout the world, been much used in sympathetic magic, usually to their discomfiture or death. In South Slavonia, for example, it was long believed that a thief, wishing to pilfer at the market-place without detection, had only to burn a blind cat, preserving the ashes. A pinch of the cat ash sprinkled over the tradesman who was to be victimized, passed to him the blindness of the cat, and made theft easy. It has also long been believed, in many parts of the world, that the gift of second sight may be achieved by sacrificing a cat, which is itself thought to be a seer. The cat was much used in divining the future by the witches of centuries ago.

There have been, for so long, so many reasons to kill the cat that one is sometimes astonished that success was not final—that the cat, as such, was not exterminated. But probably there are more cats in the world today than there ever were, since there are more men and since where there are more men there will be more rats and mice. The cat's opportunities to feed himself, enjoy the entertainment a mouse provides and win houseroom from the human are thus multiplied, and all cats will multiply with their opportunities. For the cat, in spite of being a creature from the underworld has, paradoxically, been also the "harmless, necessary" creature of whom Shakespeare wrote. He has always been a furry mousetrap, and mankind has kept the door open for him.

6

The Furry Mousetrap

NOBODY KNOWS HOW many billions of rats and mice there are in the world, all of them doing, assiduously, as much harm to man as they possibly can do. Nobody can do more than guess how much that mankind prizes has been destroyed by these small, ubiquitous creatures since first they began to pester man. Rats, it has been most reasonably contended, have changed the course of history. The plague they carry has almost wiped out certain populations and is still a smouldering menace throughout the world. The food they, and their smaller cousins, have destroyed might feed a generation and they do not limit their destructiveness to food. Mice and rats will eat almost anything, and what they do not eat they will foul. There is no excuse that man can see for rodents, and if left to themselves they would willingly inherit the earth. No other animal, except man himself, does so much harm to mankind.

There are, it is almost certain, more rats and mice in the world than there are men and women. The world's barns are full of them and the fields are full of them. Along every water front rats forage by the thousand; the great cities men have built shelter more rodents than people. Rats scramble in the walls of houses and at night emerge to eat people's food and, when the occasion arises, people. No viciousness is beyond a rat and a mouse is as much like a rat as his smaller size allows.

There are, it was recently estimated, fifteen million rats and mice in the city of New York, where there are by no means fifteen million people. Not long ago the city appropriated $100,000 for preliminary work in rodent eradication, it being thought that this money might, if carefully expended, reduce a little the rat and mouse population

in a few square blocks of one of the most infested areas. A few
tenements might be partially rat- and mouse-proofed, which could
be expected to inconvenience the rodents somewhat and might even
cause a certain number of them to move to new apartments. This is
no great chore for a rat or a mouse, who does not use his own
furniture, but that of his hosts. When, a few years ago, three old
houses were torn down on lots adjacent to the building in which
we lived, the rodents which had inhabited them were hardly at all
bothered. They moved to our building and began to eat and foul
our food. Mice and rats are adjustable.

They are also extremely prolific and the rat population of New
York apparently is increasing, in spite of all that can be done about
it. The population is either increasing, or the rats are growing more
rapacious and biting more people. In 1947, four hundred and thirty-
five persons complained to the city authorities that they had been
bitten by rats—or that their children had. The following year, the
number rose to four hundred and seventy-nine. In 1949, the incidence of rat bite apparently was still slowly increasing, perhaps
indicating that rats and mice are on their way to inherit the earth,
or at least the city of New York. If it were not for the cat they
might; if it were not for the cat they might have long since. The
cat has always been man's better mousetrap.

He has been this since the days of Egypt when he was a god,
and he was this in Europe when he was a devil. God or devil, the
cat kept his nose to the mousehole and worked for his living. Probably he did not do this because it was useful and because it pleased
the humans with whom he lived; probably he did it because, for
a cat, there is nothing quite like mouse-hunting. But it is very
possible that he recognized, as an agreeable by-product of his sport,
that his humans praised him when he caught a mouse and might
let him enter and stretch out by the fire. It would be logical to suppose it was this human approval of mouse catching which taught
the cat to bring his prey and lay it at human feet, meanwhile talking
earnestly about the accomplishment and, if necessary, attracting
further attention by hooking gently at a human garment. Certainly,
most cats do do this and expect praise for it, as they expect praise

for bringing home wriggling snakes and badly damaged rabbits and, it must be admitted, birds. (That most humans do not find his bird catching praiseworthy must a little surprise the cat, who can remember that in his Egyptian days it was thought a fine thing for a cat to do. Humans, the cat has found, are changeable and not to be predicted.)

But mouse and rat catching all men approved, all men thought useful, and it is for that that mankind has rewarded the cat with shelter and with food. (The cat has earned his caresses otherwise, by being himself; by being, himself, warm and friendly while retaining a decent reticence.) It is as a mousetrap the cat has gone on government payrolls and on those of private industry; it is because he is a mighty hunter of small creatures injurious to man that he has been introduced into catless regions—and has, through no fault of his own, there disturbed that "balance of nature" about which men talk so wisely and which they do so much to upset. As a rat killer, he has been used—and his greater use has earnestly been advocated—in the unending campaign against bubonic plague, which is a hideous adjunct of the rat.

Delightful as the cat is to those who find him so, it may be doubted whether cats would have come to live harmoniously with people if there had been no rats and mice in the world. With the dog it may have been different, since only in the most primitive times did most dogs earn their livings by doing chores for men. Most dogs now are unemployed—a few pull sleds, a few help with the herding, a few participate in the hunt, assisting men to kill inedible animals by the most awkward possible method. A few are expected to bark at burglars. A dog does not live by working; he lives by charm, and has for generations. His affections are vast and not subtly expressed; it is no trick at all to love a dog, who would slap you on the back if he could and who, it must be admitted, sometimes manages it. One of the most agreeable dogs we ever knew, a magnificent Doberman, once greeted his mistress, who had been away for a few moments, with such hearty enthusiasm that he knocked her backwards into a fireplace and broke two of her ribs. It is somewhat more difficult to love a cat, who

insists on the refinements of affection and who is, in his own fashion, intensely civilized. The cat had first to prove that he was indispensable. To the great majority of people, he did. There are dissenters.

It is because the cat is a hard worker, not because he is a gay companion, that the farmer keeps a barn full of cats—and so keeps his stored grain. Not his fetching ways with men, but his "cruel" way with a mouse, keeps the cat in the corner grocery store; he is there on business and is as useful as an extra clerk. The men and women who went out to farm a continent did not keep cats, did not buy them eagerly from peddlers, because of a sentimental fondness. They paid money for cats, encouraged them to multiply and did not drown the kittens, because there was no other way half so good to keep down the vermin—the rats and mice, the ground squirrels and gophers—which destroyed crops. And when not catching rodents, the pioneer cats were happy to make themselves useful among the snakes, which almost all cats will kill, although not many find them edible. Our cats have caught a good many, but none has ever appeared to consider a snake food, and Martini, who is as fastidious as she is crotchety, always makes a face after she has mouthed a snake, for all the world like a human who has bitten into a bad taste. She will paw at her mouth to remove the flavor and, if one of us is available, protest audibly, human again in a desire to share with others the blame for her indiscretion.

Those cats who, bought from a traveling tinker's cage, helped to subdue a continent, made an outstanding contribution to mankind's expansion and this contribution has, by at least one writer, been acknowledged almost extravagantly. "The influence of the domestic cat on American civilization has received far less consideration than it deserves," the *Encyclopedia Americana* announces, and the writer of the article on cats, clearly a man who loves them, continues flatly: "A great deal of the advance of agriculture as well as the spreading out over the vast woodland and prairies has been made possible by this much abused and misunderstood animal. How much food cats have saved, how much property they have guarded from destruction, what plagues of vermin they have kept in check, from the time America was first settled, it is impossible to compute. But for their sleepless vigilance, the large cities would quickly be over-run with rats and mice."

Since the large cities are already over-run, or near enough so, one does not need to be a cat doubter to season this encomium slightly. Cats are by no means sleepless; some cats awaken quickly from sleep, others can sleep through almost anything. When the cat is asleep, also, the mice will play; now and then they will play almost within striking distance of a cat, and more than once we have awakened a cat of ours to point this out. But the author of the *Americana* article, Ernest Ingersoll, a well-known naturalist, is no doubt more verbally than factually extravagant. Any farmer would agree with him and so, by and large, would anyone who keeps cats and hence is freed from the unpleasant necessity of keeping rats and mice. Pete dealt promptly with the migration of evicted mice into our New York apartment; he and his successors dealt with a more extensive problem we had for many years in a country cabin, which at first we visited weekends and where, toward the end, we lived for the major portion of every year.

When we first started going there, the place was in the most literal sense a rat's nest and mice raised families in all the bureau drawers. The rats occupied the premises without hindrance during the winters, and took the premises apart; each spring when we returned from urban hibernation it was to find a devastated area, the floor strewn with broken glass and crockery, everything gnawed open that could be gnawed—and rats can eat through practically anything—the characteristic manifestation of the rat everywhere. The place literally smelled of rat, and mice had dug into the mattresses to have their families.

Nor did these creatures willingly retreat as we advanced. They had the cabin in the winter and used to fight for it all summer; the scurry of rats would awaken us at nights and there were sometimes prodigious rat-hunts in the small hours, we and our guests armed with brooms and pokers and the rats armed with hatred and ugly teeth. One needed to be half huntsman to live in the place and guests became a little difficult to entice—would bring, as hostess gifts, packages of new and highly recommended rat poisons, none of which had been sufficiently recommended to the rats.

Then, after the first few years, the cats came—Pete first and after him the others. And when they came, the rats left and the mice left after them. Not only did they shun the place when we and the cats were there. They abandoned it as a winter resort, or all but abandoned it. During the last three or four years we saw only one rat, and that was during a period when Martini, then in residence, had been very much preoccupied with kittens.

Yet only once in that period during which rodents retreated, leaving this tiny portion of the world to people and their cats, did we see any of the cats actually with a rat, and that rat was a rather small one. (At their time of supremacy, the rats were almost as big as cats.) Some may well have been killed in our absence, and carried away for feline reasons; rats are not like mice, and cats know it, and do not play with them, so that the kill may be quick and secret.

But only this one rather aborted rat was presented in evidence. So far as we can determine, the rats were scared off, not killed off.

For cats have this effect on rodents: the mere presence of a cat is usually enough. Cats are almost odorless to humans; if in a house where there are cats one can smell cat—except, of course, the odor intentionally scattered by an unaltered male—the cats in the house are sick. But to rats and mice cats smell highly, possibly of brimstone, and there can be no doubt that cats frighten from barns and houses far more rodents than they actually kill. St. George Mivart, author of the most monumental, and probably most authoritative, book anyone ever composed about cats, wrote that one cat had been known to devour twenty mice in a single day "and put many more to flight." And rats seem to be even more wary of cats, and to leave even more quickly any place that cats frequent.

Mice are not nearly so intelligent about cats and have more or less to be killed off one by one. This all our cats, with a single exception, have been delighted to attend to. Pete was the luckiest of them all in this respect, coming upon an area which had not been shot over for years and hence was swarming with game. He cleaned up the resident mice in almost no time during his first visits, and thereafter found it necessary to maintain indoors only a precautionary patrol. For his real hunting, he went afield, catching the mice who lived there—and who would, remember, inevitably have come indoors as soon as they realized what opportunities they were missing. During the ten years or so Pete was with us, he caught, we suppose, hundreds of mice, and we suppose this because he brought most of them home. During part of one night, when we were up late with guests and Pete was out late as a result, since the guests did not greatly interest him, he caught half a dozen mice and laid them in a neat row on the doorstep, showing us that, although absent, he had not been idle.

Pete only now and then ate one of his mice and when he did it apparently was more from a sense of duty than from any real taste for mouse. If he had been hungry, he would, no doubt, have felt differently. But if he had been hungry, he would not have caught so many mice, the best mouser being always a well-fed cat who seeks recreation, not food. (The cat is not, to be sure, quite like a human hunter similarly inspired. The human knows in advance that he will eat only a fraction of his edible kill, and will never eat a lion. The cat, it may be assumed, discovers only after he has caught a mouse that he prefers beefsteak.) Pete's occasional nibble at mouse was a formality, to prove to mice and men that he could devour the former if he chose.

Cats subsequent to Pete never found a hunting ground so happy. Pamela, who followed with her brother Jerry, did most of her hunting out of doors, although she still found a house mouse or two each spring. She gave a good many of her field mice to Jerry, who was eager but inept; he was one of the few cats we ever saw who lost a mouse once he had it. He used to lose them regularly, being a poor judge of the distance a mouse had to go to find shelter; being, indeed, a poor judge of almost everything. He spent a good deal of his time sitting in windows and chattering angrily at birds, none of which he ever caught.

Martini, when she came along, found the going even tougher and the last year of our residence in the cabin she could not find a single indoor mouse, although she waited long and hopefully at last year's mousehole. She spent the rest of the summer in the fields, but even there hunting was not what it had been. Primarily a mouse-cat, she was brought to giving aid and counsel to Gin, one of her daughters, who—coming late to the mouse fields—chose to concentrate on rabbits. This concentration, and her considerable success, proved to us somewhat disconcerting, since rabbits scream when captured and are much more amiable than mice in action and appearance. But no gardener, whether of flowers or vegetables, can afford to be over-sentimental about rabbits.

Martini's other daughter, Sherry, is the only cat we have ever met who does not, so far as we have been able to determine, kill anything larger than a grasshopper. She is, or appears to be, somewhat afraid of mice and the other two look down on her because of this. They are fond of her, in a tolerant fashion; they sleep with her, lick her and play with her the contact games—at which, inconsistently, Sherry is formidable. But one may guess that they do not really think her much of a cat. We are sure her mother does not, since Martini is a person of decided views and had an early disappointment with Sherry. This disappointment came when Sherry was very small, still under maternal tutelage.

Martini, as all cat mothers should and as, given the opportunity, most of them do, was explaining things to the kittens. There was, Martini pointed out, this important matter of mice. This, she told Gin, laying a not quite dead field mouse at Gin's feet, is a mouse. Martini poked it, pushing it toward Gin. Mice are something all cats should make themselves familiar with, and catch when available. Martini pushed the mouse closer and made a low sound, deep in her throat. "Mouse," she said, as clearly as cat could.

Now Gin, when things were thus explained to her, said, "Oh. Mouse!" with pleased interest, batted it a little, and carried it around for a time and if, for a while thereafter, she had the notion that mice lived in Martini's mouth and were to be caught there, she outgrew this childish dream, as cats and people must, and came to realize that each cat is obligated to earn his own mice. She became a very good mouser before she went on to bigger game.

But Sherry, when it was her turn to be instructed, behaved most oddly. Martini brought Sherry's trial mouse and laid it in front of Sherry; Martini explained and explained again. But Sherry did not advance. Sherry drew back in fright, making small alarmed sounds; she drew in her feet so as not to touch mouse—it was as if she had wrapped her skirts about her and climbed to a kitchen chair. She did back into a corner, finally, saying, "No! No!" and in the end Martini took the mouse away, now and then looking back and shaking her head. Sherry has never caught a mouse since, although she will now and then play absently with one when it is safely dead. She pursues butterflies, but we have never seen her catch one.

Sherry is a cat of great charm, but if there had been many like her in the old days cats might not have come to live with man. Cats vary as mousers; being good and indifferent and downright inadequate. Some cats never actually take on a rat, the technic being different, the prey more formidable and harder to come by, since for all the rats there are in the world a cat may live his life out and never meet one, unless he is a barn cat or a store cat or a cat who makes his living along the docks, where both cats and rats grow large and of great ferocity. If all cats had been like Sherry, it is doubtful that cats would even frighten rodents away, since no rodent would have great cause to fear the cat. But Sherry is not like most cats; it sometimes appears that she is not like any other cat. (Being a blue-point Siamese, she does not even look much like many other cats.)

A race of Sherry-cats would not have been commended by Charles Darwin for preserving the English red clover; would not have been advocated as the best means of diminishing the incidence of bubonic plague; would not have been reproduced in china on the theory that even a china cat will keep the rats and mice away from silkworm pupae. It was the Petes and the Martinis, the Bosses of Morton Street, the cats who live in barns, who brought the tribe to live with man and got them endorsed by men of science.

Darwin's classic paragraph on the balance of nature, and on the cat's relation to it, is widely known and has been endlessly paraphrased. It has to do, many will remember, with mice and bumble-bees, and it reads as follows:

"From experiments which I have lately tried, I have found that the visits of bees are necessary for the fertilization of some kinds of clover, but bumble-bees alone visit the red clover as other bees cannot reach the nectar. Hence I have very little doubt that if the whole genus of bumble-bees became extinct or very rare in England, the heartsease and red clover would become very rare or wholly disappear. The number of bumble-bees in any district depends in great degree on the number of field mice, which destroy their combs and nests; and Mr. H. Newman, who has long attended the habits of bumble-bees, believes that 'more than two-thirds of them are thus destroyed all over England.' Now the number of mice is largely dependent, as everyone knows, on the number of cats; and Mr. Newman says 'near villages and small towns I have found the nests of bumble-bees more numerous than elsewhere, which I attribute to the number of cats which destroy the mice.' Hence it is quite credible that the presence of feline ani-

mals in large numbers in a district might determine, through intervention of mice and then of bumble-bees, the frequency of certain
flowers in that district."

This study of nature's balance has been amplified by one step:
The number of cats in a village varies directly as the number of
spinsters who are—in the popular mind and to some degree in fact
—the great protectors of the house cat. So the abundance of red
clover may, in or near the end, be said to vary inversely with the
plentitude of human males or directly with male recalcitrance. The
balance of nature will take one almost anywhere.

It was another British scientist, less widely known—a mere
lieutenant colonel, acting as a civil surgeon in India—who made a
study of cats and rats and plague, and as a result of it made a recom-
mendation: More cats. He made it twice, the second time a little
plaintively, in the *British Medical Journal* in the year 1908, writing
first in May and returning to the attack in October.

The lieutenant colonel—whose name was Buchanan—mentioned
that, as everyone knew by 1908, rats incubate bubonic plague and
spread it to people through their parasites. He found evidence that
for thousands of years people had seemed vaguely to suspect this
connection, knowing at least that when rats started dying in houses
it was time for people to flee the houses. He made note of the fact
that cats are sacred to Mahometans and Hindus alike. "Now," he
wrote, "when the Plague Commission were satisfied that rats are
the cause of plague epidemics, one would have expected that the
first thing they would do would be to enquire whether there is any
natural enemy of the rat and whether people would be willing to
keep this animal. The first sentence that most of us learned in
school was that 'cats kill rats.' "

But if one had held such hopes regarding the Plague Commission
one would, Dr. Buchanan admitted sadly, have been mistaken. The
Plague Commission, possibly because its members had attended
different schools, seemed not to know that cats killed rats; certainly
they did nothing to encourage cats. And cats needed encouragement; most of them were having only two litters a year, those
small, and the kitten mortality was high. Already, the need was

great; if the commission started at that moment, May of 1908, their work would be cut out for them; it would "take considerable time to get a sufficient number of cats." But the commission, in so far as Dr. Buchanan could see, was merely sitting on its theories; certainly it was not mobilizing cats. The good doctor, fighting for his belief—and for the lives of a great many people—shook his head sadly in the pages of the *British Medical Journal*. He did more than that, however. He sought to prove his point.

He made a census of cats, there in mean, crowded Indian villages. He found many villages in which, with one cat or better for each two houses, there was no plague; he found, and proved, that plague diminished as cats increased. He found that there was this difference between three villages—in Village B there were many cats; in villages A and C there were few. In Village B, there was no plague; in villages A and C there was much. He found that in one village where there were forty houses and thirty-six cats there was no plague; he found that in the village of Jasapur where there had been thirty-eight cases of plague and twenty-one deaths and where these cases occurred in twenty-one houses, all the cases but one were in catless homes. (The single exception housed a cat too young for ratting.) He found that Hindus were unwilling to trap or poison rats but had no objection to the capture of rats by cats; that most of the Hindus and all the Mahometans were willing cat keepers. And, when the Plague Commission continued inactive, Dr. Buchanan had pamphlets printed in praise of cats, and caused these to be distributed widely.

It all, apparently, came to nothing. Neither the Plague Commission nor the Indians responded. A cat-conscious visitor twenty years later noted that "few Indians appreciate the cat" and India remains one of the regions of the earth where plague still lurks, ready to spring again. We learn in school that cats kill rats; this precept is, as Dr. Buchanan morosely noted, apparently "the last thing that many are willing to put into practice." Many, in India and elsewhere, seek to circumvent this natural law. Many have sought to circumvent its since the days of the Greeks and the Romans, who tried for a long time to use martens in place of cats.

But this effort was made before the cat came to Europe; the rational Greeks abandoned the marten when the cat came.

The marten will, certainly, kill rats and mice. So will a number of animals—the owl, the weasel, the ferret, the mongoose and the skunk, among others. So, if the rats and mice can be persuaded to enter them, will traps, although rats are notoriously hard to trap. So will poison, although the victims may choose to die in inaccessible places within the house, with results which are distasteful, or may leave the poison untouched where it may, in time, be found and eaten by dogs and cats and children. Poison gas is effective but extremely dangerous, usable only under conditions where adequate controls are possible, since any gas which will kill rodents will kill people. This last fact is proved rather too frequently. Black snakes are good mousers, if one likes black snakes as pets.

It is probable, indeed, that other natural enemies of the mouse and rat—owls, particularly, and weasels and skunks—kill more rodents each year throughout the world than cats kill. "Quite naturally this is true," writes Ida M. Mellen, a great defender of cats, "since mice number thousands more in the woods and fields where these birds and animals get their prey than in the house or barn, and they must catch them to live." It is true, or probably true —nobody really knows, of course—and it is evidently beside the point. The field mouse in the field is of no great interest to anyone, except another mouse and, so long as he remains in the field, does no great harm to anyone. He will follow mole runs to tulip bulbs, and eat the bulbs, but this is more nuisance than menace. Mice and rats become the plague they are when they come into human habitations—in other words, when they leave the orbit of the preying owl and enter the territory of the cat. It is with those rodents that people and cats are immediately concerned.

And it is this situation which confronts those who would, at almost any cost, eliminate the cat. Generally, they must admit that cats are mousetraps; few quarrel openly with Darwin's observation that the number of mice is largely dependent on the number of cats. Dr. Nathaniel Southgate Shaler, sometime dean of the Lawrence Scientific School of Harvard and a great foe of the cat, went as far in challenging Darwin as he was able, and about as far as anyone has gone, when he wrote in 1895:

"Among the curious features connected with the association of the cat with man, we may note that it is the only animal which has been tolerated, esteemed and, at times, worshipped without having a single distinctly valuable quality. It is, in a small way, serviceable in keeping down the excessive development of small rodents which from the beginning have been the self-invited guests of men. As it is in a certain indifferent way sympathetic and by its caresses appears to indicate affection, it has awakened a measure of sympathy which it hardly deserves."

Admission could scarcely be more grudging; "in a small way serviceable" in preventing the "excessive" development of those "small" rodents which are "self-invited." The rodents are too small to bother with; a few billion rodents are to be expected, hence the word "excessive"; it is man's own fault anyway. But admission is there, all the same. In spite of his obvious wish that things were otherwise, Dr. Shaler was forced to admit what others learned with Dr. Buchanan in elementary school: "Cats kill rats." Of course, as Dr. Shaler points out, rats are not as big as cattle.

Dr. Shaler may, unknowingly, have seen the demon in the cat, or have been scratched by a cat as a baby. So, it is convenient think, must Edward Howe Forbush, state ornithologist of Massachusetts in 1915 and a Moses who would have led man out of the wilderness which cats infest. Mr. Forbush did not go quite so far as Dr. Shaler. By implication, in one of the most remarkable documents ever written about the cat, he admits that cats kill rodents and even that the killing of rodents is, to man, desirable. "Unquestionably, selected cats are useful in the dwellings and granaries of man, as a check on the increase of small rodents." (Rodents appear to shrink when the usefulness of the cat is in question.) Nevertheless, the cat must go—the cat kills birds, which is the theme of Mr. Forbush's protest, to which we shall subsequently return. A dilemma is presented, and Mr. Forbush wracks his brain.

Barns and houses should, to begin with, be rodent-proofed, a practice to which nobody can object except, perhaps, those who have to pay for it. Traps may be used. If animals are to be employed, he suggests the owl, the weasel, the mongoose and the skunk, among others, apparently being undeterred by the comparative rarity of the mongoose in North America and the human's irrational prejudice against the skunk. To Mr. Forbush, it is enough that the skunk is not a cat. He does not, however, insist on either skunk, mongoose or owl in house and barn. He prefers the combination of ferret and dog, an ideal ratting team.

The ferret is first procured—and the dog persuaded not to kill it. A muzzle is prepared for the ferret; both it and the dog are leashed. Then the farmer goes with this interesting team to the farm, points the ferret at a rathole and says, no doubt, "Sick 'em." The ferret chases the rat out of the hole. The dog, held in readiness, kills the rat. The farmer finds another rathole and extermination continues.

Mr. Forbush admits, without stressing, that there are certain disadvantages to this method. The period of training is something of a problem. Even when the animals are trained they must "be attended and assisted by their master." Rather petulantly, indeed, he admits that most people may continue to prefer cats, since they cost little in time or effort, hunt by themselves and "make pretty and pleasing pets." People are misguided, as Dr. Buchanan discovered; there is a recalcitrance in nature, as Martini found out when she sought to instruct Sherry. Even when one shows the way, there is no certainty that it will be followed. But the way Mr. Forbush shows remains fascinating: The farmer day by day and night by night training dog and ferret, accompanying them to the barn, finding rats for them to kill, neglecting his other work—since how could he find time for it?—growing no grain and in the end, as the rats leave for better stocked barns, starving philosophically— farmer and farmer's wife, dog and ferret all together—sustained by the knowledge that what men and other animals can do against the cat they have worthily done.

Mankind has through the centuries preferred the easier way, which is the cat. Realistic men have valued the cat accordingly, now and then even to the point of placing specific monetary value on cats known to be hunters. Like other workers, cats are most highly valued when they are scarce. In 948 there seem, in Wales, not to have been enough cats to go around freely, and King Howell price-fixed them. A new-born kitten, its eyes still not open and its mousing potentialities only to be guessed at, was worth a penny. When it could be proved that the cat had caught a mouse, its value was doubled. A cat of established reputation as a mouser, a twenty-mouse-a-day cat, was worth fourpence. And in England, when cats were scarce there, there was an appropriate penalty for cat murder. The killer paid the cat's owner, and by this method: The cat's body was suspended by the tail, the nose just touching the swept barn floor. Then over the cat, until the rising cone covered the uppermost tip of the tail, the murderer was required to pour grain—grain the cat might have saved from rat and mouse had the cat lived. Given a long cat and a smooth barn floor, the bereaved owner might show a profit. (A hunter may kill our cats today and pay us nothing, unless we can prove that our cats are valuable and breeding animals. Since they are merely pets—and companions and sources of delight—they are worthless. The best mouser is no longer worth a stipulated fourpence.)

Companionship and mousing are about all man has ever got from the cat, although this is not entirely for want of trying. The Chinese have used them, on cloudy days, as clocks, or are reported to have done so, gauging the approach of darkness by the narrowing of the pupil in the cat's eye. This seems a little improbable; certainly it is going the long way around. In the sixteenth century an inventor proposed that cats be used in chemical warfare. Small cannon "charged with pestilential odors" were to be fastened to cats and the cat set off in the direction of the enemy, providing, however, that the enemy was not Christian. It is not in evidence that cats so equipped were ever sent off against anybody, no doubt because it is traditionally hard to tell which way a cat will jump.

Cats were, Champfleury records, employed rather horribly as musical instruments in medieval times, and he tells of a procession in 1549 in which a kind of cat calliope was used. A number of cats were caged, with their tails hanging out; the tails were tied to a kind of keyboard and a trained bear pressed on the keys, so that the cats screamed "in bass or treble tones" as the float trundled through the streets. There were several variants of this diabolical arrangement but the idea did not catch on, perhaps because men's ears are more sensitive than their hearts.

Cats have been eaten for centuries, sometimes as cats, probably more often as rabbits; their bodies, and especially their livers, have been used in the preparation of many of those ancient remedies which seem so preposterous until we recall what effective inhibitors of bacilli can be made from mold; many of the cats and other animals destroyed by humane groups are rendered for their fat; catskins have been used in the fur trade, but the supply has always exceeded the demand—a catskin is not durable except when it is on a cat. The catgut which finds its way into violins and tennis rackets and surgical sutures does not come from cats but from sheep; according to Mrs. Mellen, the term may be a misusage of "kitgut," the old English word "kit" meaning a fiddle. Sometimes, in periods more recent than those of the Egyptian hunting cats, cats are reported to have brought food home to their human friends; when Sir Henry Wyatt was imprisoned in the Tower, his cat is said to have brought him pigeons. Cats have also from time to time been of service as forecasters of the weather and of such phenomena as earthquakes, or people have thought so.

But it is not these minor services and properties which earned the cat his place with people and retained that place for him. Cats and humans live together because the domestic cat is a hunter as his fathers were before him—is a sinuous stalker of small game and a pouncing thing with claws; because, as Dinictis was, as the tiger is, the littlest cat of them all is death clothed in beauty, a creature whose business it is to kill. For that purpose he is shaped, and for that purpose men have used him.

7

Cats, Birds and the Balance of Nature

PEOPLE MUST BE very puzzling to cats, since cats are above most animals rational and direct. Cats whisper to one another about people, courteously pretending that they are merely washing one another's ears. When they stare at people it is in the hope, still held although for thousands of years unrealized, that by prolonged scrutiny they may learn to resolve the obvious inconsistencies of the human mind. Our own Gin, who is fairly young and uncommonly eager to establish rapport between minds feline and human, often asks us pointed questions which we, having no good answers ready, pretend to think have to do with the imminence of dinner.

But what Gin really wants to know is why we feel as we do about birds. You praise me, she points out, when I catch a mouse; you are tolerant when I catch a rabbit. But when I bring you home a bird, which is really much more difficult to catch, you are cross with me. You say, "Bad cat!" and, "Drop it, Gin!" and you try to force my jaws open so the bird can escape. Sometimes you succeed in this, and the bird, about which I have troubled myself considerably, flies away. What is all this about birds?

Because, Gin continues—shaking her head, trying to make the issue clear even to the clouded human mind—it is as a hunter you keep me and my kind. By you, she says, keeping it clear, I mean all humans; for this discussion I am not Gin, but a specimen of Felis domestica. (We, as individuals, she adds, purring, rubbing against us, have other ties; I am very fond of you; I will follow you for long distances to be with you, and cry bitterly if you go into a fenced garden and leave me behind. But I am not talking about us as individuals. I am talking about cats and people.) We of Felis domestica are hired as hunters, but you scold me when I hunt the best.

What, she asks, is a bird but a mouse with wings—with wings and a voice which sets my nerves on edge, so that while I hunt mice without prejudice and without anger, I feel a special satisfaction when I still the raucous voice of a bird, much as you hunt mosquitoes with animus and kill them with pleasure? (This is why I often chatter when I see a bird; birds make me angry, as rabbits never do.) What is there about birds, except that they are a great trouble to a cat?

The answers are too obscure to give to Gin, so we give her dinner instead and for that, being a very active cat and hence usually hungry, she settles. Now and then, before she eats, she turns and shakes her head sadly, tolerantly. We are hers, and she loves us. We are not, however, very bright.

We could tell Gin, of course, that birds are often beautiful; that some of them make sounds which to human, if not to feline, ears are delightful; that in the flight of a bird man perceives a freedom he is denied, a lightness he covets. She could tell us that butterflies also are often beautiful and that birds kill butterflies; she could add that many birds make sounds as unpleasant to human as to feline ears, and could instance crows; she could suggest that freedom is in the mind, not in the possession of wings. As for killing birds, she could say further, men kill more than ever cats did and other birds kill not a few. Be reasonable, Gin might say—were she not philosophically eating her dinner. Try, for heaven's sake, to behave rationally.

To that we could only say that we do as well as we can, and that there are a good many people who do worse. We would not, however, tell her too much about the cult of the bird, in its most extreme form, since we do not wish to discourage her utterly with people. It is not for a cat to know that the Illinois State Legislature not long ago passed, amid catcalling, in what the Associated Press called a "kittenish mood," a Marauding Cats bill, which stipulated that cats should not be allowed out except on leash, that a roaming cat, captured, may be fined—through its owner—one dollar, and that this bill was passed at the instance of the president of Friends of Birds, Inc. The mere existence of an organization called Friends of Birds, Inc., would cause Gin to despair of humanity. (Martini, who has lived longer, would be saddened, but not surprised.)

The governor of Illinois, who harbors a cat, vetoed the bill, Gin would be pleased to know if the subject were brought to her attention, as it will not be. The magazine *Life* found space amid its pictures for an editorial article approving the veto—and then had to find space for letters denouncing *Life,* the Illinois governor and the feline tribe. One correspondent found it "disgusting how any civilized man can write an editorial in favor of lousy alley cats. One mocking bird is worth more than all the cats in the world." Another made the interesting announcement that "snakes and spiders do more actual good in rodent and insect control than do any of the four-legged, flea-bitten felines of which you write." (Gin would resent that last particularly. She has never had a flea in her life.) Yet another found in *Life*'s editorial, which had spoken slightingly of the whippoorwill, an insult to the Deep South and one more of the outraged humans concluded that anyone who approved cats must also approve "Al Capone and other gangsters."

Life's correspondents are, of course, extremists, as are many people who write letters to newspapers and magazines. But the bird-cat controversy brings out the extreme in almost everyone; there are few bird lovers as moderate as John Kieran, the authority on almost everything and most of all on birds, who likes cats well enough but birds better, remarks that "some of my favorite birds kill other birds," citing the Peregrine falcon, and adds, when we come to that, birds kill cats, too. (The cat killer is the great horned owl, a great lover of cat meat and, Mr. Kieran reports, possessed of talons "like ice picks." The horned owl has taken cats off the cats' own back porches; it is reported able to handle with no difficulty a full grown tomcat.)

Mr. Kieran is typical of the informed bird lovers and conservationists of the present, but by no means of those most commonly heard from, most prolific of letters to the editor, of articles against the cat in popular magazines and the house organs of such groups as Friends of Birds, Inc. The voice of reason is seldom heard in these matters, as in so many which concern the cat. It must be sought out and listened for. The voice of Edward Howe Forbush, the ferret and dog man of Massachusetts, still fills the land, although now it is heard in echoes. Large groups still live, or appear to live, in active terror lest cats wipe out all birds—and remain undisturbed by the fact that man has already wiped out a good many, apparently for his amusement, and recently brought wholesale death to "our little songsters" in the Middle West by indiscriminate use of DDT.

Mr. Forbush, obviously a sincere if furious man, is to a considerable degree responsible for this alarm. Between 1915 and 1918—a period during which many people were more concerned about the decimation of animals rather larger than birds—magazines in the United States were flooded with pro-bird, anti-cat articles and most of these were, sometimes admittedly, rewrites of Mr. Forbush's pamphlet, issued by the Massachusetts Agricultural Board as "Economic Biology Bulletin 1-2." As recently as 1940, a writer on the "Status of the Domestic Cat" in the Wisconsin Conservation *Bulletin* repeated, little changed, the significant points of Mr. Forbush's article, although by then considerable further study had been given to the subject. As recently as 1949, an unnamed expert of the Audubon Society was quoted in *The New Yorker* as guessing that "common house cats may take a hundred million bird lives a year" although he added, anxiously: "Please don't put me down as anti-cat. Cats are as much a part of the balance of nature as birds are."

Where the expert got his figures is anyone's guess; where he got his cat tolerance was not from Mr. Forbush.

The world pictured by Mr. Forbush crawls with cats, none of whom is needed. "The cat," he reports, in the dispassionate language of a scientist, "has disturbed the biological balance and has become a destructive force among native birds and mammals. It is a member of one of the most bloodthirsty and carnivorous families of the mammalia and makes terrific inroads on weaker creatures. It is particularly destructive to certain insect-eating forms of life, such as birds, moles, shrews, toads, etc. . . . The pet of the children, the

admired habitué of the drawing room or the salon by day may become at night a wild animal pursuing, striking down and torturing its prey, frequently making night hideous with its cries, sneaking into dark, filthy, noisome retreats or taking to the woods and fields where it perpetrates untold mischief. Now it ravages the dove-cote, now it steals on the mother bird asleep on her nest, striking bird, nest and young to the ground. In the darkness of night, it turns poacher. No animal it can reach and master is safe from its ravenous clutches."

Nor is this terrifying animal, this wild predator, infrequently encountered. In Massachusetts the Commission on Fisheries and Game reported to Mr. Forbush that there was at least one stray cat to each hundred acres in the state and that all of them, killing each a bird every ten days, exterminate two million birds a year. Twenty-six correspondents, aiding Mr. Forbush in his research, provided him with statistics showing, if conceivably not proving, that 226 cats killed 624 birds in a day, each cat getting 2.7 birds in each twenty-four hours. Cats, he reports, kill meadow larks, hummingbirds, flickers, robins, warblers, wrens, woodpeckers, woodcocks, cedar waxwings, grouse, heath hens, thrushes, bobwhites, ruffed grouse, pheasants, partridges, snipe, doves, chickens, young turkeys, squirrels, hares, rabbits, moles, shrews, rats, mice, bats, reptiles, mollusks, insects and weasels. That some of the animals in this list—squirrels for example—also kill birds is beside the point; that cats kill and eat insects (which are not too good for them) is not to be seriously considered, since a major point in the anti-cat argument must be, and is, that only birds are of value as insect destroyers.

Against the cat, few natural enemies are arrayed and if cats are to be eliminated the task is up to man. Foxes now and then kill cats, although preferring chickens; wolves and lynx may take a cat here and there and Mr. Forbush mentions, somewhat with his mind averted, the great horned owl. But if our birds—and our balance of nature—are to be protected, mankind must get to work. Mr. Forbush's article is a rallying call.

It is best, of course, to kill the cat and that simple and desirable solution appears first on the Forbush list. Failing that—and people have been failing it for many generations—he suggests: confining the cat, feeding the cat well, feeding the cat raw meat, keeping it on leash, belling it, putting cat guards on trees, putting barbed wire on trees, keeping only light-colored cats, electrocuting cats, shooting cats with air guns, hitting them with stones, throwing torpedoes at them; whipping offending cats; tying dead birds to their collars, preferably after putting pepper or kerosene on the carcasses, drenching the cat with water and setting the dogs on it. He would require that all cats be licensed and collared (which would serve his major purpose, since out-of-doors cats so equipped probably would end by hanging themselves) and urges legislation providing that unlicensed cats be killed "in a humane manner." He suggests, also, that cats have few legal rights in any case and may be killed by almost anyone almost anywhere except, possibly, on the premises of the cat owner.

The ferret and the dog, as we have seen, take care of the rat-mouse problem and, with that so conveniently solved, there would be only gain were the cat to go. The agriculturist, to whom Mr. Forbush's remarks are primarily directed, would then find, as the bird population increased, that the insects which damage crops would vanish into birds and that the world would be a brighter place.

These were, in 1915, the essential arguments advanced by the cat detesters and bird lovers. They have remained so since, being expounded sometimes with more seeming detachment—Mr. Forbush leaves no doubt as to where he stands—but at no time more ingeniously or at greater length. (They are only very briefly summarized in the foregoing.) And certainly if all these things were true they were grievous faults in cats and much could be said for the Forbush crusade as both necessary and moral.

The issues are fairly clear: How great actually is the cat depredation on bird life? Is it sufficient to reduce bird population to a point where the balance of nature is disturbed? Is the value of birds as great to the agriculturist as Mr. Forbush assumes? Is the value of the cat as slight?

The exact extent of cat depredation has usually been only guessed at. Mr. Forbush himself illustrated his pamphlet with fairly gruesome pictures of dead cats, in one instance hanging on a line with the proud killer posed alongside, and with captions indicating that the high incidence of feral—i.e., wild domestic—cats was thus proved. And where there are cats, it is flatly assumed, there will not be birds, because the cats will have eaten them.

Now it is easy to set amateur observation against amateur observation. Most of Mr. Forbush's twenty-six correspondents were people who "knew" certain things about cats, in the sense that most people "know" that cats are color blind. No scientific observation was attempted; the two million birds killed in Massachusetts are guesswork, done once over lightly—two thousand? twenty thousand? two hundred thousand? Come, let us be generous; ciphers cost us nothing. Two million is a fine round figure. Let us say, as the Audubon expert does, that cats may kill a hundred million birds a year. Who can prove us wrong?

Nobody can prove them wrong, obviously. But here and there, working without too much fanfare, writing for such publications as the *Journal of Mammology,* which is not universally read, scientists have made controlled observations. Paul L. Errington of Iowa State College, for example, made a study of cats and birds in Wisconsin in the early nineteen thirties, urged to it by reports that cats were wiping out the bobwhite quail before hunters could get to them. And Dr. Errington did not merely kill cats and hang them on a line. He took them apart to see what they had been eating. He examined the stomachs of fifty cats, of which seven had been pets, thirty-nine self-sufficient hunters and two definitely established as feral. Most of them had been eating mice.

Twenty-six of the cats had made their last meal off meadow mice and eight off deer mice. Three had found house mice which, one may assume, had wandered from houses. Nine had eaten un-identified mice and seven had made away with, and were trying to digest, Norway rats. Three had caught and eaten rabbits; one had caught a short-tailed shrew; three were attempting to ingest the heads and feet of chickens—presumably found in garbage dumps; three were full of grasshoppers, one cat had been eating crickets and another June-bugs; twenty-one had found remnants of human food and had eaten that; one had eaten a heavy cord and another a piece of cloth. (Cats notoriously eat unwisely; a cat belonging to a friend of ours ate steel wool and lived to talk of it, but he had a veterinarian for owner.)

Two of these cats had caught and eaten English sparrows; three had killed "unidentified small birds" and one, triumphantly, had achieved a pigeon. None of these cats, examined between October 15, 1929, and January, 1932, had eaten of bobwhite quail. This disturbing news had not, in 1940, reached the Missouri State Game and Fish Department, a representative of which was willing to be quoted in the Wisconsin Conservation *Bulletin* that his department "has long contended that cats in Missouri each year kill more game than do hunters." Unless mice are included as "game," Missouri cats differ from those of Wisconsin; they are no doubt an offshoot of the Massachusetts cat. This is a little odd, since cats in near-by Oklahoma are like Wisconsin cats in their food habits. A test made in Oklahoma in 1941 showed that, of the feral cats killed and examined, fifty-five percent had been eating rodents, twelve and a half percent insects; four percent birds, two percent reptiles and twenty-six and one half percent miscellaneous human food.

Dr. Errington's conclusions are, as one might suppose, somewhat less sensational than those of Mr. Forbush, possibly because he had looked more deeply into the subject matter. He "found scant evidence of adult strong winter birds suffering cat predation to any extent. Well accommodated populations [of bobwhite] lost at a low rate through winter predation; material depredations in other instances represented largely the removal of an ill-situated surplus or that part of the population in excess of environmental carrying capacity. . . . From the above thesis there is apparent the probability that any study of the house-cat intended thoroughly to divulge its ecological status would have to answer not only the question of what the cat eats but the actual effect its preying may have upon the species in question. Preying upon a species is not synonymous with controlling it or influencing its numbers to any perceptible degree. Predation which merely removes an exposed prey surplus that is naturally doomed anyway is entirely different from predation the weight of which is instrumental in forcing down prey populations or in holding them at given approximate levels."

It will be noted that Dr. Errington's investigation was into cat depredation on a game bird—on a bird, that is, not prized for its charm or its song, not of primary interest to Friends of Birds, whether or not incorporated, but dear to the hearts and guns of sportsmen. Most of the effective work at cat suppression is, in fact, being done in the interest of people who hope to eat birds, not to watch them, or listen to them. In many states—New Jersey and New York among them—any hunter may kill any cat, feral or house pet, he finds "poaching" among "any birds protected by law"; in many states, game wardens are expected to kill hunting cats on sight, and do.

Mankind, also "one of the most bloodthirsty and carnivorous families of the mammalia," has already wiped out certain bird populations even more thoroughly than he wiped out the bison and he, likewise, must be restrained by law if he is not to upset the balance of nature. Man, when not in the salon or drawing room, is also a hunter, perpetrating "untold mischief." It is clear that between the sportsman and the cat the moral issue is obscure and the dispassionate must be guided by personal preference. Ethical principles will not aid in determining whether a young bird should be protected from a small, hungry animal in order that it may become a larger bird and be killed by a bigger animal which is not hungry.

It is generally true, indeed, that nature has an excellent chance of staying in balance as long as man keeps his hand off the scales. This fact is nowadays generally recognized, as the hasty afterthought from the Audubon Society's expert indicates; increasingly (one at any rate hopes) the saner counsel of such as John Kieran prevails, and one is not forced to so drastic a choice as that between cats and birds. For the present-day view among conservationists, one may more wisely turn to such authorities as Mr. Richard Pough than to such extremists as Mr. Forbush. Cats do not greatly frighten Mr. Pough, who is curator of conservation of the American Museum of Natural History and is associated also with the Audubon Society. It is possible, Mr. Pough suggests, that Mr. Forbush was an alarmist —and that he was rather glib about the balance of nature.

There is no evidence which Mr. Pough has encountered, and it is his business to encounter evidence in such connections, that feral cats have depressed bird populations anywhere. A great concentration obviously might prove depressing; so might a great concentration of anything, including man. As concerns northern latitudes, which would include Massachusetts, the number of feral cats probably is not actually great, since the winters are too severe for most cats to endure and the great horned owl is apt to be hungry and rampant. A few feral cats make it, almost always with the tips of their ears frozen off; if they live in Wisconsin or Oklahoma, it is evident that they make it chiefly at the expense of mice.

(A black cat, or conceivably a succession of black cats, made it for several years a few miles from Brewster, New York, and there the winters are frequently severe. We saw this cat often, at a distance; at intervals with kittens; living largely on what she found in garbage pits. She would be there in November, when we returned to the city, and be there still in late March when we came back. Why she did not freeze we never knew; her ears were frozen; what she ate in the winters when the garbage pits were no longer supplied we also did not know, although she was often seen with mice. In our brief glimpses of her she never had a bird and, although our garbage pit was bordered by bird-infested trees, she never seemed to look at them. But we have no doubt she caught them, since Gin and Martini sometimes do and her cunning must be greater than theirs.)

The domestic cat who still lives at home is another matter and there can be no doubt he kills a good many birds. But it is also true, as Mr. Pough points out, that the areas where house and barn cats are most numerous—farm lands, city suburbs—are at the same time those in which the native predators are fewest, so that again nature balances. And—always as long as man keeps his hands out of it, his guns out of it—there are enough birds to go around.

There are a great many birds; in many areas there are already too many birds. Dr. Errington hints at this in his summary; to modern conservationists, if not to incorporated bird lovers, it is an accepted fact. There are enough pigeons in New York City, for example; the Audubon Society is pleased, rather than alarmed, that duck hawks have recently discovered this and are moving in, nesting on the roofs of towering buildings, diving at an estimated two hundred miles an hour on wandering pigeons. The society does not advocate the destruction of the duck hawk in behalf of pigeons, for duck hawks are, in the words of *The New Yorker*'s expert, "beautiful to watch, rare and protected by law." (Cats are only beautiful to watch.) And conservationists are by no means afraid we will run out of robins.

In the suburban and near rural area about New York, for example, there are already more robins than there is room for robins. This is because, as the most amateur observer knows, robins insist on exclusive jurisdiction over a prescribed area during nesting time. They lay out claims like prospectors; they will fight to the death if necessary against any intruder. Being easily misled creatures, they will also fight their own reflections in windows and other polished surfaces. We spent the better part of a day some years ago in trying to save a robin from what seemed a determination to beat out its brains, which evidently were not numerous, against the shining hubcap of a Buick. Frantically the bird flew at the robin in the hubcap, banging head and beak, clawing angrily until it dropped exhausted. It would rest a little then, glaring at the hubcap. When able it would rise and look again. And again that intruding robin would be there and again the indomitable, if half-witted, bird would fly to the attack. We chased it away, we tried to distract it—meanwhile locking up the cats. We moved the car into the shade. Nothing worked, until finally we took the car and drove off for an hour or two.

This in the end apparently satisfied the robin. The foe had fled; he could return, battered, to his mate, who must have thought he had involved himself in a saloon brawl. (There was great scolding from the nest that evening.) He had proved his right to nest in the area which was his by pre-occupation and beak and claw. He would have fought as angrily against a real intruder and driven it off if he could.

A good many robins are so driven off and, lacking an area of operation—a homestead—do not breed. This is true of many other common birds; in the area around New York, indeed, all common species of birds are now at the saturation point. There is simply no more room for further birds; the population is complete. And it may be expected, regardless of cat or other depredation, and short of unforeseeable catastrophe, to remain complete. Robins, for example, have a life expectancy of three to four years, although some of them live twice as long. They have two broods a year of, usually, four birds each. Thus, with normal luck, a pair of robins may expect to produce from twenty-four to thirty-two robins during their lifetimes. It is clear that, with the population at saturation point, all but two of these, necessary for replacement, are "an exposed prey surplus that is naturally doomed away," as Dr. Errington says. Nature is wasteful in achieving her balance; she provides more birds than she needs, or than the world needs. If the cat—or the farmer's dog, which, because he ranges farther and has better scent, is considered by Mr. Pough to be a worse problem to game birds than is the cat—keeps this surplus down, he is balancing, not unbalancing.

Except on a humanitarian basis, man's interest is in the number of birds which are left, not in those which are killed. "Preying upon a species," again to quote Dr. Errington, "is not synonymous with controlling it or influencing its numbers to any perceptible degree." Mr. Forbush's horrid picture of a birdless world is no more likely to be transferred to nature's canvas than is the, to him, more attractive one of a world without cats.

Amateur observation bears this out; our own observation bears it out. For more than fifteen years we spent much summer time, and most recently all of the springs and summers and early autumns, at the camp near Brewster. During most of these years we had cats—one cat first, then two, finally three. There were many birds around when we first went there; there were at least as many during the last year we spent there and in the summer before the last—for some reason a bumper bird season—there were more than we had ever seen. Always robins were busy on the lawns, pulling out of them the worms which are essential to the formation of friable soil; always catbirds were busy with catbird tasks; woodpeckers were digging holes, sometimes in the roof; crows were making mornings hideous and corn cultivation almost impossible; orioles were passing in beauty, and red-winged blackbirds and bluebirds and jays; hummingbirds were poised in dazzling flight, hanging like vari-colored sparks on the fringe of delphinium. Wrens nested under the eaves in certain years and began with the dawn that incredible chatter which is pent up in wrens and must come out when it is light. Toward dusk swallows were swift and erratic in the air and often there were owls. It may be one of them was a great horned owl and it was the end of the cat named Jerry.

From time to time the cats killed birds. We were always sorry, but we never belled the cats or poured water on them or hung about their necks bird carcasses saturated with kerosene. We scolded them; if they brought the birds home, we tried to free the birds and often were successful.

(Several times, incidentally, our intervention was not necessary; the birds freed themselves. This is not uncommon, particularly when the bird is good-sized and vigorous. Early in his career Pete —who later in life gave up birding altogether as a waste of effort— captured a thrush of considerable size. He brought it to the vicinity of the cabin, so that we could see it, and then put it down on the grass so he could look at it himself. The bird immediately took wing, gaining altitude rapidly with Pete leaping despairingly after it. When he realized it was beyond recovery, Pete sat down and looked after it. Then he began to cry. Almost he sobbed, so that in the end we had to console him as best we could. More recently, Gin lost a bird under similar circumstances. She did not sob. She swore.)

There were always enough birds around to look at and to listen to, and to do whatever services to man birds perform. Mr. Forbush thinks these services are great, but this again is a matter of opinion. They do eat insects, the harmful and the harmless indiscriminately. Undoubtedly they are so serviceable, although they are no substitute for dusting in the bean patch, and almost all of them are indifferent to Japanese beetles. (Starlings are reported to have a taste for them, but few people have a taste for starlings.) Certainly they do not eat as many insects as man would like them to, perhaps because, as Mr. Pough suggests, all predatory creatures seem by instinct to preserve the balance of nature which most concerns them—the future food supply. Birds never eat so many insects as to interfere seriously with the insect population, taking care to leave at least a breeding nucleus—else what would birds do next year? It is unfortunate that birds behave so in relation to tomato worms which, incidentally, they seem to have small taste for; it is fortunate that they are similarly foresighted in regard to earthworms, since the elimination of earthworms would be disastrous to all of us.

Birds are useful to men; they are also harmful. They eat some insects which might eat pea vines. But they also eat peas on the vines. Seeds from which the gardener hopes to achieve flowers are merely birdseeds to the many ground-eating birds and it is sometimes a question whether, in laboriously preparing a bed for flower seeds which can be covered only lightly if at all, one is planting a garden or setting a table for avifauna. With birds as with cats, one must take the good with the bad. Crows—although no less a gardener than Rex Stout defends them as potential pets and had one once which got drunk regularly on the terrace, sipping from highball glasses; finally, when too inebriate to stand easily, wrapping wings about a glass to steady it while he drank—crows seem to us altogether bad. They make mornings hideous with their squawking and when corn shoots are a few inches out of the ground they dig them up to get at the germinating seeds. If circumvented in this, if the corn is, despite them, got to grow, they begin to eat corn on the cob as soon as it is ready. There is nothing good to be said of crows, at least when they are sober.

It is conceivable that incorporated bird lovers do not consider crows to be birds as they do not consider turkeys to be birds. (The New York Audubon Society not long ago served roast turkey at its annual dinner.) But unaffiliated bird admirers, such as we are, must count the crows with the engaging catbirds—and wish that our cats did also. But none of our cats has ever caught a crow, and several have been chased by them.

If it may be argued that there are already enough birds, and far too many crows, it must be argued that the extermination of the domestic cat would upset, not redress, nature's balance—and this without regard to the resulting inbalance of rodents, which might prove disastrous. Since this extermination is unlikely to occur, one must have recourse to analogy to estimate the possible results. The analogy is not hard to find, and it concerns one of the little cat's bigger cousins—the mountain lion, known variously as the cougar, the puma, the catamount, the painter and the panther. This cat, than whom there is, in the words of one scientist, "no better example of the splendid feline race," once ranged the North American continent, from Canada to Florida, crossed the Isthmus and found habitat in much of South America. He used to live primarily on deer.

The white man exterminated him in the eastern and central parts of North America and, except for some parts of Florida, he lives now—and there precariously—only in the high mountains of the West. With him they exterminated the greatest natural enemy of the deer, a creature prized alike by those who like animals in their living grace and those who prefer them roasted. And now, everywhere in the country, there are too many deer.

Meeting in Washington in the spring of 1949, the North American Wildlife Conference took up the deer problem and worried it, and was worried by it—and did not solve it. For now the forests are full of deer, which is bad for the forests, and deer are spilling out into the farmer's fields, which is bad for the farmer. Deer, while dainty creatures, are great eaters. If there are enough of them in the woods, they will eat down the new forest growth, and in many places there are enough of them and that is what they are doing. They will also eat crops. They are eating them, at great cost to the farmer, in Pennsylvania, in New York, in New Jersey and throughout New England.

More than twenty years ago, while sentimentalists wept, Pennsylvania established an antlerless-deer season and has since had fifteen such seasons, in which a total of 566,093 deer have been killed. Farmers have been permitted to kill 17,000 more, out of season, when they caught them destroying crops. There are still too many deer in Pennsylvania. In most New York counties, landowners may obtain permits to kill deer found damaging crops, and many are killed so, in addition to those killed by hunters during the allowed seasons. There are still too many deer in New York. Driving at night on minor highways, one must be careful not to run into them. Driving along New York Route 22, a major highway, we have seen deer grazing in pastures with the cattle.

In Maine, where deer are everywhere, farmers have recently been experimenting with deer-repellent crop sprays, precisely as if deer were Japanese beetles. In Maine the state assumes responsibility for deer damage, and in 1947 it paid out $60,000 in claims. And each year the deer grow more numerous and the damage grows greater. This is true not only in the East; a federal forest preserve near the Grand Canyon was finally, some years ago, rid of mountain lions. Government conservators gratefully dusted the hands which they had been pressing down on nature's balance, and went on to other useful pursuits. The deer multiplied—they began to destroy the forest and also they began to starve since a forest has a definite carrying capacity of deer, as a pasture has of cattle. The government conservators had to go back again. They had to import and loose, at considerable trouble and expense, enough mountain lions to save the woods.

"These native cats of ours," Dr. Edwin H. Colbert writes, "play a very useful role in the workings of nature. The deer, and likewise the rabbits [prey of the lynx, also nearly exterminated] if uncontrolled multiply excessively and do much damage to the forest cover. Man can control these animals after a fashion, but efficient control depends largely upon natural agents. And among these natural agents are our predatory cats, the mountain lion and the lynxes."

Man's meddling with this natural balance has gone on endlessly and goes on today. The chain of events is sometimes amusing, and as intricate as Darwin's cat-red-clover sequence. Some fifteen years ago, for example, Europe, in one of its moments of peace, was swept by enthusiasm for leopard-skin coats. Leopard skins became more valuable. Now much of Africa is infested with bush pigs and baboons, described by Jean Paul Harroy, of the International Office for the Protection of Nature at Brussels, as two of the most destructive animals in the world. The skins of the cats who long kept these pests in check are now being worn by other animals, on whom they are seldom so becoming.

Extermination of domestic cats to encourage birds, as suggested by Mr. Forbush, might prove as inconvenient to mankind in the end as has the extermination of the mountain lion. No one, fortunately, is likely to find out, since cat lovers are also, in their fashions, incorporated, and since mankind has long disapproved of rats and mice. And birds will get along well enough, multiply sufficiently, fill the air with song and discord, vary in beauty from hummingbird to crow, as they always have.

Yet we, and most other country cat lovers, will continue to scold our cats for catching birds, so proving human inconsistency to the logical minds of cats. We will continue to try, in ways less drastic than those recommended by Mr. Forbush, to discourage cats in this natural pursuit of theirs. We will not, however, be altogether hopeful.

Some cat owners have, or believe they have, persuaded their cats not to hunt birds and it is unquestionably true that cats and birds have been taught to live together, at least long enough to have their pictures taken and probably at the cost of great mental strain, leading to neuroses. Taking birds away from cats may, in time, discourage cats, although we have found little evidence of this. Mr. Forbush's suggestion that one keep only light-colored cats is nonsense; Gin, a fairly light Siamese, is as good a bird-cat as was Pete, who was all black where it counted. Keeping cats in at night, which is not at all difficult if they are altered (as they should be, unless one is breeding cats intentionally) reduces their bird depredations and also prolongs the cats. Great horned owls come out at night, and so do great-lighted motorcars, in front of which cats may stand blinded and wait for death.

The feral cat problem could be solved readily enough by a slight increase in human decency, for which one may always hope. For the ranks of feral cats are not filled, although occasionally they may be augmented, by pet cats who have left their homes. The feral cat, ninety-nine times out of a hundred, is a cat whose home has left him.

More people like kittens than like cats; the only trouble with kittens, they will tell you, only half jesting, is that they grow inevitably into cats. This is not, of course, quite true; a kitten can very easily be prevented from growing into a cat. There are two ways of doing this: One may quickly, as mercifully as is convenient, kill the kitten when it is six months old or so; one may, avoiding so honest a course, turn the kitten out to fend for itself, thus usually achieving the same result while keeping, as man can so easily do, that valued possession known as a clear conscience.

It is not difficult, in city or country, to get oneself into the predicament which makes this choice necessary. In the country there are many kittens in the spring; in the city young cats are often willing to follow home humans who do not reject them out of hand. Kindheartedness may involve almost anyone with a young cat—that and the cat's own charm. Since the sense of responsibility is often dormant in the human race, even in man's relation with his fellows, this is not surprising. But it is apt to be rather hard on cats.

A family, perhaps with a child or two, moves to the country for the summer. A kitten, finding the house occupied, being on his own, drops in. Or the children ask for a cat, and almost any farm has a young cat to spare. And in the country, cats are no trouble—when they want to go out they will mention it, they will eat almost anything. They will let the children romp with them—usually too roughly. They are infinitely playful and engaging; they will chase shadows on the lawn and are captivating in the eagerness with which they pounce on dangled strings. A reciprocal love affair is very likely to develop in June and in July and in August.

But then comes Labor Day, that moment of exodus by summer people; that day of worried packing, of regrets, of thoughts of school and apartment house confinement. Already, the cat is in the way; now it is not amusing that the cat gets into the box, plays with the string. Now the cat is a nuisance. And if a nuisance now, what will it be in the confines of the city apartment, where furniture is to be clawed instead of trees, where toilet facilities must be provided? Anyway, it is not the kitten it was, by now; by now it is more than half cat. It may even have begun to make unmistakably clear which kind of cat it is.

The children still are fond of the little cat, to be sure. But school will distract them, new interests will come. And next summer—who knows?—there may be another cat. Meanwhile, there is this cat, and this cat—not really a kitten any more—is a problem. It is a problem which, if there is no other way, a few sleeping pills will solve, but that seems so cruel, doesn't it? Perhaps, if there were time, we might try to find a home for it, but now—now with a sudden great rush the summer is over, the country is dead—there is no time for that. It is simpler all around merely to leave the cat. Cats have nine lives, as everyone knows. Cats are self-sufficient. Cats do not really care about people anyway; they always find new homes, and one home is like another to a cat.

Across the road from the cabin near Brewster there was a large settlement of summer people and almost none of them ever saw autumn in the country—saw the soft-colored days of October, the sharp gray days of early November. On the evening of the first Monday in September they went home—and left their cats. (Their dogs, although infinitely more trouble in an apartment, they took along.) In the hot, sunny days of mid- and late September, we would see those cats, most of them long well-cared-for, still retaining confidence in people. A fine young tom would come across a lawn to one of us, crying a little, puzzled a little, more than a little hungry, but still confident, still with his tail in the air.

We could do nothing, being at the cat saturation point. We could not even be too friendly, because one's own cats are jealous creatures; we could not feed, since then the cat would think he had found a home and would abandon further search—search while days were warm still, and nights not too cold, and a cat could make a go of it. We might have been honest too, of course. During the last few years we kept available a bottle of sleeping pills which our veterinarian prescribed. But we were cowardly as the others in the end; we never used the pills. A cat always has a chance of sorts, and killing lies on the conscience. What ever happened to that fine young tom, we wonder? Perhaps he found a good home.

Perhaps, of course, he did. It is comforting to look on the bright side of things. Even now he may be catching mice for people.

But most probably he died slowly as the winter came and food became harder to get; when the nights were cruel and the days not much better. Probably, in the insufficient cover he could find (he was not an experienced cat; he had been taught cats live in the warmth of houses, eat out of dishes prepared for them) he froze to death one night. Or perhaps, since he was obviously a husky animal, he made it after all, even through a New York winter. Perhaps now he is a feral cat, running in fear from humans, facing them bitterly if cornered. He is thin and tough and his once pointed ears are rounded, because ears freeze first. He will kill anything he can find, and he hunts at night. He "poaches"; he will eat "protected" birds if he can come on them. The people who abandoned him to this will tell you that kittens are delightful, but they grow into cats; will tell you that cats are cruel and constitute a great menace to bird life.

The unwanted cat is not, of course, a problem peculiar to the country. No one knows how many homeless cats there are in a city like New York, except that the American Society for the Prevention of Cruelty to Animals knows there are thousands. They eat from garbage cans, go into "noisome" places after rats and mice, grow mangy and carry fleas. They—along with pet cats which are left free at night—howl on the fences. (They also transmit disease, to say nothing of fleas, to pet cats.) It is widely felt that they are better off dead, since their lives are miserable, and that it is humane to kill them. Presumably this is true, although the cats themselves do not think so. They are very hard to catch.

Sydney H. Coleman, executive vice president of the New York ASPCA, decided a few years ago that he and a group of agents would do something about an uncommon aggregation of homeless cats who were making nights noisy on the lower East Side. Everybody knew there were hundreds of independent cats there; everybody could hear them. Mr. Coleman and his men took along enough boxes for fifty cats, which they expected to pick up in an hour or two.

The people who lived in the area were right; there was no lack of cats. From midnight to four in the morning, the searchers saw scores. They saw them disappearing into previously invisible hideouts; they saw them going angrily over twelve-foot fences. The men were experts; they had been handling animals for years, cor-

nering stray dogs with little difficulty. And in four hours they caught precisely one cat and put it in a box and carried it away, yowling—yowling so loudly that Mr. Coleman expected at all times to be showered with old shoes and empty beer bottles. The cats did not, it appeared, wish to be destroyed, painlessly or not.

But many are, all the same. They are collected, still half alive, from ashcans in which their former friends deposit them when they begin to outgrow the kitten stage. They are picked up, still too small to go over fences, on the streets, having been carried far enough from home so that they cannot get back. There are what the ASPCA calls, unofficially, "cat women" who make it a hobby to collect cats and take them to the society. (Some of these women do this because they love cats; some because they hate them. Some are "fanatical," in Mr. Coleman's word; the society has to scrutinize each animal, since many cats brought in are obviously well-cared-for house pets who were kidnapped while out for an airing.)

In the year 1948, followers of Mr. Forbush will be gratified to learn, the New York ASPCA killed 168,029 cats out of the 168,814 it had available. It restored to their owners 115 kidnapped—or strayed—cats and found homes for 430. (Homes were found for 1,978 dogs in the same period, and 3,215 were returned to their owners and only 65,561 were killed. But only 72,035 dogs came under care.) Of the cats, 138,028 were voluntarily handed over by their owners, probably after they had lost their kittenish charms. The others came from the streets and ash cans, and from the "cat women."

A good many birds came under the care of the ASPCA during that period—robins, sea gulls, starlings, woodpeckers, a bluejay, a bluebird and a swan. Most of these were "released to freedom." The birds must have reported happily to their fellows in freedom that at the ASPCA cats were dying like worms and butterflies. White mice and white rats were also inmates of the society's shelters, but presumably they were not released. Had they been, and if white rats and mice speak to their dun brothers, the word that mankind was thus preserving nature's balance would have been a happy one to the city's fifteen million rodents.

8

The Anthropomorphic Cat

WHEN WE TELL the cat Gin she is "bad" because she catches birds, there are certain evidences she knows what we mean. Her ears may move back a little; she looks at us with what seems to be doubt in her slanting blue eyes. She does not go away, knowing that from us no physical violence will follow, but she does not come closer, rub against us purring, as she is likely to do when we say, "Nice Ginny. Good Ginny." One might suppose that the word "bad" had a special meaning for her, and even that it meant to her what, more or less, it does to us. Things far more improbable are supposed by many people about cats.

Actually, if we do not altogether imagine the change we think we see in Gin when she hears the word "bad," it is probable that she is reacting to a tone rather than to a word. Cats are responsive to the timbre of the human voice, as dogs are; if we called Gin a "bad cat" in the tones of affection we employ when we praise her, there can be no doubt she would come to us with her low-pitched remarks of pleasure and hold her head up to be stroked. It is by no means true that Gin understands every word we say to her, or even appears to. There are several human words incomprehensible even to Martini, and she may be a cat genius and is certainly of superior mentality.

But if Gin, and even Martini, actually understood the word "bad," or any of its gradations or opposites, neither would understand the concept, which is human and not feline and which is applied to cats by people with a childlike naivete which would, in itself, puzzle any cat. Almost no cat is naive; if we had not learned through long experience to be wary of generalization about these friends of ours, we would say flatly that no cat is ever naive. But that would mean only that we had never known a cat whose behavior reminded us of the behavior of a naive human being. Many cats may seem naive to other cats; the whole feline apparatus for revealing this, and other characteristics, may be quite different from the human apparatus. It is entirely possible that cats do not behave like human beings, and it is even possible that they have no desire to, although humans generally try to make them do so and almost always think of them as if they were rather peculiar and on the whole somewhat backward men and women.

This tendency to anthropomorphize the cat—to ascribe to it human characteristics and, as a logical result, to insist that it mimic human behavior in so far as it can—begins very early in the human mind and continues very late. Children think thus about the cat and so, as we presently shall see, did the late Dr. Edward Lee Thorndike, who was not in other respects notably childlike. It is an attitude of mind which is very convenient for the human, and one into which the human almost inevitably falls. Probably, indeed, it is unavoidable; probably the only tribute the human mind can pay to objectivity is a realization that it has not been attained. Even this tribute is rarely paid; there is, for example, every evidence that Dr. Thorndike not only sought scientific objectivity when he tested the intelligence of cats but believed he had found it, although almost nothing could have been further from the truth. In his whole approach to the feline mind, this very great psychologist behaved embarrassingly as did 2,835 children who, almost fifty years ago, were asked about their pets by G. Stanley Hall and C. E. Browne. The children thought of cats as small humans with fur and four legs; so, essentially, did Dr. Thorndike.

Most of the Hall-Browne children did not, as a matter of fact, write about cats at all, since 71.6 percent of them preferred dogs—a statistical indication of some interest and one of the few which science seems to have made available on the subject. Whether the ratio of preference continues into the human's later years is uncertain; probably it does to a considerable degree, although many people come to know and admire cats as they grow more mature and less in need of that assurance of superiority which the attention of a dog provides. Certainly at any age, at least in the United States, more people are dog than cat addicts and there is a social pressure to reveal that preference. This is particularly true of the male. It is "manly" to have a dog as a small boy—and it is also a great deal of fun, and dogs are durable in relation to small boys as cats seldom are. Of the 804 young cat fanciers queried by Dr. Hall and his associate, 582 were little girls and only 222 young males.

These 804, regardless of sex, liked the cat because of the way it played, were captivated by its grace in movement and the constancy of movement. (Most of the children probably knew kittens or young cats, and these are almost never quiet, except when, suddenly, almost without warning, they go sound asleep.) The movements of cats are infinitely varied; no cat does things precisely as another cat does, and few cats repeat their own movements, even when performing essentially identical actions. (Sherry, for example, has a peculiar twisting leap in play, going into the air to avoid the onslaughts of a bit of paper, turning in the air like an acrobat, as if pivoted on her right shoulder, coming down still facing the plaything with four feet planted and back a little arched. We have never seen another cat make precisely these movements, although we have seen many cats perform what is essentially the same play antic. And Sherry does not do her leap each time, or perhaps ever, with identical movements. There is nothing mechanical about it as there is, for example, about the forehand drive of a good tennis player.)

Almost without exception, the children who liked cats for these habits and accomplishments thought of the cats as if they too were children, ascribing to them the same motives, requiring of them adherence to the moral standards the children had been taught, usually—no doubt to the astonishment of the cats—feeding them the same food that children like to eat or are required to eat. Most of the children were certain their cats talked to them by purring, moving eyes and heads and tails in certain fashions, and were certain they knew what the cats were saying. The cats said, "I love you" to their young playmates; said, "I want some milk," "Open the door, please," "Don't be cross with me," "I'm sorry; I won't do it again." The cats also said, "I want my dinner," and were re-warded with some remarkable embellishments to the normal feline diet of raw meat.

The cats were fed ice cream, which most cats do like; they were also fed peanuts, candy and custard pie, all of which most children like better than most cats do. They also, in homes where the child's diet was carefully supervised, got milk and cream, eggs, cereals and meat. A few of them, the children reported, ate mice and rats and fish, but the child mind clung to the conviction that the cats really preferred peanuts and hard candy, since what child does not?

"The child's attitude toward the cat is largely anthropomorphic," Dr. Hall wrote in his conclusions, published in 1905 in the *Pedagogical Seminary*. "He attributes to the cat the same thoughts and feelings which he himself experiences and in his treatment of his pet unconsciously reveals his own standards of right and wrong, his tests of affection, his preferences and dislikes. In this connection one of the most interesting points brought out is the child's inclination to make the test of right and wrong an objective conformity to the will of the owner. . . .

"Children have the old conception of animals as moral beings fully responsible for the moral or immoral quality of their acts. In very few instances were the natural instincts of the cat taken into account; though catching rats and mice is often accounted a virtue, the catching of birds is designated as badness. It may be that in this moral objectivity there is a reflection of the regime to which the child himself has been subjected, for it is unfortunately too common to find children who regard an accident to their clothing or to property on the same plane with a moral offense, because the same punishment is meted out to both."

Dr. Hall decided also, from the data before him, that from their cats children derived a sense of authority, based largely on their superior size and strength—always desiderata when moral standards are to be established and kept in force. The investigator was left with the further conviction that keeping pets helps children develop a sense of responsibility and a humane attitude toward animals—which might, conceivably, later be broadened into a humane attitude toward humanity.

From the child to the adult mind is only a little step; sometimes, one suspects, it is not even that. Growing up, one may discover that cats prefer ground beef to peanuts; one may never learn that cats and other animals are not beings with man's morality; that to them it is naive and impertinent to apply such terms as "good" and "bad," charge such sins as cruelty. "Objective conformity to the will of the owner" may be asked and even insisted upon, although with a cat it is not at all likely to be achieved. But it cannot be characterized, cannot be called "good," unless we are willing to abandon all but the crudest standards of morality. It is obvious, of course, that in most of mankind's relations with other animals, to say nothing of his own inter-tribal relations, it is precisely these crude standards which are accepted. No doubt it is too much to hope that men will be more perceptive in their contacts with cats than they are in their contacts with other men.

But until men give over applying these human standards to cats there is little chance of establishing that confident understanding between the two orders of the mammalia which should be the goal of all men and all cats. There is no use expecting cats to behave like human beings, and in a good many areas of activity it is as well that they do not. It is, for example, no good hoping that cats will become humane and abandon practices which man, an authority on the subject, considers cruel.

It was cruel, and human, to behave as the jailers of the Inquisition are reported—no doubt libellously—to have behaved toward certain prisoners they would torment. Their unfortunate victims, long locked in darkness, hoping to see light again only in the flickering fires of the auto-da-fé, were sometimes given brief glimpses of miraculous hope. A cell door was not, perhaps, securely locked or, carelessly as it seem, an instrument was left available with which it could be opened. The prisoner, hope faintly stirring, would begin his escape and find that, true enough, the door would open, that the corridor outside it was deserted.

Then would begin a long, toilsome creeping toward the light;

a cautious movement through stone corridors, quick retreats into available niches, ascents of interminable flights of stairs. And always this flight from darkness would be aided, would seem to be aided, by many tiny miracles—by jailers who did not look when hiding was impossible and discovery would have been certain; by doors unaccountably left unlocked, chains insecurely stapled. So, with hope growing slowly, the prisoner crept toward the light— crept until finally, at the end of a dark corridor, he could finally see the light; could see it through an open door, could stumble forward, blinded by light, a little more rapidly. It was not until he was almost at the door, could feel the outer air on his face, that the men who had been waiting stepped from concealment and put chains again on the miscreant and, one supposes, laughed. It was very amusing, very human—and very cruel, this cat-and-mouse game.

It is, of course, not too unlike the game the cat plays with the mouse, although it is more ingenious in the torment it inflicts, since man is a more ingeniously sadistic animal than a cat. The only difference is that man knows better and the cat does not; that in doing such things man violates, derides, his own humanity. Man puts himself not on the level of the cat, but on an infinitely lower level, because the cat is cruel only by man's standards and not by his own. There are no humanitarian cats; none to say, as men have said when man's history was darkest, that certain things are unworthy of cats; no cat has ever formed the concept of "cruelty" and so, essentially, no cat can be cruel. When men do what cats do, men are cruel. They often do; one does not need to go back to the Inquisition to find proof of this in man's history. "Even owners of factories employing child labor and dramatic critics have told me that cats are cruel," Carl Van Vechten remarks quietly in his famous book on cats.

Many others, in more tenable moral positions, have made that charge and amplified it and always, as when they call the cat "sly" and "crafty," they have been anthropomorphizing the cat and, at the same time, sentimentalizing the cat. The two things go together; they are parallel manifestations of the difficulty men have always had in looking at the cat as a cat, and agreeing that it be allowed to remain a cat. Possibly man has been misled by his experience with dogs, because it is much easier to apply to dogs the standards to which humans verbally adhere and to get the dogs to play along.

It is easy, indeed, to believe that the dog would very much like to be a man, just as man would like to make himself over in the image of God. The ambition of a well-brought-up dog—that is to say, of a "good" dog—is to please his master before himself and the means he employs to accomplish this are commonly more human than subtle. He is demonstrative in displays of affection as many people are, and as almost all people would like others to be toward them; the dog leaves you no doubt where you stand and when he gives his devotion, as he does readily, he is apt to give it fulsomely, so that for a little while the meanest human can see himself godlike in the dog's beaming eyes. The dog is uncritical; one of the best known dogs of literature belonged to Bill Sikes, certainly one of literature's meanest men, and followed his master to death in, it must be admitted, one of the most improbable scenes of melodrama ever to come from human pen. Dogs are continually wasting away on the graves of their deceased masters, dying of broken hearts during less permanent separations and otherwise behaving with an almost human lack of reticence. If you want to go for a walk, there is nothing a good dog wants more; if you want to sit by the fire, so does the dog, looking up now and then from his sleep with tender eyes, making sure that you have not left him. If you want to play games, the dog will learn them eagerly, and play them with zest; a dog may be trained to walk on his hind feet, which makes him ridiculous, and to "speak" for his dinner. If he had the words, he would no doubt be happy to recite for company.

This canine desire to do everything the human wishes, to shape his whole life to human rather than to canine preferences, is naturally very gratifying to man. It supports man's assurance that he is in all respects superior, corroborates his belief that all animals would be simian if they could. And it makes the dog lovable to all people capable of affection; it is difficult to see how anyone can resist a dog, whose whole being is bent on proving himself irresistible.

The dog is a sunny animal; if he had ever been a god, he would have been a god of light. And if, as Nelson Antrim Crawford has unkindly suggested, he now and then reminds one of a bond sales-man, there is no harm in bond salesmen and they, also, tend to be creatures of the greatest cordiality.

It is also easy to understand a dog, at least superficially. One may assume, with some safety, that when a dog behaves as a human would under given circumstances he is feeling as nearly as he can as a human would under those circumstances. When a dog smiles, he smiles like a man. When he greets his master with bounds of delight, he clearly feels delight; he is a human throw-ing arms about a returned loved one. When a dog licks you, it is probable that he is kissing you. (When a cat licks you, it may well be to see how you taste.) A dog who is spoken to crossly sinks into shame and abasement, and does it notice-ably; a whipped dog cowers as a whipped man does—or, if the man's pride will not let him, longs to do. To a kind word fol-lowing punishment, the whole dog brightens. The authority one can exercise over a dog provides a gratification hardly to be equalled now that human slavery is, in some parts of the world, abolished.

And, because he is convinced that man knows best—is convinced, surely, that man *is* best—the dog will accept, or seem to accept, man's codes of behavior. Often, indeed, he accepts them much more wholeheartedly than man does. One can persuade a dog that it is "wrong" to eat canapés from the coffee table and it is reported to us by dog owners that many dogs will continue not to eat canapés even when humans are absent. We knew, for many years, a fox terrier who had been persuaded it was "wrong" to go to the second floor of the house he lived in and who consequently never went there, even when the family was away. (He was believed not to, at any rate, and since he was always shedding on the furniture he was reasonably easy to trace.) The same dog, who never seemed to us notable in intelligence, knew it was "wrong" to sleep on the down-stairs furniture, but that temptation was more than he could resist. He always, however, got down when he heard the family coming, and always landed on the floor with a revealing thump. He retained for some minutes after these violations of the code the expression so aptly called "hang-dog."

No cat we have ever known would have got off the chair in deference to human wishes and there is no facial expression that can be called "hang-cat." Nor have we ever known a cat who considered it "wrong" to eat all the canapés he could reach, if he liked them, although we have taught one or two that it may prove inexpedient. A cat's interests remain feline, not human, as do his habits. If he likes you—and cats often fall in love with people—it is because he approves of you as an individual; he makes allowances for your humanity, but he does not envy it. All his ways are his, and none of them are human. It is clear that he would not be a human if he could.

This refusal to fit into an anthropomorphic pattern irritates many people, and particularly those who like to keep life simple and on a plane of ready understandability. It is difficult to understand a cat, who persists in being "different," a vice which many humans cannot tolerate, even in other humans.

Now there is, evidently, no reason why any human should bother to understand a cat. It is not necessary to know cats; when one encounters them, as one is likely to in a world heavily cat-populated, one can easily ignore them. All people can live without cats; even cat addicts probably could if they tried, and this without too drastic deprivation. It is not necessary to have any opinions about cats, and having wrong opinions endangers neither one's standing in society nor one's immortal soul. It is, of course, a little silly to have demonstrably wrong opinions about anything, even about cats. It is foolish to make all-inclusive generalizations about any group merely because one finds it difficult to comprehend even one individual of the group. But foolish or not, people make almost as many ridiculous generalizations about cats as they do, for example, about women.

The cat does not, as the dog does, fit neatly into the human pattern, which is the only pattern humans at all understand. The human mind is often at a loss when it can find no pattern. Better than this vacuum is an invented pattern. For generations, men have been inventing such patterns for cats—telling one another that "all cats" do this and that, feel so and so. Cat lovers do this as frequently as cat dislikers; it was a widely known cat addict who wrote that "there is no such thing as a bad cat," using the adjective not in the moral but in the behavioristic sense. She should have met the Boss of Morton Street, who was steeped in sin. It is from cat lovers one hears that cats, in their delicate grace, are so sure-footed that they never knock anything over. Our present cats, all of whom are healthy and vigorous and two of whom are graceful, knock things over constantly and sometimes fall down themselves. They also, running after one another on uncarpeted floors, are about as quiet as horses trotting through a covered bridge—none of this silent movement on velvet paws for Martini and Gin and Sherry, or for any cat in a big hurry. Nor are all cats beautiful, although most are in their fashions; they are not even all sinuous. Sherry wobbles; she has never, we sometimes suspect, solved the vexatious problem of having four legs.

Cat addicts sentimentalize their friends; so, inversely, do opponents of cats. A good deal of Mr. Forbush's attack on them was based on sentimental, or if one prefers romantic, exaggeration of the habits, and the skill and ferocity, of these creatures who are so little human, hence so little comprehensible. Alan Devoe, writing under the title "Our Enemy, the Cat," informed readers of the *American Mercury* a few years ago that all cats are completely wild animals, that they always hide when having kittens, that their matings are carried on by preference in the depth of the woods and that they die as they live. "One day," he writes, "often with no fore-warning, the cat is gone from the house and never returns. He has felt the presaging shadow of death and he goes to meet it in the old unchanging way of the wild—alone."

This is a picturesque view to take of cats; it makes them strange and fascinating. And, as a generalization, there is little truth in it. Many cats have refused to have their kittens until their humans had rallied round to cheer; Martini, after a very terrible experience in kitten birth, had her last on a couch in a bright room, although she was almost too weak to climb to it and, presumably, because it

smelled of a human of whom she was fond. Cats mate wherever they happen to meet, as all city dwellers know, and are anything but secretive about it, and anything but modest. Some, it is true, seek out dark shelters in which to die; our Pammy, who was stricken suddenly and died in an hour or two, called to one of us in her pain, purred faintly when taken up, and, in the moments before she collapsed, tried to come closer, on legs too weak to carry her, to the person she loved if ever cat loved person.

But the cat does not love the human; any number of writers will tell you that. "In his feline heart," Mr. Devoe observes, with all the assurance of a man who has been there, "is neither love nor gratitude." "I have been unable to find any authenticated instances which go to show the existence in cats of any real love for their masters," writes Dr. N. S. Shaler, with the assurance of a man who has spent years looking.

No cat, with the exception of Saki's Tobermory, is known to have achieved human speech—Tobermory, brilliant as the famous story about him is, was a human in cat's shape, and offered no comment on the men and women he so much embarrassed which might not have taken shape in the mind of a human *enfant terrible*. (Tobermory was, indeed, the type of the anthropomorphic cat.) So no cat has ever said, "I love you," except to the sensitive ears of children. One suspects that Dr. Shaler would accept nothing less than so direct a statement as an "authenticated instance." And in a sense he is right, of course; until cats speak to humans, or write about them, no human will ever know how cats feel, and even then the cats who achieve loquacity may all be liars.

Dr. Shaler is, however, certain that dogs love people, although dogs, like cats, seldom speak good English. He is certain of this because dogs act as if they loved people. On that evidence, we are as far from doubt as he. We, also, are confident that most dogs grow deeply attached to the people of their choice, because there is no other reasonable explanation of their behavior, so often exuberantly affectionate. On similar evidence, we believe that our cats have been, in their varying ways and with differences in intensity, fond of us.

The evidence cats give us of affection is in some respects similar to that given by dogs—after all, cats and dogs both have paws and both have four of them; they both have mouths to open and tongues to lick with. They both are capable of sounds which appear to approach speech. But since most cats are not extroverts, since none of them is primarily concerned with pleasing humans by behaving like them, cats are not often openly demonstrative. There are, however, other levels of devotion than those so ably expressed in the lyrics of popular songs; other means of expressing cordiality than a hearty slap on the back. A cat will tell people many things, if people will learn to listen, and later we will consider some of their ways of telling.

But they do not speak as humans do, nor act like humans. No one learns much about cats who approaches them as the Hall-Browne children did—except that they are engaging to watch, soft to the touch and make somewhere deep in them a soft sound which, without proof, we know to be friendly. No one can learn much about them who sentimentalizes them, directly or in reverse; who asks of them adherence to human moral codes; who seeks uncritical devotion from them; who expects from them that acknowledgement of inferiority which is so gratifying to the late-model simian; who requires of his pets that they cringe for their supper. Cats are not human enough for that.

"Of all God's creatures there is only one that cannot be made the slave of the lash," Mark Twain wrote. "That one is the cat." And he continued, in that rather cross way of his: "If man could be crossed with the cat, it would improve man, but it would deteriorate the cat."

This amalgam, despite the best efforts of the anthropomorphizers, is not likely to be achieved. Both men and cats are too old to change, have grown stubborn in their ways through many centuries. If we are to take the cat at all, we must take him as he is, not as we are. He will meet us, but perhaps not quite half way.

9

The Cat's Behavior in Two Worlds

IT MAY BE that the cat lives emotionally in two worlds, the human and his own, and that this is more true of him than of the other animals who associate with man, although it is to some degree true of all of them. Even chickens, creatures of exceptional stupidity and little emotional warmth, seem dimly to adjust to man's habits. Dogs, although always knocking hopefully at the door of man's world, have also a world of their own and it is conceivable that cows, gathering at the pasture gate toward the hour of going home, think mistily bovine thoughts while waiting for the herdsman. But it may be that no other animal makes the distinction so sharply as it is made in the logical mind of the cat.

As he moves between the two worlds, the cat speaks languages suitable to the comprehension of the other denizens—speaks in one fashion to men and women and in quite another to his fellow cats, and to the mice and birds and, lamentably, dogs who share or intrude upon the feline world. To show affection for another cat, a cat licks it and the greatest affection is shown by licking the other cat's face. When a cat wishes to join another, or several others, in a preempted place—a box, a warm ledge, a cushion—the newcomer must first lick, if only in token, the cat or cats who got there first. Failure to do this is bad manners and may lead to ejection by the resident. Now and then, the cat who has been moved in on may comment audibly, giving permission or expressing disapproval, but this is unusual, even among quite talkative cats. Except in anger or other passion, and as between mother cats and kittens, audible conversation is the exception between cat and cat. Beyond hissing, which is done by curling the tongue up at the sides, making it into a kind of trough, cats have little to say to dogs, and a minor growl will do for a rat or mouse.

But with humans who, as the cat has noticed, communicate with one another by making sounds, almost all cats talk audibly and some talk a good deal. (Siamese are traditionally, and in our experience actually, the most frequent talkers.) They speak abruptly when they want out or want dinner; some of them talk uninterruptedly while their meals are being prepared; they purr when stroked (as, although more rarely, they purr when licked by one another); many of them respond, usually in a monosyllable or two, when spoken to in greeting; Martini has a special quick ejaculation used only when she wishes to jump to human shoulders—it is at once request and warning, although more the latter than the former. If offended by a human, a cat will growl briefly in admonition—as it will with another cat; if sufficiently alarmed by human, as by dog or other cat, a cat will hiss.

The cat has discovered, however, that humans are slow of understanding and so adds pantomime to words, as humans do when seeking to explain something to other humans of imperfect understanding—as, for example, foreigners. Thus a cat wanting dinner may add to his vocal announcement the pantomimic explanation of going to the place in which food is prepared; Gin, when the ordeal of waiting for food to be warmed becomes unbearable, when her most audible instructions to hurry up—can't you see I'm starving?—do not produce the speed she wishes, goes to a pile of paper plates and paws at the topmost, knowing that it is the one on which food will eventually—but how long, oh God?—be served.

All cats go to the door and speak there when they want to go out, many reach toward the knob or latch, not a few learn to manipulate the lock and go out by themselves if the door opens away from them. Gin used to climb into a chair which stood near an outer door and do her talking from there because then, since the door opened inward, she was out of the path of its swing and could go out faster. All cats know that people speak cat imperfectly and that the simplest things have to be acted out, as in a charade. Some of these performances become so familiar, and so stylized, that cats probably hardly know they are engaged in them and people take them for granted. Thus even Dr. Shaler no doubt took for granted that when a cat said he was hungry, and then acted as if he was hungry, he *was* hungry. Almost without knowing what he did, he took the cat's word for it—the cat's words and actions.

But often, in any cat's life in the human world, situations arise which require greater thought on the part of both feline and human if communication is to be established. If the thing to be expressed has to do with an objective matter, this need not long baffle an intelligent or a reasonably attentive human. Thus Martini once communicated to one of us an emergency which had arisen in connection with her toilet pan, and did it with an explicitness which no one could fail to understand.

Martini was, when living in town, "broken" to torn-up newspaper. The quotation marks are used because, as is usually true of cats, we

did not "break" her to this sanitary arrangement. We provided pan and torn-up papers and, although the result is by no means a cat's idea of toilet facilities, it was better than anything else available. Being a reasonable person, no holder-out for unobtainable perfection, Martini promptly used pan and paper and, when it became necessary, pointed out the pan to her kittens. Thereafter, all three used the same pan.

The flaw in this, from the cats' point of view and ours, was that we and our maid had always to be thinking of whether the pan was clean and dry and that our minds too often wandered from this, to the cats, essential, preoccupation. On the day when Martini explained things to one of us, we had apparently been thinking for some hours of lesser matters. Martini probably spoke about it several times and got no answer, which gave her a low view of our intelligence and also annoyed her considerably, since she is uncommonly fastidious and insists on a dry pan.

So she came to the room where one of us was working and gave that one a final chance. She got onto a couch and spoke so loudly, so insistently, that no concentration could withstand her voice. The human turned and said, "What's the matter, Teeney?"

Martini spoke again, more briefly. Then she assumed a characteristic and unmistakable position on the couch.

"*Teeney!*" the human said, very loudly, in surprise and shock. "*Teeney!*" The human also got up. "You bad—" the human began.

But then Teeney left the couch. She left hurriedly, and resumed her vocal instructions. She also went toward the kitchen, in which the pan was kept. She went hurriedly. The one of us summoned went after her and found her standing in front of the pan, looking at it, her upper lip slightly curled back, as cats curl back their lip when they encounter something unpleasant. She let the human see this attitude of hers. Then she looked up. Then she said, "Yah!"

The human changed the pan. Martini used it.

Now this, while requiring some ingenuity on Martini's part, was not too complicated for a bright cat and it does not, one would think, admit of more than one explanation. Martini wanted something done and saw it was done. Presumably a person who knows little of cat's habits might argue that she had really intended to use the couch, so that her actions were not pantomimic but real. There are several things against this. Healthy cats, except females in season, almost never break habit; Martini, locked up in the Brewster cabin for hours together—the cats reasonably enough decline to use the pan in the country and Martini, for reasons of her own, for a time abandoned the fireplace—waits until she is let out, no matter how long the waiting is. (Cats have unhuman control in such matters.) And, if she had been going to break habit on the couch, she would certainly not have announced it to one of us, nor have used a cushioned surface in an occupied room.

But often cats must talk with humans on subjects more abstract— must communicate such emotions as jealousy, hurt feelings and, most frequently of all, affection. Some of them seem to feel these emotions more keenly than do others; some are more adept at communicating them. But neither of us ever knew a cat who could not, in one way or another, express himself on these matters and who did not do so when the need arose. It seems to us, as it does to most people who have spent any appreciable time around cats, that a cat's expression of, for example, love for a human is often quite as clear as a cat's expression of a desire to go out doors.

There was, for example, the case of the cat called Pammy who, like Martini later, was a very special cat—a cat about whom one would like to write a book, as Michael Joseph did about Charles; or such an essay as Charles Dudley Warner wrote about the incomparable Calvin, who used to turn on a furnace register "in a retired room, where he used to go when he wished to be alone" and when he required more heat. (Any writer would like to have done either of these perceptive pieces, as a craftsman even if not as a cat lover.)

Pammy, who as we have said is dead now, was a longish gray cat, with a white collar; her mother was Siamese and her father anybody, and she came to us years ago with her brother Jerry. Of these two, and of other cats of ours, we may tell more on later pages; what is significant here is that, from the time she was a small kitten, Pammy formed a special attachment for one of us—the one, as it happened, the more aggressive Jerry did not prefer. He would

slap her down if she approached Frances. All the affection of a very gentle cat was thus channeled toward one human, and it was shown in soft sounds, in purring, in a desire always to be close—in all the little ways which are convincing to those less adamant than the Dr. Shalers.

But then the war came and for a couple of months it became necessary for the one to whom Pammy was devoted to be away. The room in which he worked, and in which Pammy tried, with soft paws, with endearments, to keep him from working, was temporarily otherwise occupied. And Pammy was brokenhearted—one does not like to use terms so extreme, but other terms are inadequate. The bottom dropped out of Pammy's life.

She would go to the door of the small room in which the man should have been, had always been. She did not need to enter to know that he was not there; there was another smell there, even when the room was empty. She would look into the room and raise her head and give a small, hopeless cry. Then she would turn away and wander the apartment restlessly, and return to the room and again find it empty—find it worse than empty, because someone else was occupying it. She would turn away again and then, perhaps, she would hear the front door opening a flight below. Then, instantly, she was all a listening animal, but only for an instant. The sound of footsteps was as wrong as the scent had been and again she would cry, and begin to wander.

For the first few weeks she would have nothing to do with the one who remained. She displayed the detached courtesy she always showed; she was never a rude cat. But the affection freely offered by one who was lonely too, in a human fashion, was accepted only absent-mindedly, did not touch the cat. Pammy continued to eat; there was no change there, except that she seemed to eat with no great pleasure. (The one who was gone had almost never fed her.) But she did not play with her brother; she merely drifted through the apartment, searching; merely listened at the door, hoping.

Finally, she appeared more or less to give up, but that was after weeks. She began to look up into the human face which remained and, although she still expressed her loneliness with a little cry, it was clear that she also sought friendship and reassurance. Finally, after about six weeks, she appeared to accept her loss and to make the new adjustment. When the wanderer returned she was clearly very glad to see him and sat as much as possible on his lap. But she was never again a one-man cat; she had learned, as humans most often have to, that there is danger in channeling love too narrowly; she had widened her emotional field.

But if, during those weeks, she did not feel deeply the loss of someone she loved, then the actions of cats and men make no sense at all, and the words we use have no meaning. We may guess that emotions were inchoate in her mind; that she did not form an "idea" of her loss, although in this we may well be wrong. But she did all a sentient being could to reveal that underlying disappointment, that feeling of depression, which, for some time after an affectional trauma, also underlies the human consciousness, is never quite absent even when the surface mind is busiest.

Martini, in all respects a more violent person and not a cat to take anything sitting down, showed a similar response when it was necessary for both of us to leave her at a crucial time in her life. We had to go away for ten days or so when the kittens were very small and she was their only source of sustenance. Martini merely quit eating and, since she continued to provide food, she faded alarmingly. The person who was, very generously, acting as cat sitter became alarmed and summoned the veterinarian. Martini retired to an inaccessible position, prepared in advance, and growled and hissed. She would not allow herself to be touched; she met coaxing with angry warnings. And, since she had never been a cat to fool with, she was allowed her way, which was to continue to refuse food. When we returned, she swore at us for a couple of days, and would not let us touch her or the kittens, but she ate.

Obviously, if one of the things so many people "know" about cats had been true of Martini, none of this would have happened. She was in a familiar place, and places, many people tell one another, are all cats care about. She was not even with a strange person; her sitter was one she had known and liked since she was a kitten. She had been deserted by people she loved and, being the kind of person she is, this made her furious; Martini is of a temperament to kill the things she loves; she is very proud and one rejects her at his peril. Her love is violent.

It is more violent than that of most cats we have known even when nothing in particular has happened to upset her, even in its day-to-day expression. When she chooses to express affection—usually toward Frances, whom she owns—there is nothing half way about it. Lap sitting, quiet purring, is not enough. She lies up a chest, with her whiskers tickling a cheek; she puts paw to face, and arms about neck. When she is in this position she expects to be talked to, touched gently, to hear her name often spoken in a soft voice. During this period, the occupied person must sit quietly, must not try to read, must not answer the telephone if it rings. A movement, any wavering in concentration on cat, and Martini is down with an oath, is on the floor, sitting with back to the offender, not answering if spoken to. She is not to be lightly wooed, our major cat; she has no patience with casual affection.

She and her daughters always greet us when we return after an absence; they are always sitting at the door before we reach it. Martini usually moves a little away from the others and rolls over on her back. She expects to be greeted first; it is wise not to notice the others until her emotional needs are gratified. Then one may speak to Gin and Sherry, who are rubbing against legs, purring furiously. (Martini herself has a very small purr; often it is almost soundless, and merely a matter of vibrating cat.)

If we have been gone for some hours, the cats—after being greeted—usually run excitedly through the house, wrestling with one another, leaping onto things and off of them, emitting sharp cries of excitement. Martini at such times, and often at other times, forgets the dignity of a matron and romps furiously, leaping half across a room, her tail bushy, to land almost upon another cat, to lock with it and roll it on the floor, pretending to tear it apart with tooth and claw. Both of them are larger cats than she, and stronger; both have been under her paw since they were kittens.

Not all of our cats have been so demonstrative in the world they share with humans. Pammy was, in her fashion. She, also, met us at doors. Jerry did sometimes, when he happened to think of it, but perhaps only because Pammy did, and he wondered—in his rather vague fashion—what she was up to. Jerry liked attention well enough, but he did not seem to be a deeply affectionate cat. Pete was wont merely to look up when we entered, smile faintly, and go back to sleep again. Sometimes he would roll over to be rubbed, but not always. But he was a great cat to follow us around, as Martini also is. Pete kept an eye on us and did not let us wander far afield. One night, when we stayed too long with friends at a near-by cabin, Pete came across the fields after us, looked in the window, opened the screen door, and entered to tug at our clothing and to tell us it was high time we came home with him.

Pete lived longer than the others a semi-migratory existence between town and country, since during the earlier of the ten years or so he lived with us we stayed most of our time in New York and got to the country only for weekends and for vacations. Pete traveled, usually by car but now and then by train, always in a carrying case which he hated thoroughly. But he never showed any signs of a place fixation; if he was in the apartment, that was all right; if he was in the country, that was fine. After his first visit to the country it never seemed to surprise him, although for some time, of course, it required investigation. There was never any thought in our minds, or apparently in his, that he might try to walk back to New York. Home was where we were; he might have been contented in the traveling box if it had been convenient for one of us to ride in it with him.

The more recent cats have all shared his indifference to places and addiction to people; we have, indeed, never known a cat who felt otherwise, nor have we ever heard of one at firsthand. (If cat stories have any value—which many dispute—they have it only at firsthand; what somebody has heard about somebody else's cat is seldom instructive and never evidence.) But the cats we have known, and know most about, were cats who, in their homes, were treated as persons, not as furniture. Presumably a cat treated like a piece of furniture would begin to act like one, at least to human eyes. He would not feel like one, but he might come to feel like part of the house.

Cats appear to recognize their people by sight and sound, rather than by scent, although they do a great deal of smelling of their friends and more—sometimes embarrassingly more—of strangers. Apparently they tell a good deal about people by the way their fingers smell, and a good deal of where people have been by the way their shoes smell. Probably their sense of smell is highly selective rather than keen, but of course it is infinitely more acute in all respects than that of a human. We have seen a cat who had had, during his absence, a dog visitor, trace the every movement the dog had made over the floor of a room half an hour after the dog had left. The cat's lip was curled throughout, perhaps in contempt for so smelly an animal.

A cat will, normally, recognize a friend as far as he can see him, which is a good distance. Now and then, for reasons not entirely clear, recognition may be uncertain until the cat is spoken to. Then the cat is usually very chagrined—an anthropomorphic word; they cannot be avoided by anthropoids—at having been caught out. They are also chagrined when, as sometimes happens, they stalk cautiously a familiar object which happens to be in an unfamiliar place; Martini once with the utmost gingerliness stalked half across a lawn a cushion which was drying in the sun and was six feet from it before she found out what it was. She stopped in her tracks, then, and looked off to one side, as if the whole approach had been an elaborate feint, and the real object of her interest had all the time been elsewhere. She rather spoiled this pantomime, however, by looking back over her shoulder to see how we were taking it. We were amused; she recognized this instantly and went off with slow and rather contemptuous dignity. And familiar persons in unexpected postures—such as standing on the head—may frighten a cat.

Cats go by shapes and positions, and show little interest in color, probably because they are largely color blind. That they are completely color blind is something which everyone "knows" about cats; the cat's-eye view of color—shades of intensity in a primarily monotone world—is frequently pictured in books on color blindness although, so far as we know, none of these pictures was ever painted by a cat. Investigators constantly remind one another, and their readers, that no one can get inside the mind of a cat, or see with a cat's eyes—and many of them are as constantly doing what amounts to precisely that. The degree of color blindness in the cat can only be guessed at by those who are not cats, and that rather haphazardly. Of the two best planned investigations of the cat's color vision, one proved conclusively that it did not exist, the second that it was very acute. Anecdotal evidence from lay cat owners does little to resolve this scientific confusion; some people are sure cats are sensitive to colors; some that they are not. Our own experience has been that color, at the best, means little to a cat; they are attracted to flowers, as most of them are, by the scent, not the color. Most cats evidently enjoy smelling flowers; some of them like to eat flowers. Almost all, incidentally, like to drink water in which flowers have stood, and this when much fresher water is available.

Dr. Georgina Ida Stickland Gates, a psychologist who has gone into the matter—but evidently with a volume of Thorndike propped between her and the cat—is confident not only that cats do not see color but that they do not see much of anything else, and hear very little. Her cat, she writes, "probably sees me as a vague form. Just as she does not distinguish the color of my dress, so it is improbable that she perceives slight variations of facial expression or that she notes changes in costume. She probably feels me in gross, as a large total thing, the parts of which are but vaguely apprehended."

One man's probability is another's unlikelihood; to us it does not seem at all probable that the cat does not notice changes of costume, chiefly because our cats so evidently do. Pete knew in town when we changed to clothing we wore to the country, and hid at once to avoid the carrier, which we never touched until the last possible moment. But when we packed suitcases to go somewhere in city clothes, he paid little attention, being well able to tell the difference. And all cats examine the costumes of people they propose to occupy; when either of us is wearing shorts or other tennis clothes, the cats, after a quick examination, decide we are not dressed to be sat upon.

It was also Dr. Gates's conviction, based on heaven knows what evidence, that cats have little or no tonal perception, although all the cats we have known seemed to show a good deal—very evidently responded favorably to soft tones of the human voice and unfavorably to harsh or high-pitched voices. There is a considerable body of evidence, largely anecdotal to be sure, that some cats enjoy music, although none of ours has ever seemed to pay much attention to it. Martini did, on one occasion, respond angrily to the sound of an Egyptian flute which emerged, rather unexpectedly to us also, from the radio, but otherwise she can take music or leave it, even when she happens to be sitting on the radio. But she hates whistling, as has every cat with whom we have been associated.

Dr. Gates also questioned whether cats know their own names, which is merely arrant nonsense. Cats who are always called "kitty" presumably think "kitty" is their name. Other cats know their names about as well as people know theirs; many will answer when spoken to by name and all will come when called by name if, at the moment, coming seems like a good idea to the cat. It was perhaps Dr. Gates's careless observation in this particular which led Nelson Antrim Crawford to characterize her cat book as "a dull and dubious study of feline psychology."

It is difficult for the human not to assume that obedience is synonymous with comprehension or should be so in the case of small and admittedly dependent animals. It may be that Dr. Gates, and others who have questioned whether a cat ever learns his name, subconsciously assume, although they may consciously know better, that if a cat recognizes his name he will come running when it is called. A dog does; why should a cat differ from a dog?

And, quite often, cats do come, often at breakneck speed. They will do this most often, of course, when it is near mealtime, since then it is almost always worth the trouble. But they are quite likely to do the same thing at other times, if it seems a good idea. What makes it seem a good idea no human knows, or is likely to know. We have no idea at all why, one day, Sherry will come across a lawn as if blown by a high wind, her hind legs clearly moving faster than her front, to her evident confusion, when we call her name; why, the next day, with conditions apparently almost identical, she will merely look around languidly and go back to eating grass, which we have never been able to convince her is bad for cats. It is not true that she knows her name one day and not the next, but beyond that the human can only vaguely speculate.

It is this exercise of judgment, this apparent consideration of and response to only the specific circumstances of a certain time, which gives the cat its rather exaggerated reputation for independence— that and, of course, the fact that a cat will not be bullied by anything, on two legs or four, or on multiple legs or no legs at all.

The cat will come or not come as suits the cat, the cat will with-draw if it grows bored; no cat would ever suffer politely at a cock-tail party. Because of this attitude, the cat is "independent"; he may be termed "anti-social" or even, by some, "stupid." Perhaps it would be more accurate to say that, instead of being primarily any of these things, the cat is selective and that the bases of his selection are not always clear to the human mind.

All, or almost all, cats who have humans to depend upon become dependent on them—for affection, for an emotional center, as well as for their obvious needs of food and warmth and shelter. They are to a considerable, although as we have seen seldom to a com-plete, degree capable of fending for themselves, but they much prefer not to. With humans most of them are anything but anti-social, although among humans many of them make sharp selection, and again without always making their reasons clear. As people move from room to room of a house, staying now in one room and now in another, most cats will follow them; all our cats habitually, when we lived in the city, stayed in the living room with us while we remained there; moved with us into the bedroom when we went there, as we often did, to read in bed. They did not do this for any discernible reason, except that they preferred our company to our absence. They did not always do it at all. They did it if they felt like it; they felt like it, at a guess, two times out of three. All of them would show attention when spoken to by name, sometimes they would come and sometimes not, and they varied in this from cat to cat; Martini almost always answers whether she moves or not, but she will not continue to answer if spoken to repeatedly, declining to labor the point.

Their choices among people are often entirely inexplicable. For many years in New York we had a maid of whom we, and all our cats but one, were fond—she was as gentle with the cats as she was expert and faithful in meeting our needs; she often fed them as she for years fed us. Pete openly adored her and used to play games with her; Pam and Jerry seemed fond of her; Sherry liked her from the first and Gin, who makes friends slowly, came to approve her and to sit watching her by the hour. Gin was particularly entertained when she mopped the kitchen floor, and would lie across the threshold, one paw in the kitchen, and raise the paw to be mopped under.

But Martini, who knew Elizabeth almost as early in her young cathood as she knew us, could never abide her. She would run from her sometimes; other times, she would stand in a doorway and, hissing, refuse permission to cross. During several years of acquaintance, Martini never altered her views about Elizabeth, although in many ways, because of a change in her life, Martini did alter her views on other matters. Neither we nor Elizabeth ever understood why this was, and we all regretted it. Since she had kittens, and then was spayed, Martini has not been particularly bad-tempered with other people, although it would be absurd to contend that she is an especially amiable cat. But she never liked Elizabeth.

Sherry likes everybody and, although afraid of mice, was only mildly alarmed when she first met children and soon came to be fond of them, although most cats who grow up with adults are greatly disturbed by small humans who must, to a cat, seem an unnatural compromise. Gin likes almost nobody the first time, but relents to a degree later, although without ever approaching Sherry's cordiality. But even Sherry likes some people better than others, and not always merely because she knows them better. Nor does she always show herself most friendly to those who most readily offer her friendship. Like most cats, she picks and chooses.

Cats so much insist on this prerogative of selection that all experienced people in meeting unfamiliar cats wait to be chosen, usually with fingers dangled, as if by chance, near a cat's nose. The hand of a wise human is, at such times, held near the floor, or near whatever the cat happens to be on, and not above the cat's head. Cats do not like to have things come down on them from above; their invariable habit, in environments not tested and found safe, is to get under something and look around. For all the cat knows, any strange object descending from above may be a great horned owl, and a nervous cat may act accordingly. A cat wants to see the proffered fingers as well as smell them; he will then make up his own mind as to the human's acceptability. He will not necessarily

like a person because other cats like that person and this is sometimes confusing to people who are sure they "have a way with cats."
Martini, in the pre-operation days when she was not well and very
nervous and irritable, once rather thoroughly scratched a visitor
who, in spite of warnings—not from us; we probably could have
controlled the cat, if not the person—chose to prove that there
wasn't a cat in the world he couldn't handle. Perhaps Martini resented being placed in a category, knowing indignantly well that she
was a person.

Unaltered cats are, generally, more insistent on making their
own choices, as they are, again generally, more insistent about most
things. Martini's attitude toward life has not, to be sure, appreciably
altered, but she is less violent in her means of expression. And we
once met a large and beautiful tom who, in spite of living with an
extremely nervous collie pup and another dog who talked a good
deal, was calm and placid and would lie relaxed on almost any lap
offered, beaming up at the lap owner and purring loudly. But a
human can never tell about a cat he doesn't know, and can tell
rather less if the animals are fully sexed. Cats one knows well, cats
one lives with, are generally as predictable as most individualistic
creatures, and rather more predictable than people. Cats also, of
course, seem sometimes to have got up on the wrong side of the bed,
as is said of people; some cats, like many people, appear to be mildly
manic-depressive.

When they are feeling a little grumpy, cats will reject attentions
they at other times enjoy and may even warn a human off, either
in pantomime or vocally. None of our cats has ever offered to do
more than this to us—except, of course, when being held for examination by a veterinarian or, as has now and then been necessary,
while hypodermic injections were administered. Cats are not
tolerant of pain and, if being tormented, will bite the tormenter
if he is within reach, and more or less without regard for his identity.
Now and then, a male may grow entirely disenchanted with life and
people as he grows old; we knew one, Deuces Wild, a delightful
fellow in his prime, who became too difficult for anyone to handle
in old age and had finally to be killed. Humans also sometimes

become personality problems as they approach senility, but human ethics do not permit their destruction. Also, of course, aged humans have neither such dangerous claws nor such sharp teeth.

But cats in health, when treated with consideration and rudimentary courtesy, are almost never entirely unpredictable in their dealings with humans, and only an occasional cat is at all difficult. Now and then, of course, one encounters an apparently psychotic cat; we have heard of, but not met, one who is clearly a homicidal maniac, seeking only to kill all living things—with the single exception of a pet human he keeps as an attendant. Our own Jerry, although quite harmless, was clearly a neurotic, probably suffering from a manic-depressive psychosis. But most cats probably are saner than most people, which is possibly not high praise. Although they live in two worlds, they are infrequently schizophrenic.

It is, of course, difficult for a human to examine with any exactitude the cat's life in his own world of other cats and other non-moral creatures. If the human is present to observe, the human becomes a condition of the problem and so modifies it. Now and then one may eavesdrop, but may not end up the wiser. When one cat sits on a stone wall and another on the ground near by, and when they converse lengthily in wails, yet without apparently meaning either to fight or to love, the human is apt to remain baffled. It is fairly evident that the cats understand each other, that they are abiding by certain feline conventions. If one cat is a resident and the other an intruder, the home cat may be warning the other off. (Such encounters do, indeed, seem frequently to have this purpose, since the visiting cat often turns away toward the end, although clearly not in fear, and permits the occupying cat the satisfaction of a token chase.) These discussions may, incidentally, take place between neuters and spays, neuters or spays and un-altered cats of either sex, and it is reasonably certain that there is no question of mistaken gender. In such matters, cats do not fall into error.

Cats are not, by nature, gregarious with others of their kind; stray cats meeting do not romp and play together. One who has cats already may add to them and many people do constantly, but rather careful introductions usually are necessary. But to this rule, as to all rules about cats, there are many exceptions. Now and then cats do meet and make friends with other cats; there are many stories of well-cared-for cats who brought home strays to share their good fortune. Now and then, without human intervention, cats and dogs similarly make friends; we were once acquainted with a fine German shepherd bitch who more or less adopted, apparently from a Baltimore sidewalk, a large black tomcat and brought him home to live. The cat, although not accepting entirely the sanctuary offered—the cat was a wanderer and had been for years—nevertheless used the dog's home for some time as a base of operations, and was clearly devoted to the big shepherd. The dog used to walk slowly across a room, and the cat would walk, more rapidly, in and out between the large canine legs. Both seemed to enjoy this pastime, which was engaging but rather meaningless to human observers.

With human intervention, on human insistence, cats and dogs often live happily, and even affectionately, together; almost any animal "family" can be artificially created by those who find it worth the trouble. The chief reward, presumably, is that such odd assortments may be pictured in the newspapers, or even in *Life*. But no cat would choose to live in friendship with a bird and most would rather have nothing to do with dogs. Now and then a cat may enjoy teasing a dog; one of us watched such an intentional badgering a few years ago from the windows of a second floor apartment in downtown New York.

Across the street, there was a row of houses with old-fashioned "stoops"—stair flights running up to entrance doors some feet above street level. A large black cat was sitting in front of one of these stoops, washing himself. He looked up the street and saw an approaching dog, running illegally free with a master sauntering at some distance behind. The dog was inquisitive; as he came along he looked around each stoop to see what might be there. The cat watched this for a time with interest. Then, thoughtfully, the cat withdrew out of sight behind his own stoop.

Dramatic comedy then built to climax with almost classical inevitability. The dog came to the fourth stoop up the street and looked behind it and found nothing and bounced out; the dog looked behind the third stoop and then behind the second. He went into the matter of the stoop beyond the cat's, and found nothing and bounced out. The cat, now, could hear the scratch of canine nails on the cement. The cat gave a final casual lick to one shoulder, as if he had been adding a touch of makeup in a dressing room, and crouched. The dog reached the stair flight and the cat waited; the dog turned around the stoop.

The cat did not really try to harm the dog; the cat did not even leap at him, but merely started up, black and threatening, and jabbed once at the dog's nose. It was almost make-believe, but that the dog could not know—he knew only that death confronted him, he could only brake frantically with all four paws, could only yelp his terror and anguish. And get out of there. He got.

The cat watched the dog, scampering with screams back to his master, and then came out and sat again on his sidewalk. It seemed to the human onlooker that he then looked up toward the window—as toward a balcony seat—and took a bow.

Certainly, even if this last is not precisely true, the cat had been engaged in play; had been producing, with some care and a fine sense of timing, what was essentially a practical joke. He had not been afraid of the dog, he had not even particularly disliked the dog. He had merely enjoyed scaring the dog and making it ridiculous, the butt of a jest. He would have liked applause, of which cats are fond. But if, as was probably true, he was unaware of the onlooker, the knowledge that he deserved applause was sufficient—that and the game itself.

It is because of this feline consciousness of the human onlooker that one can never be sure how much, in the play of friendly cats with one another, the cat's two worlds may overlap. Cats may not play together, indeed, when no humans are present; it would be hard for a human to say. Their play with one another may be always partly play to an audience.

This cat play—the big game of the cat—is a spectacle of which the owner of a single cat is, of course, deprived. Basically it is mimic warfare; it might be thought of as a feline encounter in a prize ring, except that cats do not hurt one another or intend to. It is also a wrestling match and often includes, at one or more stages, an obstacle race. Apparently it is played according to certain established rules; one cat watcher, a reformed sports writer, thought he had worked out a point-count which determined a winner, but he was either more observant or more imaginative than we have ever been. The game is, certainly, played to a more or less fixed conclusion; it may be called off at any time by the defensive cat.

Recently, in a manner not apparent to us, Sherry violated one of the rules—apparently an important one—in playing the game with Gin, and thereafter Gin would not play it at all with her, although continuing to play it with Martini. When Sherry suggested the game, Gin jabbed at her, not intending to land but in warning, and hissed. Sherry did not appear to know what she had done, and it may be that, since she has grown heavier than her sister, it is her weight rather than her methods to which Gin objects. But the game has never been a great favorite of Gin's, who would rather be out hunting. Often, after a day in the fields, she regards the other two with weary forbearance as they romp, a business girl home from a long day at the office, too tired for the frivolity of those who do not know what it is to work for a living. When she plays at all, Gin is usually in the defensive position.

The cat on the offensive gives the preliminary signal for the game. That much is clear. If Martini wants to play, she crouches to leap, makes stalking movements and bushes her tail in excitement. The bushed tail, the rising fur along the backbone, are her idiosyncrasies; the others bush only when dealing with dogs. Sherry observes these preparatory motions and crouches in her turn. There is then, often, considerable stalking, usually ending in a chase. The chase may take both cats over chairs and sofas and, not infrequently, over the people sitting in them. Martini, as the instigator, is most often the pursuer, but at a certain stage she may permit herself to be pursued.

In the early stages, these activities may be interrupted, apparently on the choice of either cat, by brief rest periods, during which the cats will sit, paying little attention to each other, and wash up. One might think the game over, and now and then—for reasons never apparent to us—it actually is. Usually, however, it is merely that they are taking a break between rounds, changing courts after odd games. Usually, one of them—Martini most frequently—starts it up again.

Eventually, the contact stage is reached. At this stage, the defending cat lies on her side, feet extended, claws exposed, mouth open and teeth ready, and the offensive cat circles for an opening.

The attacker also has claws exposed, ears laid back and mouth open, the incredibly sharp canines in readiness. There is, at this stage, considerable maneuvering for position, and if Sherry is the defender, not a little cat talk indicative of fear and pain. (This is no more to be taken seriously than a professional wrestler's groans and cries of anguish.)

At a certain stage, the attacking cat leaps in. If the defender can hold her off with stiffly extended legs and avoid being otherwise touched, it may be assumed the defender scores a point. If the attacker can break through the guard, she may pretend to tear at the unprotected belly, as in an actual fight she would seek to rip it with the claws of her hind feet; she may bite at the other's ear, she may merely circle the defender's neck with both front legs and apparently try to choke her to death. The distinction between defender and attacker is obscure at this point, the cats roll furiously in combat.

Either cat may break this off, but it is usually broken off by the original defender. There may then, apparently at the election of the defending cat, be another chase and another tussle or an end of the game. The game is ended when either cat merely walks away, or sits and looks at something else, or goes for a drink of water. If the game is resumed it is, almost always, with the roles as they were before; seldom in any given series of contacts do the cats reverse position.

This much can be observed and certain of the rules may be guessed at. It is, for example, not considered good form to jump another cat who is seriously washing up. It is not cricket to attack a cat who has no room to maneuver; if a cat runs under something, as a sofa, the other cat seldom follows; if a cat indicates that he is actually hurt, the game ends at once. No cat ever is hurt, although the breath may be knocked out of him.

This is the way it is played. One must watch it to discover how exciting, how essentially gay, how amazingly dextrous it really is.

Cats in movement are always delightful, and during the game cats are constantly in movement—the game is an amazing spectacle of lithe grace, of dazzling acrobatics. The human, with his spine stiffened, his muscles unbalanced to make erect stature possible, cannot at his most flexible achieve a fraction of the agility of the least graceful cat. Martini is a little chunky for her breed, and slightly overweight. But it is nothing for her to leap into the air sideways during the game, to land on a sofa tiptoe with back at once arched and longitudinally curved, to dance thus for several steps while looking back over her shoulder at another cat, to take off then through the air, twisting in flight and landing not upon, but within grazing inches of, her adversary, to roll in a single motion as she lands, over and to her feet again—and then, perhaps, in what seems the same instant, become a sitting cat again, reflectively washing her right shoulderblade. When this is multiplied by Sherry, is on occasion multiplied still further by Gin, when all three cats at once are leaping and twisting in the air, each in her own fashion but each incomparably feline, there is no other pattern of animal movement approaching the game in grace and essential excitement. The human ballet, the best of ice skating, the most perfect of human play with balls, whether on court or diamond—

all these activities, in which man most nearly shows grace, are heavy and contorted by comparison.

Man, slowly, effortfully, learns to do such things as these, achieving a partial triumph of imagination over rigidity. But he learns them arbitrarily, not from inner necessity; it is not required of man that he contort to live. Not even a Nijinsky can outjump a bullet; DiMaggio cannot hit an atom bomb out of the lot; pretty Miss Henie cannot skate her way out of danger.

But the game is part of the cat's life; in a sense it is practice for his life, as kitten chasing of a string is practice for hunting. Martini's life may at any moment depend on her ability to leap sidewise to a wall, land there in perfect balance on her toes, ready instantly to continue in another direction. No doubt it often has so depended. Cats play the big cat game for fun; there can be no doubt they enjoy it. But they play it also to keep their muscles supple and their reflexes almost instantaneous. Instinct—a human word for a complex of stimuli about which the human knows practically nothing—instructs the cat to keep his paw in, not to forget his tricks. If he ever goes out of a city apartment he may need them all.

It is when he goes out the front door that the cat most truly enters the non-human of his two worlds, and his every movement shows his knowledge of the risks involved. He shows it on the doorstep; not only Mr. Warner's inimitable Calvin, but all cats, stand on the sill, as Calvin always did, looking about the sky as if "thinking whether it were worth while to take an umbrella." Little as cats like being caught out in the rain, it is not likely that they hesitate to observe the weather. Danger may come from the sky on wings; it is wise to be sure before venturing farther. (Cats are most concerned about danger from above, since it is from above they are most vulnerable.) With the sky established as free from menace, the cat surveys the land about, checking for dogs and other dangers. This whole survey may take from seconds to several minutes; only when it is completed does the cat go about whatever his business of the moment is.

Unquestionably, the wandering dog is the most common danger to the cat, and this is particularly true of the suburban cat. A good farm dog expects cats to be around and expects to leave them alone; even when he is out hunting on his own, he recognizes cats as out of season. We have seen good farm dogs stick to this rule under the greatest provocation; one, whose ancestry had been lightly brushed by collie, allowed himself to be chivvied out of our yard one day by Martini, whose simple purpose it was to kill him. He made no move in self-defense, although he could—if luck had been with him—have killed her with one snap. He merely looked around at us, beseechingly, as if begging that we remove this annoying creature who was getting very much on his nerves, but still was sacrosanct.

But by no means all dogs are so trained; many dogs are cat killers. And almost no cat of any spirit recognizes at the start that he is outmatched. Against a medium-sized dog with no training against cats, the cat is quite right, of course. Either Martini or Gin would probably fare excellently against any but a large, tough dog; the dog might well be blinded. But neither seems able to tell a large tough dog from any other and Gin has had several bad experiences with dogs she thought she was going to chase off the premises. Too many cats—Gin is one of them, and Pete was another—willingly attack almost any recognizable dog. Pete once took on three, all of them large, and leaped for the eyes of the largest, but that time he was trapped and needed to create a diversion in order to reach a tree. Even he, who had a great contempt for dogs, probably would not voluntarily have taken on so many. (He had been spoiled by long association with an incompetent fox terrier, whose life he made miserable. It was an association Pete thoroughly enjoyed, but not one which taught him the facts of life.)

The facts of life are that dogs are very dangerous to cats and that the greater the cat's courage the greater the danger. Every cat who runs at large has many moments of peril when to escape with his life he needs all there is of feline skill at acrobatics, all that cats are provided with in reflex response. The cat cannot afford to grow rusty in a world of dogs and owls, of motor cars and, of course, other cats. He must practice constantly, and much of his play is practice.

Yet much of it also is clearly fun and some of it plain puckishness. When a cat lies crouched, tail moving slowly from side to side, ambushing a favorite human on a country path, leaps out at the human, touches a human shoe lightly—for all the world as if playing tag—it is hard to believe that his primary purpose is to keep in training. When a cat comes when called, and when wanted in, and then crouches until fingers brush him before leaping away, and when he continues to do this time after time, never really leaving, not trying seriously to avoid eventual capture, the cat is surely merely teasing, since this procedure has no apparent utility in the non-human world.

It is when the cat invents such games as these last—and any cat watcher has seen many such inventions—that the barrier between the feline and human mind seems thinnest. In such games there seems to be, on the cat's part, a kind of humor which, although physically expressed, is essentially not physical and certainly is not a practical joke. (A cat is quite capable of practical jokes, however, as the story of the cat on the stoop indicates.) One might almost think the cat capable of a concept of the ridiculous, which is certainly exemplified in the effort of human fingers to close upon a cat who, by perhaps no more than a foot or so, is no longer there.

Much of the cat's behavior, indeed, would seem to show something which approaches, if it does not reach, abstract intelligence—an ability to put two and two together; to perceive, if only dimly, causal relationships; even to form "ideas." One could almost swear, watching it, that in Martini's comic elusiveness there is not only a game, but the *idea* of a game. It is something to which she is not, at least in any obvious way, conditioned, as all cats are, of course, conditioned to certain actions which appear to bring them food; as they are conditioned by trial and error, and an accumulation of successes, to opening doors through which they want to go. (In the less obvious sense, it can be, and has been, argued that humans as well as cats are but aggregations of conditioned reflexes.)

It would seem, watching cats—and in this chapter, as all cat observers will agree, the vagaries of feline behavior are hardly more than suggested—that much of what they do results from the working of intelligence. Since no human has ever been a cat, no human knows. But, in their inquisitive simian fashion, humans have tried very hard to find out. This human study of feline intelligence is one of the most fascinating, and sometimes one of the oddest, episodes in the ancient association of cats and people.

10

The Mind of the Cat

"CATS ARE A mysterious kind of folk," Sir Walter Scott wrote of them. "There is more passing in their minds than we are aware."

Sir Walter felicitously paid a tribute. He also noted a problem which a good many men and women—writers, naturalists, psychologists, people who merely watch cats with affectionate interest—have tried to solve. The simian resents a mystery not of his own making; it is not proper for the four-footed to keep secrets from the biped. Man's conscience is uneasy; if cats and dogs think, they may think about man and, since they have many opportunities to observe him, this possibility is disquieting. "We cannot, without becoming cats, perfectly understand the cat mind," St. George Mivart warns, but the warning is disregarded.

Man is man and therefore, *a priori,* capable of understanding everything. He is, at any rate, capable of worrying about everything he does not understand, and of inquisitively probing into it. Since animals are abundant, and subject to man's control, man has diligently probed into them, proving that rats can be driven mad, that dogs' mouths can be made to water by conditioned reflex and that cats are very intelligent, not intelligent at all, capable of ideas and incapable of learning their own names, familiar with a vocabulary of six hundred words and unable to remember anything for fifteen minutes. Man has also proved, in carefully controlled experiments continuing over a couple of years, that some cats are brighter than other cats.

In general, this enquiry into the cat mind has been conducted in two ways. One, the simplest, has been to watch cats, observing their actions, and to reach conclusions by inference. This is the oldest method and, of course, the most common, since the only equipment needed is a cat. The second, or scientific, method requires anything from half a dozen boxes to an electronic device so complicated that only a reasonably bright human can make anything of it and only a mathematician understand the results. This latter method, which has been employed often during the past fifty years or so, has resulted in many interesting findings, most of them in conflict with one another.

As one would expect, anecdotal evidence is overwhelmingly pro-cat and has produced characterizations of animals who make Tobermory, the talking cat, seem a dullard by comparison. People who do not like cats seldom have stories to tell about them; people who do like cats do not, naturally, often tell stories about stupid cats. Thus Mivart repeats the fascinating tale of an accomplished cat who, finding that starlings he would catch in a field took wing at his approach, but were indifferent to the cattle grazing near them, rode a cow into the middle of the starling group and then alighted among the deluded birds. This ingenious cat was obviously of super-feline intelligence, but his ingenuity is of the kind which gives cats a bad name, proves them "sly" creatures—hardly superior, indeed, to men, who invented the Trojan horse and who uses decoys to lure ducks from the safety of the sky.

Such stories have been told, no doubt, by proud humans since humans first kept cats. Did we mention how bright Martini was when she told us about the condition of her toilet pan? Surely there, if ever was, is evidence that cats can think.

Charles Dudley Warner's Calvin not only opened a hot air register to warm his retiring room; he opened all the doors of his house with latches not beyond his reach. Mivart heard of dozens of cats who did as much; that hundreds of cats have is incontestable, and this ability is offered as proof of intelligence—and argued away as the mere working of conditioned reflexes. The late W. H. Hudson once watched a cat stalk a bird until within six feet of it and then suddenly, for no reason, abandon the whole idea and go home. Conditions had not changed; Mr. Hudson was convinced that the cat had simply thought the matter over, thought, "Shucks, what am

I doing this for? They always fly away," and changed his mind, which would indicate he had a mind to change. And it is Mr. Hudson, also, who tells one of the most charming cat anecdotes, a delightful little story worth retelling whether or not it proves a point and, indeed, whether or not it is a true story. (Mr. Hudson got it secondhand which is, unfortunately, where many of the best cat stories come from.)

The cat of the story was a small cat and had lived almost all her life in close association with a dog, the two having met as kitten and puppy. As they grew up their friendship grew closer, the little cat affectionately ordering the dog around, as is usual in such relationships—scolding him now and then for his stupidity but nevertheless relying on his protective largeness and his, to a cat, rather ungainly strength. The cat had kittens, then, and introduced the dog to them, explaining, no doubt, that he was to look after them in the event she had to be away.

But while the kittens were still very small, the cat discovered that they were not in the safest place for kittens. Cats are always discovering that; for many cats, early motherhood is one long moving day. She looked around the house she and the kittens and the dog shared with a few humans, and found a fine secluded place on an upper floor. She started to carry the kittens there, and at once a difficulty arose—she was a very small cat and the kittens were too bulky to be transported. She turned at once to the dog, who was easily large enough to carry kittens; who was built to be a moving man among dogs.

She took the dog to the kitchen box, pointed the kittens out to him, and then took him to the new place she had chosen. Then she returned him to the box, picked up one of the kittens as well as she could, carried it a step or two, put it down and looked pointedly at the stairs she would have to climb. Then, figuring it was clear enough, she went up to the new place and prepared to receive.

The dog did not get the idea at once; she waited but he arrived with no kittens. She found him, took him back, explained the whole thing over again, as patiently as a cat might under the circumstances. And finally, as Mr. Hudson heard it, the dog got the idea. He picked the kittens up gently, one by one, and took them to the new nest and thereafter, when the cat wanted the kittens moved, she had only to mention it to her dog and transportation was arranged.

It is an engaging story and perhaps, of course, not completely factual. But there is nothing essentially improbable in it, assuming intelligence in both the animals. Martini is also a very small cat and her kittens were too heavy for her to carry; she could not lift them clear of the floor, as a cat wants to do; part of the carried kitten was always dragging. She always tried, when the kittens strayed, to carry them back where they belonged, but it came to seem to us that, after the first few times, she gave it more or less a token effort. She would lift a wandering kitten, start back with it and then pause and look at whichever human was nearest. She always got the help she wanted and, we thought, came in time to rely upon it. It is not inconceivable that she might similarly have educated and relied upon a dog, had one been handy.

Such stories convinced Mr. Hudson that cats do think and similar stories, corroborated by a few simple experiments, were similarly convincing to George J. Romanes who, in 1883, published one of the earliest semi-scientific discussions of animal intelligence. In collecting material for his book, Romanes, "considering it desirable to cast as wide a net as possible, fished the seas of popular literature as well as the rivers of scientific writing." He came up, Thorndike was to think later, with some very odd fish.

The Romanes study, although in some respects pathfinding, is not entirely scientific. He encouraged people to write to him, telling stories about their pets, and there can be little doubt that, particularly with cats and dogs, he started with an unscientific predisposition which his correspondents—all of whom knew amazingly bright animals—did nothing to dissipate. When one is informed, for example, that there was a cat once who, noting that birds like crumbs, got crumbs and scattered them to attract birds for his own nefarious purposes, one can hardly avoid being impressed by the acumen of the feline. Romanes heard of such a cat, although his informant did not tell him precisely how a cat goes about scattering crumbs. He heard of another who, finding that crumbs humans had scattered for birds had become buried under snow, dug them out and put them in sight, for all the world like a human feeding deer during a bad winter to keep the game supply alive.

The author lapsed now and then into scientific detachment. "It clearly becomes a matter of great difficulty to say in the case of the lower animals whether any action which appears to indicate intelligent choice is not really action of the reflex kind," he dutifully notes, but his heart is clearly not in it. He is happier, one feels, when he can retell stories of cats and crumbs, although it is only fair to say that he was mildly sceptical of the crumb-scattering cat. He appears to accept, however, the story of a cat who, given to catching rabbits, found a black one and brought it to his mistress "clearly recognizing it was an unusual specimen" and, one may assume, hoping that his mistress would have an interesting explanation of the phenomenon.

His own experiments, which were not as extensive as some made later and even less carefully controlled, were fairly simple ones, done with strings and levers and the like, and with food as the incentive. They convinced him that "in the understanding of mechanical appliances cats attain to a higher level than any other animals, except monkeys and perhaps elephants." He shrewdly enough observed that this might be expected since "the monkey in its hands, the elephant in its trunk, and the cat in its agile limbs provided with mobile claws all possess instruments adapted to manipulation with which no other organs in the brute creation can properly be compared." He may have been less shrewd in regarding, as he apparently did, the cat's paws as comparable to the monkey's hands as instruments of manipulation, but this is a mistake easily made by an animal which is so used to hands that he is no longer able properly to appreciate them. Certainly it is a mistake which has been made, almost without exception, by the investigators who have followed Romanes.

Romanes did note the probability that "the higher aptitude which these animals display in their understanding of mechanical appliances is due to the reaction upon their intelligence by these organs of manipulation," a statement which, carried to a point by no means illogical, might well explain why there are super-monkeys but no super-cats. And his final conclusion was that the cat is "highly intelligent . . . though when contrasted with its great domestic rival, the dog, its intelligence, from being cast in quite a different mould, is frequently under-rated." He also thought that the cat has "never in any considerable degree been subject to those psychologically transforming influences whereby a prolonged and intimate association with man has so profoundly modified the psychology of the dog."

This statement, in addition to being grammatically rather baffling, is psychologically confusing. The cat has certainly been in "prolonged and intimate association with man" if a period of four thousand years or so may be considered prolonged. Why he has not been subject to the "psychologically transforming influences" of this association is not clear, unless it is because he is a cat and not a dog. This simple solution is one not greatly attractive to psychologists, whether they are considering men or other animals, since it implies that individual differences may outweigh environmental similarities, a scientifically unsatisfactory postulate. No cat would so lose himself among words.

But Romanes was a friend of cats, and thought well of them. Nathaniel Southgate Shaler was certainly no felinophile, and there is a note of reluctance in his observation that "in the matter of intelligence, cats appear to rank almost as high as dogs." A little bewilderingly, he continues:

"Cats are even quicker than their canine relatives in discerning the nature of man's artful contrivance; they readily acquire the habit of opening doors which are closed by means of a latch, even when it is necessary to combine strong pull on the handle with the push that completes the operation. Feats of this kind are rarely if ever performed by dogs. . . .

"While considering the inelastic quality which is exhibited by cats as compared with dogs, the naturalist notes with interest the fact that the former creature belongs to a family which has never been accustomed to any social life beyond the limits of the family. Moreover, all the cats have the habit of hunting in a solitary way, each for itself in the achievement and in the result. It is otherwise with dogs. They belong to a group which hunts in packs. For ages they have been used to communal life. Their minds have become accustomed to social intercourse; they are used to having their excitements of the chase in comradeship and generally they are accustomed to the rough and tumble fraternity which we behold in a pack of wolves."

The naturalist might also note with interest the strange case of the fox, whose hunting habits and social life are more feline than canine, who is nevertheless unmistakably of the dog family and whose intelligence is proverbial. It is also interesting to note that the human, to whom gregariousness often seems a proof of intelligence, calls the reserved fox "sly" as he does the cat, and "crafty." There is obliquity in refusal to join the lodge, whether the divergent one is man or other animal.

This comparison of cat and dog, to the disadvantage of whichever the investigator does not prefer, has long been a mainstay of studies into animal intelligence. It is, of course, seldom made entirely without bias, since, although the world of humans is by no means divided into those who like dogs and those who like cats, most humans do have a preference in the matter and some have a preference which falls just short of hysteria. Even Dr. Wesley Mills, a professor of physiology at McGill University, had some struggle with his bias when, at the turn of the century, he observed a kitten and a puppy for some months and noted down, day by day, what he saw. He was, one suspects, a dog man at heart, yet few experimenters, including several more famous, ended with a clearer perception of the nature of the cat.

Dr. Mills seems, during the period of his enquiry, to have had a good deal of time on his hands, and he spent it watching the little animals. At a certain age the kitten opened his eyes; at a certain age so did the dog. The kitten and dog both learned to turn their heads in the direction of sounds; in time they learned to coordinate their movements; they learned or did not learn the toilet habits humans prefer in animals. Through all this process of growing up they were under the observant eyes of the physiologist, who was a qualified veterinarian as well as a physician of humans, and who was a master of arts to boot.

He found, as this went on, that "the cat was greatly in advance of the dog of corresponding age in co-ordination of voluntary movements" and that the cat was also superior in the speed with which it adapted itself to its environment—Dr. Mills and Dr. Mills's study, for the most part, to say nothing of a toilet pan and a spot on the lower shelf of a bookcase which the cat greatly preferred. In this last connection, Dr. Mills noted, with almost super-human forbearance, that the cat displayed "strong will power, intelligently expressed." By the time he had finished, he thought that the cat is "greatly misunderstood and its intelligence greatly under-rated" and that: "If intelligence lies in adapting means to ends, in a more or less conscious way, including the adaptation of its own organization to the environment, then the diary of the cat will be found an interesting record bearing on the subject. In fact, from this point of view, the cat during the first three months of its life is decidedly in advance of the dog."

It is obvious, of course, that Dr. Mills's investigations were of too limited a scope quite to justify generalization. He may merely have happened on a bright cat and a dog who was not so bright; the intelligence quotients of both animals varying widely among individuals. Or, the cat may have been precocious, without being essentially superior; the dog may have been embarrassed by the scrutiny and ill at ease, reactions which child psychologists always try to take into account when making human I. Q. tests—with the result, of course, that the subjective element is re-inserted into a situation contrived primarily to eliminate it. But whatever he learned on the comparative basis, he learned a good deal about cats and became, in a fashion, the cat's champion.

"Unlike the dog," he wrote in his conclusions, "the cat has received very little attention and consideration from man. There are many reasons for this neglect, but not least in significance is the fact that puss is no flatterer; the dog adapts himself to every caprice and whim of his master, but the cat is always herself. To understand her at her best, she must be manipulated as a delicate piece of mechanism and treated in the very kindest fashion. When so dealt with, the cat proves to be by no means only a comparatively untamed embodiment of certain strong instincts."

But Dr. Mills concluded, also, that the "nature of the dog is much nearer that of man's than is the cat's," possibly not intending to sound quite so misanthropic as he did.

At about the time Dr. Mills was watching his kitten and his pup, and learning that, if one wants anything from a cat, one must handle him gently, with delicacy and kindness, a psychologist who was to become much more famous was conducting a series of experiments on cats—and other animals—on the simple theory that "never will you get a better psychological subject than a hungry cat." The scientist who approached his subject matter with this almost childlike ignorance of its essential nature was Edward Lee Thorndike of Columbia University, whose contributions to human psychology were many and important, whose scientific methods perhaps should not be challenged by a layman.

Dr. Thorndike's experiments were made in 1898 and were, so far as we know, the first to be conducted with regard for modern scientific methods. He made them partly in answer to Romanes, whose anecdotal method he—rightly of course—thought haphazard. He noted that if you asked people for stories showing animals to be intelligent you were unquestionably going to get the stories; that you would get reports showing the animals only at their best. "Human folk are as a matter of fact eager to find intelligence in animals. They like it," Dr. Thorndike comments, with shrewd accuracy.

His shrewdness continued, to a degree, in his general design for the tests. He had prepared certain boxes, from which an animal might escape by certain manipulations—in the basic case, by pulling on a loop of cord. When the animal pulled the cord, so freeing itself, the animal was rewarded by food. There were variants to this basic device which, by adding complications, tested the animals' ability to adjust to more difficult environments. With these boxes, and ten cats, Dr. Thorndike conducted a series of experiments which led him to the conclusion that cats do not think, do not imitate, do not reason; that they, and other animals "have no images or memories at all, no ideas to associate." He added: "Perhaps the entire fact of association in animals is the presence of sense-impressions with which were associated, by resultant pleasure, certain impulses and that therefore, and therefore only, a certain situation brings about a certain act." He found, for example, that a cat has a "sense impression" of itself pulling a loop, seeing "its paw in a certain place" and of using its body in a certain way. Result: Food.

He reached these and other conclusions by, in the case of cats, keeping them in a condition of "utter hunger." (In a late edition of his book on the subject, Dr. Thorndike rather indignantly denied that in this instance he meant what he obviously said. Keeping cats in "utter" hunger was not, he assured some indignant correspondents, at all the same thing as starving them.) When a given cat was hungry enough, he was put into a box and left to get out. He was timed; when he solved the problem he was fed. Later he was returned, timed again, fed again. Each cat was given many tests, in the simplest box and, when he was able to escape without delay, moved to another box. The speed of escape formed the basis for conclusions; if, for example, there had been a sudden acceleration after a certain number of experiments, Thorndike would have assumed that at that point the animal had thought the problem out. He found no such sharp advances.

"The time curve," Thorndike explained, "is obviously a fair representation of the progress of the formation of the association, for the two essential factors in the latter are the disappearance of all activity save the particular sort which brings success with it and the perfection of that particular act so that it is done precisely and at will. . . . The combination of the two factors is inversely proportional to the time taken, provided the animal surely wants to get out at once. This was rendered almost certain by the degree of hunger. . . . The gradual slope of the time curves, then, shows the absence of reasoning. They represent the wearing smooth of a path in the brain, not the decisions of a rational consciousness."

What actually happened to establish these convictions in Dr. Thorndike's mind was rather odd. In the first place, the cats were obviously very odd—or very badly frightened—because, during the experiments, all but two of the ten behaved in a fashion which the experimenter describes in these words:

"When put into the box, the cat would show evident signs of discomfort and of an impulse to escape from confinement. It tries to squeeze through any opening; it claws and bites at the bars or wires; it thrusts its paws out through any opening and claws at anything it reaches; it continues its efforts when it strikes anything loose and shaky; it may claw at things within the box. It does not pay very much attention to the food outside, but seems simply to strive instinctively to escape from confinement. The vigor with which it struggles is extraordinary. For eight or ten minutes it will claw and bite and squeeze incessantly."

It is precisely at this point that people who know cats at all well part company with Dr. Thorndike. And, less subjectively, it is at this same point that those who have tried to repeat the Thorndike experiments have also parted from the master. Nobody else has ever been able to get cats to behave toward boxes as Thorndike's cats behaved—or all but two of them behaved. One of these two was "an old cat"—it was actually about a year and a half old, or just out of cat adolescence—and the other was "uncommonly sluggish." Both these cats were discarded early in the experiments.

And these were, of course, the cats who behaved as cats normally do behave when not mishandled, because if there is one thing a cat likes better than another it is a box, and being in a box. The cat's instinct is to find a box if possible; to go into it and pull the roof over his head; to sit in it and wash up. Almost the last thing a cat wants to do is to leave this delightful box, where he is safe and protected. Almost the last thing a scientist should do would be to gauge an animal's intelligence by the speed with which the animal does something he doesn't particularly want to do.

But that was what Dr. Thorndike did, and it was on that he based his conclusions. Carl Van Vechten, who cannot, to be sure, be considered dispassionate in any matter involving cats, calls the conclusions "absolutely valueless" because of this and other aspects of them and adds: "The experiment seems to me entirely analogous to that of putting a hungry and terrified Cherokee Indian into a Rolls-Royce and asking him, in a strange language, to run it if he wants his dinner." More quietly, but to the same point, a later scientist expresses the view that, judging by the behavior of the cats, Thorndike's "animal psychology is like a physiology written solely from observation of diabetics."

What precisely was wrong with the Thorndike cats has never been determined; it is conceivable, but unlikely, that he merely chanced upon eight hysterics out of ten. That the cats he used were essentially peculiar is further suggested by the fact that, so far as he indicates, food provided to all of them the necessary incentive to escape. He does, to be sure, admit that when in the box most of his cats did not seem to pay much attention to the food outside, but the importance of this indifference escaped him. The importance is that, even in the case of a very hungry cat, food is always secondary to safety, often to the need of affection, now and then merely to the urge for cleanliness. It therefore provides a very inadequate experimental incentive; one is inclined to think that the cats would have got out faster if Dr. Thorndike had merely promised to go away.

Cats are eager eaters, when in health. If they are talkative cats, they will even yammer for their food. Yet the cat who demands most ardently will frequently, when the food arrives, leave it to scout a possible danger or even to seek a caress. We have never encountered, or heard of, a cat who would eat when frightened, as all the Thorndike cats evidently were. Many cats will vomit food eaten while they are no more than mildly nervous; almost no cat will eat in a strange place until it has been thoroughly investigated. That the Thorndike cats did not end the experiments by starving themselves to death is remarkable; eating must have been among the least of their desires.

It would be unfair to suggest that the cats were in any way mistreated and in his footnote on "utter" hunger Dr. Thorndike took pains to point out that they were not. "Not one of the many visitors

to the [experiment] room mentioned anything extraordinary or distressful in the animals' conduct," he protests. "There are no signs of fear or panic."

But during the experiments, the cats were clearly, on his own description, in a state of panic and that fact alone, whatever its cause, would seem enough to vitiate his experiments and, resultingly, cast doubt upon his conclusions. One may assume merely that he was the wrong man to handle cats; that he would not have known what

Dr. Mills was talking about when he advised that they must be "manipulated as delicate mechanisms."

It is true that Dr. Thorndike himself suggested further investigation into the cat mind by people who "think they know cats," implying possible self-doubts. Nor did he claim nearly as much for his experiments as has since been claimed for them; to Thorndike the beginning made was "meager" although he also thought it "solid."

Further investigation has been made, as we shall see; much of it casts doubt on the solidity of the Thorndike beginning. Yet he was an important psychologist and he cast a long shadow, particularly over the laymen's conception of animal intelligence. One can still find his influence in much that is written about cats; almost everyone feels he knows, vaguely, that cats have trouble in getting out of boxes and that they finally learn only to repeat, precisely, a successful movement, with no "idea" what they are doing.

It must be remembered, also, that Dr. Thorndike, as a psychologist, was not interested primarily in the minds of non-articulate animals. As a psychologist, he was interested in mind, including the human. From his cats—and his dogs and his monkeys—he sought indications of the way the mind works, as mind. One can only hope that his methods were more adroit with, for example, monkeys. Probably they were; monkeys always get the best of it.

11

Monkeys Get the Best of It

In CONSIDERING NOT only Dr. Thorndike's tests of feline intelligence, but also the more convincing tests which have followed it, it is well always to remember one essential thing—the tests are devised by the simian mind. With the best will in the world, and men of the greatest good will have worked in the field, this limitation cannot be escaped. Having hands, we think in terms of hands, as we think in terms of certain desires and certain fears which are indigenous to creatures who walk upright and have a habit of using tools.

Let us try to imagine how things would be were the positions reversed, were cats—super-cats, of course—testing the intelligence of men.* It is difficult because, as Mivart pointed out, it is difficult for a human to become a cat. We must start with an assumption which may not be true: That to a super-cat a human would seem a creature which wished to be a cat and could not. If a cat felt so, he would attribute to the human the characteristics of a cat; would felinomorphize man. As the human assumes that a cat must want to escape from a box, a cat might assume that a human's greatest desire—particularly with large cats around—would be to get into a box. We may guess, then, that the cat's experiments would be conducted in a large room, or cage, with a smaller room inside it. Inside the smaller room there would, as further incentive, be a fat, appetizing mouse or rat.

(It may be argued that we go too far here; that any intelligent cat would discover that few humans are fond of mouse. Yet the incentive food usually provided cats in experiments is liver, and by

---

* Michael Joseph made a similar attempt several years ago.

no means all cats like liver. Two of our present three abhore it; Martini considers it offal, and tries to cover it.)

The human under test would be placed in the larger room, and would be expected to attempt immediately to get into the smaller, and at the mouse. He would not at first understand this; he might scramble meaninglessly around the walls of the outer room, trying to get out of it. The feline Thorndike with a stop watch would grade the human down for this; but if the human merely sat and cogitated he would probably be discarded as "a very old human"— of, say, about age eighteen—or a "sluggish" one. But we may assume that superior humans would get the idea—thoughtful feline experimenters would purr at him encouragingly and give advice in cat.

Now to the inner room the human would find no door with a proper latch, suitable for grasping with the human hand. Instead, let us say, he would find—after prolonged and at first fruitless search— that a panel which could be clawed down was set into the wall of the inner room. The panel would be flush with the wall, of course; since cats do not grasp, no handhold would be provided. It would be expected that the human would sink his fingernails, and perhaps his teeth, into the panel and pull it down, in the fashion of a higher animal, i.e., a cat. That he would not be so adept as a cat, the intelligent cat would expect. But the cat nevertheless, if we are not to assume infinitely greater intelligence in the feline than the human shows in similar circumstances, would think as an animal with claws and would find it very difficult to think in any other fashion. To the super-cat, the human would be merely a creature with aborted claws, as to us the cat is a creature with inadequate hands.

The human under test might eventually claw the panel down; might well prove quicker than, say, the bear in discerning the nature of the feline's artful contrivance. He would then be expected to leap through an opening, set perhaps twelve feet from the floor—what cat cannot easily leap twice his length?—and pounce on his mouse. But how cats would shake their heads at human pouncing! How they would write, summing up gravely, of the human's "useless movements," of the slowness with which, even

after repeated trials, the human caught on; of the essential indifference many of the subjects, although kept in a state of utter hunger,
showed to the incentive food. "The possibility is," the feline Thorndike concludes, "that humans have no images or memories at all,
no ideas to associate . . . only certain sense-impressions . . . certain
impulses. . . ."

Big cats would, of course, make no such errors in testing little
cats; super-cats would be astute enough in their enquiries into
felines who had not evolved. And man is astute enough, generally,
in testing monkeys, who are also creatures with hands. It may be
largely because of this that men commonly set so high a regard on
the intelligence of the lesser simians. L. T. Hobhouse, also a
psychologist of note, thought as much, observing in 1901 that "ape
intelligence lends itself more readily to the kind of experiments
which human intelligence most readily contrives," and suggesting
that this was not necessarily an evidence of qualitatively superior
intelligence.

Hobhouse was one of the first experimenters to criticize sharply
both Thorndike's methods and his conclusions, doing this partly
on the basis of logic and partly on that of his own experiments.
Hobhouse was particularly doubtful of the validity of the primary
conception on which his predecessor operated: roughly that intelligence can be correlated inversely with the time required to achieve
success.

"Mr. Thorndike does not seem to recognize at all adequately
the very rough and ready character of his statistical methods," Hobhouse observes with, it seems to us, considerable restraint. Hobhouse was also puzzled by the time curves themselves; to him they
did not, by any means, seem always to show the gradual advance
which Thorndike believed they did. But the curves were, Hobhouse
noted with weariness, very difficult to understand, as indeed they
are. Possibly no one, except Thorndike himself, has perfectly
understood them—Thorndike and Dr. Georgina Ida Stickland
Gates, who, thirty years after Thorndike first wrote, and almost as
long after Hobhouse and several others had criticized, wrote a

book about cat intelligence based almost entirely on the Thorndike findings.

Hobhouse, who had cats of his own, and dogs too, was conscious of the individuality of the animals and treated them well; none of his cats, as a result, became panic-stricken. He found, among the animals he tested, no "essential difference in capacity to learn between dogs, elephants, cats and otter"; he concluded that: "What the animals learnt was not merely to respond in a particular way to a particular object but to produce a certain change in that object as a means of securing food." With his animals, that is, it did not seem to be a question of "paw here, body so, pleasure" but of "move string, pleasure," a basically different thing. "If this view is correct," Hobhouse wrote, "we have here in an elementary form the equivalent in action of the practical judgment—idea." He believed that animals use experience intelligently, which is about all that can be asked of any creature, and more than is often got. He is at once observant and dryly rational in his comment on Thorndike's statement that, if three cats out of eight learn to get out of boxes, three in a thousand put into a room might learn to use a latch by the same methods.

"That is, I suppose, by jumping and scratching all around the room," Hobhouse writes, and then goes to the root of the matter: "But the reply is that a thousand cats do not spend their time jumping and scratching around a room."

Cats were not let alone in the years which followed Thorndike and Hobhouse; experiments went on, both in the United States and elsewhere. V. Teyrovsky conducted experiments in Poland and "proved" selective imitation in cats and also "practical judgment" and "articulate ideas," all of which Thorndike was confident he had disproved. C. S. Berry investigated in 1908 and also "proved" that cats imitate not only one another, but also humans, and that cats do not instinctively kill and eat mice, but learn to do so by imitation. In 1909, two experimenters found fine color discrimination in cats and in 1915, two more observers found cats entirely color blind. Dr. Gates wrote in 1928 that "other investigations may be made tomorrow which will overthrow these theories," a re-

markably temperate statement, since the theories were largely
Thorndike's and quite a few people were convinced they had been
overthrown already.

Donald Keith Adams, almost as if he had heard Dr. Gates, published in 1929 the results of experiments carried on at Yale. These
experiments—although much that has been said of the inadequacy
of the box method applies also to them—seem to us to throw more
light into the mind of the cat than any others. Mr. Adams had the
experience of his predecessors on which to build, he brought to the
task considerable lucidity of mind, and his cats liked him. They
liked him in spite of rather trying times cats and scientist had
together and in spite of the rather horrid food the cats were fed.

Adams's purpose was to recheck Thorndike's experiments and to
continue from them; Adams used eighteen cats over a period of two
years, keeping them in a converted stable where they had nothing
to sleep on but the floor, no straps or ropes to play with and were
fed, at first, a mixture of flour, water, beef and bone meal, essential
salts, sifted alfalfa meal, powdered brewer's yeast and a dry milk
product, these ingredients being cooked together in water and made
into a "stiff paste or cake of relatively low energy value." Subsequently, for reasons known only to Mr. Adams, lard was added to
this unpleasant substance, which the cats nevertheless ate. Now and
then, when liver was left over from the experiments, it was added
and "seemed to possess some mysterious property even beyond its
value in replenishing the supply of erythrocytes and vitamines. It
certainly enhanced the attractiveness of the food for the cats."
Nevertheless, the cats did not thrive on their food and, at the close
of the experimental period, Adams was forced to report that "the
diet described can no longer be recommended" because the cats
were getting mange, losing weight and now and then merely dying.

The cats were badly fed and uncomfortable, physically and emotionally below par—and one of them proved what he thought of the
whole business when Adams conducted one experiment to test
the cat's homing power. This cat was taken in a box to a point two
and a half miles from the laboratory and there released by means of
a string device, Adams remaining hidden. The cat left the box,

looked around for ten minutes or so—probably to be sure Adams had not hidden under a leaf—and then walked off hurriedly in a direction at right angles to the direction in which the laboratory lay. He never came back, either; proving a good deal about one cat's intelligence if little about homing powers.

But the need for economy caused most of the rigors to which the cats were subjected and there was no Thorndike about to accentuate the discomforts. Adams was gentle with his cats, he was fair to them; one may infer, although the experimenter judiciously does not state, that he grew fond of them; one of them, at least, fell in love with him. And only one of the eighteen behaved, when placed in the escape box, remotely as had all but two of the Thorndike cats. The other seventeen of the Adams cats behaved precisely like cats, except that at least one behaved a little like a genius.

Adams searched for, and generally got, cats who had had little experience of home life and were, as a result, less familiar than the well-cared-for house cat with human devices. Our Gin, for example, gave every indication, when she and we were living in the camp near Brewster, of knowing that movement of a latch on the front door was an inevitable preliminary to the door's opening. She could not reach it effectively herself but she always got as close to it as she could, and looked at it, and reached toward it. In almost any escape test devised by a human, she would start with an advantage. Adams sought to avoid cats so educated. He used, also, young cats, of little experience with any kind of life.

He studied diagrams of the boxes used by Thorndike and, in so far as the diagrams were clear—they were not always—duplicated the Thorndike boxes for his first experiments. It was into one of the simple Thorndike boxes that a cat named Ace, who was six months old, was put. What she did was, generally, typical of the Adams cats in the Thorndike boxes.

She did not kick and scream in a paroxysm of anything. She was, on her first time in the box, there for twenty-eight minutes, twenty-six of it she spent sitting and looking around, washing up and, no doubt, enjoying intensely the fact that she was in a box. Two min-utes she spent in not very excited activity, which was entirely with-

out result. She was taken out. After a time she was put back in
again and sat in the center of the box looking around. Then Adams
and the cat were both "startled by a loud commotion among the
apes upstairs. She moved and reached through the front of the box
to the pan, (containing the incentive food) which I had inadvertently left just within reach." She upset the pan, but drew it closer,
clawed up the food and "pulled the food—not the pan—through the
bars." She ate the food.

Adams entered the experiment room, replaced the pan at a greater
distance and Ace "immediately tried to reach it again, but quickly
desisted and sat quietly in the center for five more minutes. She
then pawed the pulley casually, caught a claw in the string, released
the door and came out." After ten trials—during one of which she
reached over the top of the door and raised the latch without aid
of the string, went out and spent thirty seconds in apparent thoughtful examination of the whole contraption—after ten trials she got
out whenever she thought it was a good idea. She got out, that is,
the first time she tried to get out, and with no useless motions, no
fumbling. Now and then considerable time elapses before she tried;
sometimes she came out at once.

Ace was tested thirty-one times. She had four "failures," that is,
on four occasions she made no effort to leave the box. And—she
used eleven methods. She did not, so far as Adams could see, form
any sense-impression of paw in a certain position, body making such
movements. She formed, apparently, an impression of pulling a
string. At first, she pulled the string most often with her teeth;
later in the experiments she used a paw. The last time she was tried
in the box she pulled the string to her mouth with a paw and then
gave a brief tug with her teeth.

It had been Thorndike's custom, when a cat eventually solved a
problem, to vary the problem. Most simply, the box was changed
so that, while it still opened from within when a string was pulled,
the string was now in a different place. Thorndike's cats made
heavy going of this. Ace, who was generally typical of Adams's
cats, was put in a changed box about a week after she had completed her first tests. She found the loop of string almost at once,

pulled it, got out and ate. She was tried twenty-three times in this box and always opened the box at once—opened it, that is, as soon as she was ready to do anything but enjoy being in a box.

One cat did have a tantrum when put in the box, continued thereafter to prove intractable and was finally discharged as incurable. Another appeared to be similarly psychotic, scrambled frantically in the box and, when let out, tried as desperately to escape from the experiment room. Adams went in, spoke to the cat and petted it. The cat, who had until then entirely ignored the incentive

food, thereupon ate. He afterward learned the escape routine quickly and well but *never ate the incentive food until Adams entered the room.* As soon as Adams did go into the room, and whether or not he petted the cat, the cat purred and ate, commenting unconsciously on feline motivation.

But a male cat named Pete was Adams's prize. Pete was put into one of the preliminary boxes; like Ace, he at first sat, spending ten minutes in what seemed to the observer to be "leisurely inspection" of the entire situation. Then he took hold of the loop in the string, pulled it, watched the door open and came out. "The act could not have been performed with greater economy of effort," Adams comments.

Three minutes later, Pete was put back in the box. He washed up. Then, without ado, he reached up, pulled the string, and left the box. Thereafter, during many tests, Pete always pulled the string, always got out. Sometimes he was quicker than other times, but Thorndike could have looked in vain for a curve indicating the slow, irrational, wearing of a pattern path in Pete's mind. Sometimes Pete wanted and got out at once; sometimes he had washing to do first—or thinking or day-dreaming. Many things, as Adams acutely observed—and devastated the whole Thorndike crude time theory by observing—may have entered into the time differences which "may have been due to variations in the apparatus, to the host of internal conditions that we commonly lump and call motivation, to some inaccessible and non-inferable mental process not subsumed in this category, or to all these things." But when Pete wanted out, he knew how to get out.

"The cat," Thorndike had written, "does not look over the situation, much less think it over, and decide what to do." Adams shakes his head. "In the descriptions of the behavior of my cats," he observes correctly, "it can be seen that they did look over the situation with every appearance of 'thinking it over' and then deciding what to do. Indeed, it was the typical rather than the exceptional procedure. Further, one of them, Pete, after ten minutes of looking it over did the correct thing. Presumably, if one of Thorndike's cats had been in a box ten minutes without doing anything but looking around he would have taken it out and labeled it an 'uncommonly sluggish cat.'"

It became clear to Adams in repeating the Thorndike experiments, as it becomes clear to anyone who reads of the Adams experiments, that to the cats "the loop was the thing to be pulled, and the how of the pulling was a secondary matter." And this, of course, strikes hard at the center of the Thorndike theory.* If the cat has a perception, however unclear—and Pete's seemed anything but confused—of the bringing about of desirable change through certain actions, it may reasonably be argued that the cat "thinks."

Adams went on to other experiments. He hung liver on a string inside a box, and the cats had to pull it up to get it. Most of them did; one, named Tom, pulled on the string with his paws, making it into a loop. He put the loop into his mouth, holding onto his gains, and pulled again with his paws until he got the food. "In a human," Adams comments, "this behavior would inevitably be called ideational and I can see no escape from the conclusion that it was ideational in the cat."

The experimenter put food in a dish inside a box and fastened a string to the dish, the string dangling outside the box so that, if it was pulled, the food would be brought within reach. He tried this on Taps, who played with the string, moving the dish accidentally. She stopped, hearing the movement of the dish, and looked thoughtfully at the contraption. Nothing further happened and she walked around the room, investigating. She hit the string in passing and again the dish moved. "This time, after looking only two seconds at the liver, she went to the grill front of the cage and pulled out the liver hand over hand. Five minutes later she did this at once, and in subsequent trials never took more than twenty to twenty-five seconds."

A cat named Chip also learned this trick readily. Then Adams made it more complicated; he arranged three strings dangling from

---

* It does not, as we have indicated, strike hard enough. As recently as January, 1949, a writer for *The American Magazine* accepted a large part of the Thorndike theory although, seeking that freshness so desirable in magazine articles, he managed to imply, without precisely saying, that it had just been formulated.

the box, only one of which was tied to liver and it the only string of the three which had not been used before, and hence did not have a familiar scent. Chip started to take the nearest familiar string but did not take it. Instead, he looked "toward the far end of the strings" and then went at once to the loaded string, pulled it out, and ate the liver. This took him twenty-five seconds. Chip went on to higher things.

Adams tried on some of his cats the memory test which has been used on various animals. The subject animal is placed, in a cage, in the center of the experiment room. In each corner of the room there is a box, and into one of these boxes, while the animal watches, the experimenter puts food. The animal is allowed a couple of minutes to think it over, then taken from the room and kept out of it for periods ranging from a few minutes to several hours. The subject is then returned and released; does he go to the right box for food?

The results with the cats varied, but many of them had perfect scores and many of the failures, Adams felt afterward, "might better be attributed to my stupidity than to that of the cats." Adams was an unusual experimenter, willing to share blame; willing to make allowances. He tried for a considerable period to set up an experiment comparable to one performed with monkeys who— sometimes—learned to move and pile up boxes to get at food hung beyond their reach.

A good many experimenters, one unhappily suspects, would suppose that, if equally bright, cats could pile boxes as well as monkeys could and, when the cats failed, ascribe failure to stupidity. But Adams was aware that "a foot is an awkward substitute for a hand." Adams worked long and diligently to establish conditions which would give cats an even break with monkeys at box piling, but he was never entirely successful. The experiment remains open; any cat owner is free to try his cats on it. But it is hard to think as a creature without hands thinks; monkeys always get the best of it.

Adams came to doubt, as a good many did in the years when cats were used extensively in psychological experiments—as they no longer are; monkeys are much more convenient—that the inherent mental difference between the cat and the simian is as extreme as is generally thought. He thought that "the limits of adaptation in cats may be much nearer to the performance reported for primates, even anthropoids, than has hitherto been supposed." Now and then, indeed, he found his cats almost comparable in method and time to children, who are often similarly tested—but are not commonly, during the tests, asked to sleep on the bare floor of a barn or to be at their best on a diet of flour and alfalfa meal and lard.

Adams ended, after a couple of years with cats, thinking well of them. He attributed to them, as few had before him, "continual use of tried ideas, common use of explicit ideas and occasional, but rare, use of free ideas"; he was inclined to think that since "the frequency of free ideas is a function of a number of associations the cats probably use such ideas in their normal environments of which they have numerous associations much more commonly than could be inferred from their behavior in experiments"; he thought some of the cats revealed "perception of similarity in difference" which is a threshold to inference and hence to rational thought.

Cats have been tested also in an effort to determine why they "home"—it may be that they have a highly developed kinesthetic sense, "the primitive muscle sense which experiment has shown to be of far greater delicacy in many animals than in man" or "homing" may, in some obscure fashion, have an electronic basis. They have been dropped upside down, being allowed to prove that they turn over—because of the use of their tails? because of the balance mechanism in their inner ears? A series of experiments was, as this was written, being conducted to find out why tomcats howl, but conclusions were not yet reached. Science is often interested in obscure matters. It will also, on occasion, go to considerable lengths to prove the unchallenged.

No more elaborate series of experiments has been conducted on cats than that undergone throughout 1929 and the first four months of 1930 by Audrey M. Shuey and eighty-two kittens in the animal laboratory of the Department of Psychology of Columbia University. Miss Shuey felt that previous experimenters had erred in using too few cats, and she used plenty; she found something haphazard in earlier tests, and there was nothing haphazard in hers, which were monitored by electricity which, to people who do not happen to live in the country, seems infallible.

Her device consisted of two round cages, one set within the other like the hole in a doughnut. The incentive food was in this inner cage. In the floor of the runway in the rim of the doughnut, three plates were set equidistant from one another, raised slightly from the floor but otherwise indistinguishable from it. Depending on the whim of the operator, pressure on one or more of these plates—and if on more than one, then in a determinable order—would open a door in the inner cage, thus making the food available. At various times, forty-five male kittens and thirty-seven females, all from eight to nine weeks old when they started, were put into this contraption while Miss Shuey, one supposes with her mind on a doctorate, looked on.

After a few animals had been pre-experimented with, it was decided that the test series would run thus: At first, the door to the food would open if any plate was stepped upon; next, if any two; finally, if all three. The kittens were allowed five minutes for any one test; failure was punished by confinement for thirty minutes without access to food. A good many of the kittens, of course, made no effort to do anything during the first five minutes; a number "failed" by "sitting or washing, playing with tail, pawing at shadow, jumping, rolling over, rubbing against the walls." They also showed a tendency to go to sleep from time to time, a practice frowned upon by the experimenter.

But they all learned the first three steps. It took them from nine to 136 trials to learn the first step—to press on any one plate; from one to seventy to learn the second; from one to 121 the third. "The wide variability in the several criteria of learning was greatly increased by a few individual animals," Miss Shuey comments, a shade morosely. And she writes also:

"No kitten was noted as having learned a step 'suddenly' in the sense of having made a series of perfect performances following a first chance success. In a few cases there were, however, as few as six to ten random successes preceding a series of from five to nine perfect trials. In all these situations, the kittens were facing the inner door as they touched the plate accidentally and probably saw the door slide back."

The last sentence might well be set in italics, although Miss Shuey did not, at least typographically, so recognize its importance. Obviously, if a cat does something with its feet and, at the same time, sees something happen at a distance, and connects the two, the cat has made an inference. (It must be remembered that a cat has no experience with remote control. The "idea" of relationships distant in space or time is the product of man's ability mechanically to create such relationships.) Inadvertently, as it appears, Miss Shuey happened upon, and perhaps did not notice, a rather remarkable example of deduction in the feline mind. It seemed to her reasonable that cats should learn more rapidly if they saw what happened and this is precisely what it was. It was reasonable of the cats. But Miss Shuey was, if her publication correctly reflects her deductions, equally interested in the fact that eighty percent of her cats stepped on the plates with their forepaws or merely walked across the plates, although it is difficult to see what this suggests about the cat, except that it wears its forepaws on the front end. Some cats did, to be sure, sit down on the plates.

To learn all three of the steps in the first series, three kittens required from twenty-one to thirty tests; fourteen from fifty-one to eighty; seventeen from eighty-one to 120; fourteen from 121 to 170; three from 181 to 230 and one poor dullard 271. After they had gone this far—Miss Shuey did not wait for the backward—the kittens were given more complicated tests: to get the food they had to step first on all three plates and then on one of the two not last stepped on; then on all three and two others; finally on six, still without immediate repetition; then, for the survivors, a plate was added with each test, until to get the food on step twelve it would have been necessary to touch each plate four times. No kitten mastered this; two, one of each sex, did get up to stepping on eleven plates. One, in the middle of this, gave the whole business up and took to chasing his tail, a somewhat more reasonable activity.

After that, the kittens—cats by this time and cats with a strange view of the world—were required to step on plates in a certain order and in this, too, "individual differences were extremely large." In this, too, a pair of cats got further than the rest. Three of the four brightest cats were males; females averaged better on the basic tests; the experimenter did not find any consistence in ranking on the basic tests and the more complex problems later assigned.

Never, one supposes, has the fact that some cats are brighter than other cats been more elaborately proved. What else was proved—except, accidentally, that cats appear able to connect cause and effect—is not clear. It is mildly interesting to learn that cats vary in intelligence much as humans do: a couple of geniuses at the top, an idiot or so at the bottom; a statistical bulge in the middle, where most of us live. It is instructive to discover that science now and then, like a kitten, chases its own tail. . . .

Of all cat tests, that of Mr. Adams seems to us the most productive; seems, with all its obvious imperfections—the quantitative inadequacy of the sample; the unfortunate physical environment of the cats—to have come nearer getting into the mind of the cat than science had done before or has done since. This is, of course, a matter of opinion purely; human preference as clearly enters in. We are, it goes without saying, more impressed with scientific evidence which shows intelligence in cats than with evidence which does not. This is partly because we like cats; partly because we have known a good many cats, almost all of them apparently intelligent. The cats we have known were, in almost all respects, like Adams's cats and unlike Thorndike's; in this our observation is overwhelmingly supported by all that has been written about cats by those who knew most about them. The human knows most about that with which he most associates, and one does not commonly associate with an animal one dislikes.

"You can learn nothing about cats unless you first establish friendly relations and that takes time, sympathy and patience," Michael Joseph, one of the most astute of modern cat addicts, writes. "A detached and objective attitude toward cats is likely to yield very misleading results." And so, of course, is a sympathetic and subjective attitude. The impasse is very nearly complete.

We can, and have, learned much of the intelligence of smaller simians and it seems to be generally like our own. The cat's mind is guarded from us and, as Mr. Adams freely admitted, the barrier between may be built as much of our stupidity as of the cat's. One can only guess that the cat does not think as we think, and this not only because the cat thinks less. He can adjust to our ways, and in his adjustment we may glimpse, obliquely, what goes on in his mind. But it may very well be that of the two worlds in which the cat lives ours is the lesser and that in it he uses only a little of his mind, engrossing himself only in his own world of the four-footed. He may reveal himself fully there, but not to bipeds, whom he likes but does not greatly strive to please, whom he respects but always a long way this side of idolatry.

Yet even of this last, which is one of the things all humans "know" about cats, we are not entirely certain. Now and then, when Martini sits and looks at us out of round blue eyes too large for her head, when she blinks a little, gently, as we speak her name, it would be easy to think that there is a kind of adoration in her mind. If a dog gazed so, no one would doubt him. If Martini at all adores there is in her feeling a kind of detachment, almost of elevation. It has nothing to do with any practical matter; as animal to animal she will continue to behave as she chooses, not as we direct. Her attitude is, one may suspect, that of a philosopher.

It would be gratifying in the extreme to believe that Martini so regards us; if the cat admires the human, there must be more in the human than meets the eye. But we have not, any more than the late Dr. Thorndike had, a way of getting into her mind. We know better than to test her by human standards. Unfortunately, we know no other.

Martini lives in our world, but we cannot enter hers.

12

The Multiplication of Cats

IT IS A major purpose of all animal life to reproduce itself, filling the world with dogs, rabbits, cows and Japanese beetles, and some animals carry this activity to ridiculous lengths. Almost anything living would, if left to itself, become the only thing living, occupying all available space, ingesting the entire food supply until there was no recourse save cannibalism. Cats are particularly interested in the multiplication of cats and they do not make any bones about it. Their love affairs are filled with sultry violence and much screaming; if super-cats wrote love songs, all would tell of the dark despairs of love, none of its brightness.

We went walking once in the country and for several miles a herd of dogs went with us, since it happened to be going the same way. There was a handsome bitch, looking a little smug, in the forefront and a fine large male trotted beside her, also looking not a little pleased with himself. Behind these two, who obviously were lovers, there was a congregation of dogs—big dogs and little dogs, of all breeds and partial breeds, and at the very end, a quarter of a mile behind, panting although the day was cool, came the littlest dog of all—a tattered remnant of dogdom, a dozen times outclassed, yet with hope brimming in his eyes.

All of the dogs, although they had a single purpose and were hence competitors, trotted together amicably. The chosen dog did not mind the followers; the followers did not mind one another, nor try in any fashion to molest the object of their desire. It was the friendliest multiple courtship imaginable and it was also, of course, more than a little absurd. It was agreeable to see such cheerfulness and comradeship, but wanting in the spectacle was the dramatic intensity which the human likes to find in affairs of the heart. And lacking, too, was any suggestion of dignity.

A cat, seeing such an amorous parade, would be shocked to the innermost recesses of his violent heart. Placidity is no part of a cat in love; group courtship is unthinkable. If it is the object of the cat, as such, to fill the world with cats, it is equally the object of the tomcat so to live that he will become the only tomcat in the world, and at any moment he is ready to do what he can to further this ambition. In the presence of a ready female the tom will eagerly murder for love; no rival is to be endured.

Nor is there any doubt—there is no doubt for miles around—when a female cat is prepared to mate. As in most four-footed animals, and unlike man, this readiness is not continual in the cat, but comes on her at intervals. In some placid cats this receptiveness, if one may use so mild a word for so great a passion, may occur only a couple of times a year. In other cats it is much more frequent, so that, if unchecked, she will have kittens continuously—or, at any rate, as continuously as a sixty-three-day gestation period allows. And a few, but they should see a veterinarian, are almost never out of "heat" or, as it is more politely but less accurately said, of "season."

One has never known cats until one has lived for the week or ten days it lasts with a female cat in search of a mate. She is revealing then and, to the squeamish, not a little embarrassing. That spinsters should, as so many of them do, associate with cats proves them more tough-minded than the non-continent habitually suppose them to be. No one who has lived with an unaltered female cat can have any real ignorance of the facts of life.

No animal, save possibly man at his least restrained, so lacks reticence as a female cat—sometimes called a "queen"—when it enters her mind, and every fiber of her body, that it is time to become a mother. She was a gay thing yesterday, with no thoughts beyond the chase, her food, a little play and a good deal of sleep, the caresses of the human. Today she is gay no longer; today all the darkness of her race has entered into her soul, and all the determination which has made that race so enduring. Today she is haunted by desire, she rolls insanely on the floor and performs other gestures which perhaps are better observed than described. One may not, on the printed page, be as forthright as a cat is on the living room carpet or, for that matter, on the human lap.

And then she "calls," as they say—as they say with that studied mildness which is part of the polite vocabulary humans employ in an effort to modify nature, to bring it within the scope of good manners. She does not, in heat, call constantly. Even in heat, the cat does other things a little—she sleeps, but minimally; usually, but not always, she eats; almost always she drinks water. She also, at such times, urinates very frequently and, in spite of her training, may do so almost anywhere. And she will pad a room in circles, as if the room were a cage and she a tiger as indeed, for all she knows of it, she is. Around and around she will go and then, at a certain place on the circuit, she will stop and scream.

Her cry is wild and almost frightening; although one knows her well, knows that even now she is a gentle cat, her claws sheathed for the human, one involuntarily shivers, particularly if she calls at night, calls into the darkness. This wild, undulating cry, this desperate cry, is of the darkness of the jungle and is echoed in the darkness of man's fears. When we clung to trees, wrapping prehensile tails around convenient branches, such cries, many times magnified, must often have filled the jungle and little monkeys must have shrunk into themselves, cowering from a monster only too well known and from a passion beyond conception. Still, obscurely, that cry, although it may echo now only in the living room of a city apartment, is harrowing to human ears, and not only because it is discordant. It is beyond description wild; it reminds us of our tameness, our easy acceptance, perhaps of our superficial responses to matters of the utmost importance. The calling cat may be living excessively, and certainly she is making an excessive noise, but heaven knows she is living fully, or trying to. And any male within reach of her voice knows where she is and what she wants, and males will gather—snarling, ready for the combat which precedes delight—to gratify her need.

If she is an apartment house cat, her dark cry may be trapped

within walls; only the neighbors may respond to her entreaty, and they unsatisfactorily, with thumpings on the ceiling; with telephone calls enquiring, more or less politely, whether there isn't something—*anything*—to be done about that cat? But the cat does not give up, while her season lasts, and sometimes it seems to last forever. She *knows* there are tomcats in the world; the very violence of her need assures her of this, although it may be she has never seen a male. She has none of man's doubts. Great aspirations make certain the existence of the object aspired to. Somewhere in the world, the apartment house cat knows, there is another cat, like yet unlike, capable of assuagement.

Martini used to roam the New York apartment, calling now at a window, now at a door—now and then, when she was very inexperienced, merely at one of her humans. Surely, she seemed to be saying, you who have given me so many merely pleasant things, can give me this, without which I will die. Right here in front of you, she would add, lying down on the carpet to writhe. We, not wanting kittens at the moment, knowing further that she was too young for motherhood, could only talk to her—which made her worse—and avoid touching her, which always threw her into ecstatic spasms, as it commonly does females in her condition.

Toward the end of her expectant life, before she finally got her kittens and was then surgically relieved of desire, she hit upon one device which, while intelligent of her, made matters worse for us and for the people who lived above us in the house. Martini fell to doing her calling in the bathroom, out of which—since it was an old house, with a latch which did not work well—we could not keep her. Off tiled walls and bathroom fixtures, her screams reverberated incredibly, and there was a ventilator to carry them to the floors above and, doubtless, to a considerable part of downtown New York. The roof, we often thought, must have become saturated with snarling tomcats, particularly as Martini, with her Siamese voice, made even more—and more anguished—sound than the average female. No one has ever heard a cat cry into the night until he has heard a Siamese queen.

In the country, Martini was, if anything, rather more of a problem. If we were to have kittens—and Martini weakened us rather rapidly—we wanted kittens of Martini's kind, although we had known and been devoted to Jerry and Pammy, who were Siamese hybrids. This meant that we wanted to choose Martini's mate, which also meant that she had—if it killed all three of us—to be kept indoors during her periods of calling. Those were desperate periods and now and then she did get out, although we always caught her before a tomcat did. But we and she were harried when she was in season and, as she eventually spent most of her time in season, we were harried most of the time.

In the country, of course, she did attract males, who would sit outside the cabin and yell back at her. Once she almost got one of her own. A large tawny cat leaped to the woodbox outside the closed window through which Martini was screaming to the world. He took a look at her, apparently was startled either by her appearance or her voice, and went on up to the cabin roof. Then Martini was beside herself. Calling frantically, with new desperation, she leaped to the mantel shelf and, from it, tried furiously to go through the ceiling to get to her tom. It was shortly after this episode, which for some reason left us feeling a little shamed of ourselves, that we arranged for her to meet a chosen tom under, as it were, legalized conditions.

Anyone keeping unaltered cats, whether in country or city, must be prepared for a life in which feline sex plays a considerable, on occasion a major, part. Admittedly, Martini was more violent than many queens—she was, and is, an extremely intense cat about everything and she also had cysts on her ovaries, which was the reason she had so little time off. But the gentlest and most normal female is almost as determined—she is going to have kittens, or else.

An unaltered male presents a problem, or series of problems, less climacteric but more continuous. The major problem, and generally the most difficult, is that the male cat, whether confined or not, does a great deal of what is called "spraying." He does this on walls and doors within the house, and on anything available outside the house. He does it by backing up and ejecting urine which has an offensive and unmistakable odor and is presumably used by him to indicate to other cats, of either sex, that he is around, ready for love or combat. This habit, plus the fact that a tomcat's sanitary pan smells exactly the same way, makes the occupancy of a city apartment by a tom very trying; everything smells "of cat" as people say who have never noticed that most apartments occupied by cats and humans do not smell at all of cats. Female cats, whether spayed or not, and altered male cats, leave no odor. Their excrement is, of course, odorous, but in that they are not peculiar.

The male cat in an apartment is, further, so determined to get out that he usually wins over any but the most adamant human—and adamant humans are not, generally, humans who like cats. Napoleon, for example, hated cats almost insanely. Once out, in the city, the tomcat will come back when he likes, usually late at night, and the chances of losing him by accident are obviously high. It is true, of course, that he will not come home to have kittens; it is also true that he may not come home at all.

Our Pete was an unaltered male for about a year and a half, and a very vigorous one. We used to let him out when he insisted unbearably, as he almost always did—and for a good many months he would be sitting on the stoop in the late evening when we returned from the theater, to which our lives were then professionally dedicated. Then one night he was not on the stoop, and calling did not bring him and the next day did not bring him. Nothing brought him for a fortnight, and we had given up hope. And then, one afternoon, the cat did come back—came streaking blackly up the stairs to scratch at the kitchen door, to argue briefly with Elizabeth because she was slow to let him in, to eat enormously and to fall asleep almost as he finished. From the looks of him, he had not eaten the whole two weeks, but we were sure he had had himself a time. And it was after that, reluctantly, that we for the first time robbed a cat of sexual power.

We did not do this willingly, and did it at all only after considerable troubled thought. One of us had said, often enough, that he would never be responsible for the de-sexing of a cat; the other, more moderately, felt much the same way. Theory met circumstance, and theory was the loser—as, of course, was the cat named Pete. But Pete lived for many years longer, happily for the most part, and was a charming pet and also, to the end, a great deal of cat.

Our scruples, which we have now overcome, were those very widely held by cat owners, to whom the problem is far more acute than it is to those who own dogs. A bitch may be shut up when she wants to breed and, although she will not like it, she will not scream about it. A male dog goes about his occasions quietly enough and does not smell any more than he usually does, which people more accustomed to cats are likely to think is enough. So only now and then does a dog owner face, and assume or reject, this admittedly considerable responsibility.

Striking at sex potency is actually striking at life, and at the communal life which we feel—deeply, for the most part unconsciously —to be of infinitely greater importance than the life of the individual, since it is permanent while that of the individual is transitory. Fear of impotence, and to a lesser extent even fear of sterility, is deep in the human mind; perhaps nothing else goes more deeply. By the male, particularly, loss of potency is tragically feared; almost as much as fear for life, the soldier carries that related fear to the battleground. A good many men would, or think they would, as lief die as be eunuched before their time, and this to a considerable degree without regard to whether they actually wish to father children or are, in fact, deeply driven by desire. The potentiality is the thing.

Women, perhaps because the physical risk of such impairment is less and for other and obvious reasons, are not so much subject to this haunting fear. But they join with men in the pity which is part contempt for those of either sex who have been neutered; the eunuch is a figure at once of tragedy and of jest, and at the same time a source of uneasy embarrassment.

Feeling so strongly on the matter, and feeling so deeply in the subconscious, the human hesitates to inflict on other animals the fate he so much dreads. This hesitancy is humane and admirable, although it is not, of course, permitted by the human to interfere with more important things, like the human food supply, as every steer notices long before he is ready for the slaughter pen. It is an attitude from which it is not easy to escape; even now we are sometimes saddened that Martini can have no more kittens and that Gin and Sherry, who have never been mothers, never can be. We recognize, however, that these belated scruples are both sentimental and anthropomorphic.

They are both these regrettable things because they are based on what is, so far as we know, an entirely erroneous assumption. We assume that the cats feel the sense of deep loss, of irretrievable frustration, that humans would feel under similar circumstances. Unconsciously, we assume that Martini thinks with painful nostalgia of other days and broods despairingly over her present limitations; that Gin and Sherry, perhaps without knowing quite what it is, are unhappily aware that they have missed something. And we think this, not because the cats show any indication whatever of brooding, but because we cannot get entirely out of our human minds that cats must be as nearly like humans as they can manage.

The effect, on cats, of either castration or hysterectomy is, as a matter of simple fact, generally very inconsiderable. It is more marked in the case of the male than of the female. The male cat, particularly if neutered young, is likely to grow fat and, in growing fat, become somewhat more lethargic. They may take on a somewhat eunuch-like appearance. A good deal of this can be avoided by anyone who goes to the trouble, often considerable, of not overfeeding a neutered male, but there is no doubt that the whole structure of the cat becomes softer. To some cats this is becoming and to none who are not grossly overfed is it seriously blemishing. The other changes are slight; one may imagine that the voice becomes a little soprano, but most cats, always excepting Siamese, are more or less soprano to begin with. The cat continues to hunt as assiduously as ever, which with Pete was almost constantly. They continue to fight other cats they meet and toms, rather unaccountably, continue to fight them, although there may be more of the scuffle in the engagement than of dueling to the death. Freed from the preoccupation of sex, they remain playful long after the unaltered male has put aside such childish things, and they are, probably, somewhat more gentle. Pete was a gentle cat before his operation, and continued to be gentle afterward, although he was one of the few cats we have ever known who was careless about his claws while playing with humans. Great friends of Pete, and he had many—more than any other of our cats—used to shake the blood from the hand they had used in tickling his belly, which he loved to have humans do. They continued to think him a great fellow, as indeed he was; they continued to play with him, knowing what was bound to happen. They assumed, as we did, that he was merely forgetful.

In our experience with spayed females, which is considerable, we have found no change in the cat which was not for the better, both as to us and the cats. Martini, who was so near to a nervous break-down during the last months of her life as a queen that she became unpredictable and was always miserable, is now as gay—in, to be sure, a rather sudden fashion—as kitten ever was, and plays like a kitten. She also hunts, fights when it is necessary and is rather less sedentary than most cats, although she is nearing five as this is written. She is heavier than she was before she was spayed, partly because she is of chunky build—a grave show fault in her breed, but one that bothers neither us nor her—and partly because we feed three cats together and she, although the smallest, eats as much as either of the others.

The other two, who were spayed young, showed no effects of any kind, except those we desired. They are extraordinarily healthy cats, carrying no fat to speak of and, particularly in the case of Gin, trim and well-muscled as even a Siamese can be. They take out in romping the energy they would otherwise expend on childbearing. They seem, except when not allowed out the moment they choose, or when out of temper with each other, exuberantly and innocently happy.

We feel, indeed, that the spayed female makes the ideal cat asso-ciate. Females are generally somewhat more ebullient than males, somewhat daintier in their movements; they seem to us rather more affectionate and, although we have inadequate evidence of this, slightly more intelligent. (Miss Shuey, it may be recalled, found little or no evidence of sexually keyed difference of intelligence in her cats, which came out at the top of the ladder two by two.) There is a certain freedom about the spayed female, no doubt because she has escaped from the compulsive responsibility to fill the world with cats.

For, whatever the dark ecstasies the female cat may know, the compulsions which drive her also prevent full development of personality. She is likely, if not watched, to spend her time in a maelstrom of desire, then in a longer period of feeling heavy and awkward, then in a shorter period of, often, great pain, and finally she has kittens hanging onto her tail long after she is ready to start the series over again, and kittens can be a great hindrance to romance. The breeding female has very little time to be herself—to be a free cat with tail waving, to dash headlong across lawns, to leap in rabbit-like lunges through tall grass or a thick bed of autumn leaves; to touch a zinnia lightly with a paw, setting it to bobbing. A breeding female has her work cut out for her, and a good many of them show it, appearing rather drawn and haggard, like human females who have taken overzealously the injunction to replenish the earth.

Short of complete de-sexing there is, so far as we know, nothing to be done about the male cat, who is all or nothing. A female may surgically be rendered sterile without being unsexed, but all either she or her human associates escape in this case is the presence of kittens, who are the only good things—for the humans, anyway—to come from the whole process. It would seem more sensible to let nature take its course.

To many people who want cats around, that seems, in any event, the wiser attitude. To those who cannot bear to deprive the cat of a full life, however inconvenient that may be all around; to those who have unlimited room for kittens or no deep-seated objection to destroying those who cannot be placed; to those who keep cats as utilitarian animals, so that the more cats the better, it may often seem, and sometimes actually be, preferable to leave the sex in the cat. If you merely want friends around you who are cats, it clearly isn't; if you do not want your cat, or cats, to take up a disproportionate amount of your time, it isn't. It is better to stifle scruples, have an end to anthropomorphizing, and call the veterinarian.

Both male and female cats can be altered at almost any time even, if this is unavoidable, when the female is in heat. Other things being equal, and the owners able to make up their minds, most veterinarians prefer to operate while the cats are young, although the change in the male cat castrated early may be more marked than if the operation is postponed until he is fully grown. Martini was spayed when she was about two; her daughters when they were about six months—by which time, incidentally, both had been in heat. In Martini's case the operation was necessary, was done while she was in season and, in effect, saved her life. Her daughters were spayed for our convenience, although they had early shown symptoms of the cystic condition which made their mother's life a burden for almost a year. As it turned out, the operations would have been necessary in their cases also; Siamese females, or perhaps only those around New York, seem uncommonly prone to ovarian cysts.

The operation on the male, at more or less any age, is not particularly serious, if competently performed. Cats have a certain tendency to hemorrhage, but almost any veterinarian—even the country vet whose major experience is with big animals—can castrate a male. Spaying a female is, admittedly, a different matter; the operation is major and, as in all major operations, there is an element of risk. The risk is enhanced, of course, if the cat is in a condition of lowered vitality, from prolonged calling or other cause, and if she is in heat when the operation is performed. If the surgeon is skilled, the risk of losing the cat is not great; admittedly, it is still there.

But the bearing of kittens, whatever is lightheartedly said by those who have never helped a cat through it, is also a risky business. In taking her course, nature is notoriously wasteful. Impartial as among individuals, nature is by no means averse to risking one for the sake of several; the death of one cat is nothing compared to the probability of life for half a dozen. In general, as regards his own tribe and the other animal families as well, one must, naturally, accept this order of things. But in particular, as regards a loved human or an animal of whom one is fond, one may try to circumvent it.

It is proverbial that cats have kittens with little trouble—"as easily as a cat has kittens" is a catch-phrase. Some cats do have kittens very easily; some have them, but with great trouble; some die having them. In general, short-haired cats have less difficulty than long-hairs, but it is by no means safe, in dealing with a cat who is a person to you, to rely on this. Nobody knows how many domestic short-hairs, unconsidered barn cats, casual kitchen cats, replaceable store cats, die in kittening; the human community has more important things to worry about. But a great many of them may.

Professional breeders, whose pocketbooks are involved, do not go about the production of kittens haphazardly, trusting to luck and old sayings. They do not breed cats too often or too young, they do not breed cats when, for whatever cause, the cats are physically below par; they do not breed cats—or, of course, continue to maintain cats—physically so constituted as to make bearing impossible or extremely difficult. Mere affection is often not so compulsive a force as money, but it might lead cat owners to take similar care of their cats. That it does not always do this is probably more often due to ignorance than to any other factor—ignorance and that bright fondness for kittens which, even among people quite familiar with cats, leads to such insouciant carelessness with four-footed life. "Female cats are no trouble at all, if their folks let them have kittens whenever they're minded to," writes the author of one recent book on cats, with characteristic verve and casualness about relative pronounce. "Anyway, kittens are fun. They're uproarious, they're delightful, they're wonderful."

Kittens are indeed a great deal of fun. So are cats. And it is arguable, not only in this connection, that we are too much inclined to consider the next generation. There is no assurance, as regards either cats or people, that it will be an improvement upon our own. Martini is, to our minds, more cat than either of her daughters, and we came within a thin edge of losing her to acquire them. We did this because we were ignorant; because we accepted what we heard and read, instead of going to the slight trouble of finding out where we, and Martini, stood.

We were not, as has been indicated, altogether casual about breeding our cat. We did not, at any rate, let her have kittens wherever—or with whomever—she was minded to. If we had, she would have started kittens when she was about six months old, and with the first tom she met, who might have been a sick cat, one with congenital deformity or one of notoriously bad disposition. Hers was planned parenthood. The planning was ours. It was little better than half-witted and it almost killed her.

We went to considerable pains, which was mildly to our credit, to find an appropriate father for the kittens. We found him in a recommended cattery, made the arrangements and, subsequent to the mating, paid the fee. Martini's husband, whom we never met, was a fine cat and a very adequate one. Martini went to her tryst in a box from Grand Central Terminal, was met at Grand Central on her return and was brought home in good order. She looked, we

thought, a little surprised; we heard that she had been very surprised and very shy, and that the tom had had some trouble with her before he had his way. She was also still in heat when she returned, still called for several days. Queens do this, and we were not surprised. We settled back, feeling we had done all we should, and waited for kittens.

We also fed Martini powdered calcium with her food during the late stages of her pregnancy, having been advised to do this. She was very hungry, of course, and we fed her lavishly on the very best beef; she became heavy and dreamy-eyed and we counted days. We promised people spare kittens.

But what we did not do was to have a veterinarian come to take a look at her. We did not do this before we sent her to be bred; we did not do it during her pregnancy. Bearing kittens is perfectly normal; short-haired cats have no trouble at all; it is all as easy— well, as easy as a cat having kittens, which is, everybody knows, as easy as rolling off a log. We had read this in the best cat books, as well as in the one from which the above quotation is taken.

We prepared a place we thought would be a good maternity ward and subsequent nursery, and we tried to get Martini interested in it. She did not get interested in it. Nor did she, as cats "always" do, look around for a place of her own. She merely ate, grew heavier, seemed entirely at peace and contented.

Then one day, near the end of the gestation period, she tried— unexpectedly to us, and before we could stop her—to perform a favorite, and always rather annoying, gymnastic trick of hers: climbing the curtains of a high-ceilinged room until she could get onto the valance board, and sitting on it and looking proud. (It may as well be said now that it is practically impossible to keep Siamese cats from climbing things.) This time she got a little way up, and clung there, and cried until she was lifted down. She was very thoughtful the rest of the day, and the next morning she tried to have her kittens. It was still two or three days short of the stipulated period.

She did not go to the box we had prepared; she went, strangely, to a place on the kitchen floor near her toilet pan. By the time she was found, one kitten had been born dead. She was laboring with the second.

The one of us who happened to be in the apartment was not the one better adjusted, by sex or temperament, to midwifery and, although he had known many cats for many years, he had not before seen kittens born. Perhaps, he thought for several minutes— although the dead kitten had disturbed him—perhaps this dreadful writhing of a small and pretty cat, this incredible distortion and evident pain, is the usual thing. Perhaps this is what is meant by "easy." And finally, to be sure, another kitten was born. It was a large kitten, strangely large. It gasped convulsively, trying to live. But Martini, who should have succoured it—should have licked away the membrane which was stifling it, should have dried it with her tongue so that the flickering warmth of life did not evaporate —could hardly move herself, but merely lay quietly, spent. Then— then finally—the one who was there began trying to get a doctor.

The doctor got there about two hours later. He was not a veterinarian we had ever used before, we had only a few days before happened to hear of him—happened to hear, from another cat owner, that he was the best man in New York with cats. By that time the second kitten was long dead, although we had tried to keep it warm and alive. (We had not known enough to give artificial respiration, which, even in our clumsy fingers, might have saved it.) And by that time a third kitten was half born, and had been for upward of an hour.

There is nothing pleasant about this clinical description, as we are entirely aware. It is a far cry from the pretty thought of romping cats, from the gay kittens who are so delightful, who "keep you young," "restore lost youth" and "scamper over a typewriter" while you are trying to work on it—something no cat of ours will do while we maintain sanity and strength. But it may be a part of owning cats who are, as we are, animals, and so subject to disease and death, and to all manner of unpleasantness. One has not really associated with a cat until one has been worried to death about a cat; cherished it, also, in sickness and in health.

The third kitten was half born. That is meant quite literally.

It was half in and half out. Martini had given up laboring; she was lying in a dark place, her eyes open, but seeming sightless. She was not crying, as she does over little things. She was waiting, silently, to die. It is possible she could no longer see us, in those last, long minutes before the veterinarian came.

He took the partly born kitten and it was dead. While we held Martini, he began to deliver the fourth. One of us went for a drug which, injected, helps to induce labor; the same drug is used, in similar emergencies, on human mothers. It helped, a little; the veterinarian helped, while we held Martini—and now she was screaming in pain. With the deftest fingers either of us had ever watched, he manipulated the cat, urging the kitten downward, easing its head out finally; with Martini helping as much as a dying cat could, he took the fourth cat. It, too, gasped convulsively for air.

And it got air, because the doctor blew air into its nostrils, stripped the membrane away with quick fingers, pressed in and out on the tiny chest. It was dead and then, suddenly, very rapidly, it was breathing.

Martini, who had been on a sheet on a table, was released to the floor, now. She did not try to do anything; she merely lay there. There was still a cat to come, the doctor said. He tried to interest Martini in the living cat, because there was still much only she could do for it. But she did not seem to see us, she shrank away from the veterinarian, had just strength to growl. The struggle on the table—during which, incidentally, she had in a paroxysm of pain, bitten through a finger of one of us, her teeth meeting on the bone—had left her her fighting spirit, but not much else.

The living kitten was put in warm towels and in a box in a dark place. It hadn't, the veterinarian thought, a chance in a hundred, and he was rather put out at Martini. It was then midafternoon, and he had been there for two or three hours. We had one apparently dying kitten and a cat who might, with great luck, live to produce another.

There was nothing more immediately to be done, and the doctor had other cats to see, so he left, telling us he would be back as soon as he could, and that we could merely hope about the kitten. Martini, he thought, had a good chance of coming through.

Martini went, very slowly, into a bedroom and we sat for an hour or so and worried, but left her alone. Then she came out of the bedroom, even more slowly, and crossed a hall—and once again, dreadfully, a kitten was half born. She went into a small room which was at once the study and dressing room of one of her two humans, and for minutes—still knowing our own helplessness, perhaps avoiding an issue we felt incapable of meeting—we did nothing. Then we went into the room.

Somehow, Martini had climbed to the couch where one of her humans commonly spent more time than was easily defensible, and where she spent as much of hers as she could on him. There, this time alone, she had born her fifth kitten. She was holding it between her forepaws, licking it, and purring. She glanced at us quickly and went back to her task.

We brought the other kitten, still alive and put it by her. She paused to push it away, and what was in her mind is beyond guessing. It was connected with pain, of course; with the indignity of manhandling, which more than any other cat of our acquaintance Martini resents. That entered into the rejection. And perhaps, to her, all kittens, except this last which she had produced as a cat should, were dead kittens, as the first had been.

The rejected kitten stirred a little when we put it back against Martini's fur, tried feebly to reach a nipple. Again Martini pushed it away, and again we placed it against her. Then, with what seemed to us a start of surprise, Martini got the idea—*another* live kitten. She licked it then, pulled it close, put the other down beside it to nurse, and then two small cats, looking like white rats, were suckling, uncertainly at first and then with confidence. So we had three cats, none of them very healthy, all of them needing for days the care of the veterinarian, but three cats.

Martini accepted the box we had prepared and the place we had chosen for it, deep in a bedroom closet. And all the first night, showing more resilience than we were capable of, she awakened us to observe the miracle she—assisted by an accomplished veterinarian, her two owners and their maid—had achieved. She would jump on one bed and awaken its occupant—awaken him thoroughly. She would then go back to the kitten box, making sure her human was following; she would jump into the box, arrange the kittens for us to see, and purr. "Nice kittens," the awakened one would say. "Wonderful kittens."

Martini would seem content and return to nursing cats. The human would return to sleep. Half an hour later, Martini would awaken the other human, repeat the whole performance. "Duh babies!" the other human would say, half in sleepiness, half in language deemed appropriate for any creatures so small and helpless. "Duh *babies!*" Martini would purr. The human could go back to sleep then, but half an hour later it was the first human's turn again. This went on all night, providing a happy, if not restful, ending to a disturbing episode.

It may, of course, be argued that the whole affair turned out well, since now we have three cats, and it is always well to have three cats. Had we behaved with ordinary consideration, we would have had one cat only, since Martini would not have been bred. Her pelvic girdle is too narrow for normal kittening—"whelping" is the breeder's word. If we had not been fortunate in her doctor, called, as doctors so often are, when it is almost too late even for skill, she would have died. The world would have continued to wag, of course, and so would we; we have lost cats before and no doubt shall again, and Martini herself is not immortal. But it is not pleasant to cause the death of any creature of whom one is fond. Clumsiness and ignorance may be venial sins, although this seems to us doubtful; they do need expiation. Through ineptitude, we did a bad turn, and almost the worst turn of all, to a charming little animal who had not asked us to assume responsibility for her, but who was our invited guest.

Since cats are so stubbornly independent about their sex life, and so obviously regard it as a thing the human should stay out of, it is easy for the human to let nature take its course. No decision is necessary, except the simple one of opening a door. For the rest, the cat will provide. What happens thereafter is the cat's responsibility; if the cat is out of luck, well everyone's luck sooner or later runs out. If the cat's luck is in, kittens are a great deal of fun, and one adds to one's supply of cats. The cat could have stayed in if it preferred, failing to keep the tryst. Natural instincts should not be curbed.

This is an entirely reasonable attitude. But the keeping of pet cats is not, obviously, an entirely reasonable activity. Cats are valuable as mousetraps; in general terms, that is their reason for living with humans. But it is not specifically the reason Martini lives with us; at any time in the past or in the foreseeable future, it has been and will be true that she brings in more mice from the fields—dead, or thereabouts, to be sure—than she takes out of the house. She lives with us as a friend and, more simply, as a pet. To make her a suitable pet, we curb many of her natural instincts. It is no idea of hers to stay in at night. Ground round steak is a fine food for cats, and what Martini and family receive, but it is not "natural" for a cat to grind up a cow.

Because she lives with us, as a pet and house cat, Martini lives to a considerable extent an artificial life and this life is largely conditioned by what we want of her. It is we, not Martini, who have decided that she shall live in this fashion. As a result, she is not so self-reliant as the black cat who haunted the garbage pits outside Brewster; not so hardy nor so tough. She is, to a degree, a civilized cat and is entitled, since civilization was forced upon her, to such comforts and safeguards as it provides—to proper food regularly provided, to pills when she needs them, to a fire or heater to lie in front of. She is also entitled to protection from her own natural instincts, in so far as full expression of those instincts would be unsuitable to her present estate in life.

If we are going to keep cats at all, an activity which is not forced upon us either by human or feline society, we assume a responsibility to keep them as nearly as is possible adjusted to the artificial environment we provide, and it seems to us that this responsibility devolves upon all cat owners. Opening a door to a cat's demand to multiply, then losing patience with the cat, perhaps even to the point of discharging it, because it does, is irrational to the point of feeble-mindedness. It is also mildly immoral. It is also very common.

It requires a decision to have a cat castrated or spayed, and it is always easier not to make decisions; there is always an excellent reason not to make decisions. But most pet cats—as distinct from working cats, or show cats—are better fitted to their lives if they are neutered. They are also, particularly in the case of females, much more fun. And certainly they are a lot less trouble, and not being a trouble is, when one comes down to it, the best position a cat can occupy in his relations with people.

13

The Cat's Great Expectations

No DOUBT THE cat feels he has given up much for humans—the freedom of the night and of the trees, some part of the wildness he prizes in his heart. That he relinquished these things for certain prosaic advantages, for warmth and food and shelter from the rain, the cat may recognize, being a realist, but not care to stress. It is animal to put one's best motive forward when motives are several, and possibly mixed. One may assume the cat feels he sacrificed much to befriend man.

In return, and in addition to scrupulous observance of his physical needs, the cat expects much from humans. He anticipates that he will have a lap to sit on, and that it will be properly arranged, so that a cat-sized space is available when the cat elects. He expects that the lap, once provided, will not prove transient and is annoyed when the lap gets up to turn off the radio or answer the telephone. While on the lap, and at certain other times, he expects that a place behind each ear will now and then be scratched tenderly, and that gentle fingers will massage the long delicate bones of the feline jaw. It is well, the cat thinks, if in addition to these caresses there is a reasonable amount of back stroking, amplified on occasion by a a little belly rubbing. These things should be done without fumbling, preferably without molesting whiskers and, in the case of some cats, without touching tail.

But the cat's great expectations from the humans with whom he associates go considerably beyond these things and now and then may not even include some of them or, in rare cases, any of them. Not all cats are lap sitters; a few, reserved even beyond the average of their breed, prefer to have a minimum of physical contact with human animals, no doubt considering that the laying on of hands is well enough for dogs, but destructive to the dignity of the cat. A cat will let a human know how he feels about such matters, and will expect his preferences to be observed. If he wishes to be touched he will mention it, and if he does not wish he will mention that also, and more loudly. One cat's caress is another cat's indignity.

But however they may vary in their individual preferences, all cats expect from humans behavior which is in a cat's eye mannerly; which is gentle and is considerate not only of the cat's special dignity but of his unique physiology. Cats expect humans to be quiet in voice and deft in movements, so that they will not hurt cats' bodies by rough handling or cats' ears by the sound of crashing objects. They do not expect abrupt movements, which startle cats, or to be laughed at or to have their tails used as convenient handles, or to be approached precipitously, without invitation. In general, they disapprove of that form of behavior which may be summed up in the word "heartiness."

Cats who are very fond of humans for whatever reasons persuade cats to fondness may overlook certain lapses in human manners, but no cat regards such lapses as other than defects. A cat too often stepped on—all cats are stepped on sometimes, and this cannot be avoided by humans without cat cooperation, which is never given—may continue fond of his clumsy friend, but he will never grow fond of the clumsiness. Clumsiness is, to the cat, a major sin; he is predisposed to abominate particularly those offenses of which he knows himself guiltless, as people well-off from childhood wholeheartedly deprecate theft. In a properly constituted world, all the humans with whom cats are required to associate would be gentle, tranquil of movement and voice, considerate always with hands and, one may suppose, have eyes in the soles of their feet.

Some of these attributes people who much associate with cats do acquire, or try to acquire, since they smooth the way between cats and people. Attaining the mannerliness cats prefer does not, of course, do much to advance a human in the human world, where there is little to suggest that quietness and gentleness are of value or that hearty violence is not a fine thing. It is probable that people

who like cats, and learn from them, are not going to inherit the
earth or have much to say about who does; it may well be a canine
world, or on its way there. Warriors almost never like cats, and
warriors are clearly taking over, establishing their standards as they
advance and bringing to everyone an enhanced respect for stern
forthrightness and the let's-have-no-nonsense-out-of-you attitude.
Cat people may become second-rate citizens yet, and even cats may
suffer, although, being less gregarious, they will presumably suffer
less.

There can be no doubt that prolonged association with cats does
alter people, and to their disadvantage as things go presently. A cat
man, however much he may like other men, can seldom bring himself to slap them on the back or even to call to them across a street.
Observing the individualistic behavior of cats and seeking to please
them, he may find himself emulating them, and so joining fewer
and fewer of the arbitrary comradeships, fraternal organizations and
affiliations of the like-minded, to which the proper human is addicted. He may find himself, as time and cat association go on, more
likely to smile than to guffaw and little inclined to show approval
by jumping up and down. These habits constitute an antiquated
way of life, as one would expect: The cat is an ancient animal,
and his ways are set. Cat people often come to value manners
esteemed by their great-grandparents. In the end such people no
doubt will approve only of one another, and be otherwise approved
only by cats.

But cats will approve and will feel that they have remoulded the
human into a pattern of civilization. They will have taught people
that violent noises are hard on nerves. (Unless, of course, the noises
happen to be made by cats.) They will have established that, in
their environment, jerky movements are anathema and that one
does not pick a cat up by the shoulders and dangle it, elongated,
undignified and at a disadvantage, before one—and that one does
not pick a cat up by the scruff of the neck, either, whatever mother
cats may do with kittens. A cat prefers not to be picked up at all
but, if this is an ideal impractical of attainment—as it is—he will
countenance being gathered up, supported fore and aft on hands

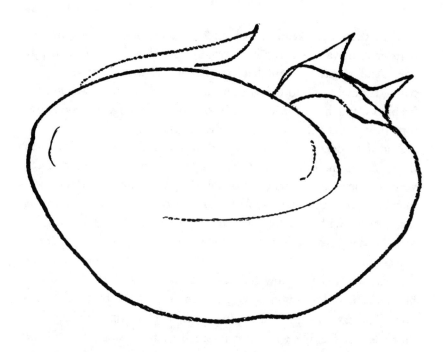

or arms and, of course, being kept right side up. There is nothing a cat finds more rude in a human than a habit of carrying cats upside down in the arms, as if the cat were a baby and had not, for millions of years, known enough to keep his feet under him.

Himself a purrer, sometimes so softly as to be almost inaudible, he likes being spoken to in a soft voice, and a human voice discordantly raised brands its user as a boor. A human who suddenly grabs at a cat, or wakes one suddenly when it is asleep, is not worth sitting at table with; the canapés he leaves within reach probably are poisoned and he is almost certain not to provide an open fire for a cat's pleasure. Such a rude human may not even have a wide window sill in his house, with a radiator under it and sun streaming on it, and what is a house without such a place for cats? (There are substitutes, of a sort. A cat one of us owned many years ago used to sleep with head and shoulders in an old-fashioned hot air register and was, as a result, a groggy cat all winter, but a happy one. And electric radiant heaters—heating elements between glass panes, framed to stand upright on the floor—are good substitutes for fireplaces and have the advantage of not exploding, as wood fires sometimes do, to disturb the dreams of cats.)

And if he does provide all these things, and does not gentle a cat, then what is the human for? He may be tolerated, if he serves the very best beef, but he will not be loved. Then, and only then, a cat may come to think that comfort is an attribute of a dwelling rather than of life with humans, and so may become a cat who belongs to a house—a cat doing well enough in a way, but not really a successful cat.

A cat will tell you how he wishes to be treated better than any human can, and a person new to cats can only learn by this instruction. The cat will not want to be hurried in making friends; that much is certain. He will want to smell first—to smell around the locality and, most assiduously, to smell the human. After these preliminaries, a cat may tell an accepted human that he is a lap-sitting cat, and that he will expect laps made ready either occasionally, often or all the time. (He will not, if his manners at all match those he prefers in humans, insist too vigorously on the ever-present lap; cats are philosophic. They know that people cannot at the same time make laps and feed cats.) A cat who is not a lap sitter may be a leg rubber, as most cats are. He may, of course, be both. He is almost certain to want his ears scratched, but jaw rubbing is not so universally approved.

But whatever his idiosyncrasies, he wants gentleness; delicacy in caress and not too much violence even in play. (He will provide the violence there, if encouraged; the human may not retaliate.) Neither his body, which is fragile—the cat is prodigiously armed, but very lightly armored, and is never sturdy as a dog is—nor his nerves will stand the playful roughness in which any good dog delights. A slap on the back or side which a dog would greatly appreciate might injure a cat, perhaps seriously. It would certainly affront him, perhaps to the point of arousing fury. A cat is not to be squeezed, either, and this makes him a somewhat chancy play-mate for very young children, who habitually squeeze things they are fond of. A small, untrained child may permanently damage a small, untrained cat and may, with unusually bad luck, be consider-ably damaged by a full-grown cat, although most well-dispositioned cats who are at all familiar with children treat them with tolerance, not expecting as much as they expect of adults. Children may also

be trained, although perhaps with greater difficulty, so becoming suitable playmates for cats.

Playmates of some sort cats do expect and a healthy, altered cat will expect all his life that someone will play with him. The play of human and cat may take many forms, always within the limitations of the cat's physical structure and temperamental preferences, and not a few of these forms the cat will himself invent. He will, for example, find many places in which he may hide, or think he hides, and from which he then may jump at the passing human. Almost no place a cat and a human can share will prove too small or too sparsely furnished for some such improvization of the jungle; if put to it, a cat will consider himself hidden behind a chair leg, and this fiction he apparently expects his human to accept. (Even in actual hunting, many cats seem to think themselves concealed behind a few blades of grass, if nothing better offers, but birds seldom enter into the spirit of this charade.) Many cats enjoy being pursued and hide and seek is a favorite pastime with almost all who are really fond of their humans. This game becomes particularly interesting to the cat when the human is trying to shut him up for the night and he prefers, as he commonly does, to remain at large.

When we lived in New York, and Martini was an only cat, this game often went on almost endlessly in the late evenings. Except during the early kitten period, Martini has never been allowed to sleep with us, which of course she would prefer to do, and in New York it was the order of the nights that she be locked in the kitchen, which was warm if not commodious, contained her toilet pan and also a bed to which she was supremely indifferent, preferring the top of the gas range, no doubt because in its innards a pilot light burned, faintly providing warmth. She had no objections to the kitchen, as such; she spent much time there voluntarily, when Elizabeth was absent.

But at bedtime it was as resolutely her determination to stay out of the kitchen as it was ours to put her in it, and this determination —on her part—was obviously three-fourths joke. Certain human movements gave her the cue, and no amount of assumed casualness, no pretense that it was really not bedtime at all, ever deluded her in the least. All evening she might have remained within reach; at this moment she disappeared.

Sometimes she merely hid behind a chair in the living room, encouraging a little preliminary dodging around it, properly certain that, nine times out of ten, she would be too quick for human hands, would slip under reaching fingers, race through the hall, and reach the bedroom. When she reached the bedroom she went, of course, under one of the beds.

Getting a cat out from under a pair of twin beds is great fun for a cat, but very nearly impossible for a single human—and by the time this part of the game began, one of Martini's humans was usually already in bed and disinclined to get out again. There are several spots under an ordinary twin bed in which a cat is entirely out of reach unless a human lies down on the floor and wriggles under the bed after him. This, of course, is what the cat is waiting for. He then goes under the other bed. There are practically no limits to this game and it is terminated only when the cat relents or, as less often happens, the human is reinforced. Martini always allowed herself to be captured in the end; she always made it clear that the decision had been hers; she was always obviously laughing. It was, everything she did made clear, pure play, not serious hiding, as it became when we took out her traveling box for a trip to the country. When we did that, Martini really hid, and no fooling; often, for half an hour or so, no finding either.

Chasing and being chased are fun for cats; so, as we have suggested earlier, is retrieving. (The sound of a crumpling cigarette package still brings Martini running, although the other cats have spoiled the game.) Most cats like playthings—small objects which can be batted here and there and, commercially, are usually made to resemble some small animal, bird or fish or mouse. Cats do not care what shape these objects are—no cat ever mistook a celluloid fish for a fish fish—nor what color. They like table-tennis balls, although they quickly lose them under furniture. They like catnip mice, some of them extravagantly, and these, before they are shredded on the carpet, as inevitably they finally are, are good retrieving toys. And as much as anything in the world, a cat likes a piece of string.

The string should, of course, be kept in motion by a human, and may have a small wad of paper knotted into it. With string, a human may even play with a cat and remain seated, although this is seldom the cat's preferred method. What the cat prefers is to have the human use the string to tie up, or try to tie up, a package. There is no better way to give a cat a good time, while personally achieving a mood of complete bafflement and a new appreciation of the underlying futility of all human effort. A cat expects that his humans will often try to wrap packages in his presence.

From all these games, and the many others he will think up, the cat of a one-cat family derives entertainment, which makes him a happier cat, and exercise, which makes him a healthier one. An apartment house cat, particularly, needs a good deal of playing with, since he commonly has neither the incentive nor the space for the rapid movements to which his structure is adapted and which his health requires. Humans who lack the time for playing, or are themselves disinclined toward beneficial exercise, should keep more cats than one. Two or three cats cannot, certainly, live as cheaply as a single cat, nor as quietly, but their reliance on human participation is less. They are also, it seems to us, even more fun.

We are cat people only by avocation, if that can be said of any humans addicted to cats, and have never harbored them in numbers. As this is written we have only three and even so many, inconsiderable as our flock is by the standards of a real addict, we acquired inadvertently. It had been our plan to keep Martini (of course) and one of her, presumably numerous, children. When only she and two, and we, survived the ordeal of her kittening we could not bring ourselves to give away either of such hard-won mites, much as they resembled not very vigorous white rats. As they grew, developing very differently, parting with either became hardly thinkable and so we became three-catters instead of two. We moved to larger living quarters, also, but that was more or less incidental.

That we have now come to think of three cats as a fairly ideal number may be, probably is, merely rationalization; it may be that, granted room for them and the money to feed them, there is no limit to the number of cats one should have, as there is no limit to the number of diamonds one would like to have. Since cats are so individualistic, the variety and hence the interest varies directly with the number; each of a dozen cats, one supposes, would establish himself as a person to be observed with enjoyment and to be made friends with. But associating with a dozen cats, or even half a dozen, requires more time than most humans can allow to avocational pursuits, and it is difficult enough to keep three cats out of rooms in which they are not wanted. It is difficult enough to keep one cat out of a room in which he is not wanted; a closed door is an almost desperate challenge to any cat. And there will always, in any house, be rooms in which cats are not desired. Our cats are not permitted in bathrooms, since in bathrooms they delightedly unroll toilet paper. Nor are they allowed in the rooms where writers are writing; Henry James is reported to have written with a cat sitting on his shoulder, but his power of detachment was notable and beyond achievement by lesser writers.

Two or three cats can, more or less, be kept under control; in three cats one finds much variety, and three cats can eat from a single dish and use one toilet pan. They can also, when we are not available, entertain themselves, either with what we have called the "big game" or in some more quiet fashion. They get exercise by chasing one another and, should they need it, warmth by sleeping in a heap. They thus remove from our shoulders to their own some of the responsibilities which inhere in the care of cats.

But whether this communal feline life is what is expected by a cat who has consented to live with humans is a question we cannot surely answer. It may well be that each cat expects humans who are uniquely his, held in his sole possession; that, although Martini and Gin and Sherry get on well together for the most part, and Sherry weeps bitterly when the others vanish as, being more venturesome, they often do, each cat in her secret heart resents the presence of the others. Martini often does, we are almost sure. For long she was the cat, and to be now merely the major cat marks a diminution in rank. If now we throw a plaything for her to return to us, the others get there first, so confusing the issue that she loses interest; if she gets a lap properly arranged, Sherry is quite likely to come and lie on top of her. Now and then, although always through inadvertence, we notice one of her daughters when she would be noticed, and when there can be no doubt that she is angry and would wish—if she could connect concurrences so separated in time and space—that she had never met the pedigreed blue point who caused her to add these interlopers to the family. She, we are almost certain, would gladly be again the only cat, although she plays with her daughters, licks them and sleeps entwined with them when the temperature goes below seventy, the point at which a cat—whose body temperature is several degrees higher than the human's—begins to feel a chill.

Gin, too, might prefer single occupancy, although she greatly admires her mother, and is under her mother's paw; although she has a milder, often irritated, affection for Sherry. Sherry, on the other hand, probably would like not only more cats around, but more humans also; she is oddly gregarious for a cat.

The relationship of our three may be complicated by the fact that they are mother and daughters; the tie uniting them, since Gin and Sherry have never lived without their mother's guidance and since Martini, at odd moments, still appears to consider them her kittens, may be closer than it would be were they merely three casually acquired cats. Martini might not so dominate two cats not her children, although it is hard to believe that Martini would not order about any cat up to twice her size.

We have never thought of adding other cats to the very closed cooperation represented by the Martini tribe, needing no further cats and doubting that good would come of any such experiment. We have, living in the country, often thought of adding a dog, but shrunk away from the problems which surely would be involved. Would the cats take to a puppy? Or would they take the puppy apart? Authorities we have consulted are of several minds. If it were only the younger cats, some say—but there is always Martini. Martini would not like a dog around; already, to her mind, our affection is spread too thin. We probably shall not take the chance;

after all, cats can keep down the population of rabbits which seek to consume the garden, and only a gigantic and fearless dog can do much about woodchucks. We would like a dog like that; Martini would not. And Martini was here first. Already, she has made concessions enough. Even her scratching post is no longer uniquely hers.

When it was, she was somewhat inclined to use it in preference to, but by no means to the exclusion of, the nearest piece of upholstered furniture. It was a sturdy post, set firmly on a wide base, covered with carpet which had—the manufacturers hoped—the balance between impenetrability and flimsiness a cat expects. It was also, at the beginning, impregnated with catnip, a substance to which Martini is largely indifferent. But it did provide, and now and then still provides, a fairly suitable place for a cat to perform that operation which humans call "sharpening the claws." Some such place a cat expects in any house in which he lives, and a number of such places he will certainly find.

Whether claws are actually sharpened by scratching fabric, carpets, the bark of trees and, in the absence of anything better, the wallpaper, has always seemed to us a little doubtful. The explanation is human; the activity relentlessly feline. Cats vary in many particulars, sometimes to the point of caring little for many of the things to which cats are traditionally devoted, but they all insist on, periodically, getting their claws firmly fixed into something and pulling at it furiously. Anyone who harbors cats must count on this and resign himself to it. Short of furnishing his house entirely in metal, in which case his cat probably would leave, there is nothing a human can do about it.

Those who write manuals on cat care are commonly blithe about this feline habit, insisting that it is all a question of training the cat. Get a good cat post, even so reliable and fine an authority as Miss Doris Bryant advises, speak to the cat firmly when he uses anything else, and the problem disappears. The slip covers remain as they came from the loom, instead of turning shaggy; new carpets are not burrowed into; interior decoration remains decorative.

We cannot, from long experience, share this optimism; we would

not be parties to deluding prospective owners of cats. Line your living room with cat posts, which are themselves starkly utilitarian in appearance; dust the arms of chairs and sofas with powders which are supposed to repel cats, and hope for but do not expect the best. The cats will get at the fabrics and, as time goes on, rend them. A cat expects you not to mind this, and there is no use telling him that he is being bad. He is not being bad. He is merely being, from the human point of view, annoying. He has few other annoying traits—he does not have to be walked, he does not smell, he will give you devotion and he is gay to watch. But he will scratch.

He prefers loosely woven fabrics, into which claws fit well and which may be counted on to give. Leather he will avoid unless nothing else is available. But cotton, silk and wool—he takes them all, and scratching post to boot. He may, as some suggest, be given a room of his own, containing none of these things, and kept in it, but that is another, and rather expensive, way of not having a cat. He may be given a cage to live in, but he does not expect to be caged. He expects to live with people, on even terms; to share their furniture as he shares their lives. To us a cat is worth a good deal of furniture, and ours have certainly used up a good deal. We do not insist that this scale of values is, or should become, universal.

It is not much good to clip a cat's claws and it is demeaning to the cat. He is a clawed animal; claws are as essential not only to his physical actions but to his inner assurance as fingers are to humans—more, indeed, since humans can bring to almost any physical loss whatever palliation philosophy may provide, and cats presumably cannot. A claw-clipped cat is an unhappy creature, slipping on surfaces where he should be sure of paw, uneasy in all his leapings until his claws grow back again. This they quickly do, so that they must be clipped frequently, if any good is to come of it. And not much does in any event; he will continue to scratch furniture and there will be enough rough claw left for that. The clipping operation is in itself resented by the cat and difficult to perform expertly; claw clippers rather than scissors must be used and considerable care taken lest one cut into the quick and cause bleeding which may be difficult to control.

It is obvious, or should be, that no cat who spends any considerable part of his time out of doors can be clipped of claw, since his life may depend on climbing and his dignity on being able to fight if climbing is impracticable or seems to him unnecessary. Our own cats, who go in and out as often as anyone will open a door for them, are long-clawed. They were long-clawed when they lived in a New York apartment; so far as we are concerned they always will be.

It is true that they now and then use the scratching post, if they happen on it on their way to the back of a chair. Martini still uses it more frequently than the others, from old force of habit, but it is no longer all hers and she does not really care much about it. At first she tried to keep her kittens away from it, but in the end found this not worth the trouble.

Another concession she has had to make, and one which now and then still seems to bother her, is of exclusive access to the plate of food which, twice daily, goes down for all the cats. Some cat authorities feel that cats, if there are several, should be fed separately, some even advocating separate rooms, the theory being that, if fed en masse, they may eat competitively, upsetting their digestions. But there are limits to the concessions a human may make to cats, and feeding three on separate plates, each in her own room, seems to us to exceed them. In any case, our cats are not particularly competitive.

Martini, indeed, when not extremely hungry often refuses altogether to enter into competition with her daughters. She joins them in the morning clamor and again at night; she curvets under foot as the plate is put down. But then she may well withdraw and merely watch until the others have finished. Now and then she waits too long and the food is finished too, but she is a little plump nowadays and can miss a meal or two. Oddly enough, and one may explain this as one likes, she is more inclined to eat at second table if the food is a special treat—if, for example, an extra snack of cooked steak or chicken or some morsels of cooked lamb is provided. It may be that she is still partly mother at heart, although cats are supposed to lose their maternal feelings as the kittens grow up.

Cats expect such occasional treats of special food, but as a basic diet they expect raw beef, which we and most cat owners—there are exceptions—believe should be ground, and which certainly should be served at about room temperature. This beef should be as free of fat as the butcher can be persuaded to grind it and it should be entirely fresh—fresher, that is, than would be necessary for human consumption. Cats do not appreciate well-hung beef and some of them will not eat it—Martini is one such.

Raw ground beef, which is difficult to keep, runs into money and, since cats will eat a good many other things, not all cat owners are able, or willing, to provide it. A good many cats live, therefore, on table scraps, which are seldom very good for them; on fish, which is all right if carefully boned and not fed raw, but which is inadequate as a basic diet; on canned foods—usually mostly fish—and on anything else they can find, including raw potatoes, bread and butter and asparagus. Veterinarians generally frown on so variegated a diet; a good many cats do not. Cats should have no starch; this is generally agreed to. But several cat observers over the past fifty years, writing independently and with no correlation of their findings, have reported cats of remarkable age who seemed to have lived most of their years on a raw potato diet. One of them specialized even further. He ate only the parings of raw potatoes.

Liver is a traditional cat food and many cats are fond of it; it provides vitamin E, but is generally not considered an adequate basic food. Cats love chicken, and all fowl; it is good for them, if the small bones which they will crunch and swallow, and which may perforate their intestines, are removed. It is also laxative for many cats, which is generally a good thing, cats tending to be a somewhat constipated crew. Lamb, not fatty, is highly prized by all the cats we have ever met, and is a pleasant and healthful change for them; horse meat is all right, although not as good as beef and most readily procurable overcooked, which isn't good either. And some cats do not like it.

"Vegetables are wholly unsuitable for cats," Frank Townsend

Barton, a firm-minded veterinarian, wrote in 1908 and, although human views of feline diet have altered somewhat since he took his stand, most cats would still agree with him. There are exceptions, but if you want your cat to have vegetables, you will probably have to feed them mixed with meat. The average cat's indifference to vegetables is on a par with that of the average child, or the average gourmet.

But vegetables, in extreme moderation, have some regulatory value and so now and then most cats who live under watchful human eyes are subjected to green stuffs. Ours have been so subjected from time to time, and it has recently seemed to us easiest to buy the strained vegetables put up as baby food, these being thoroughly chewed in advance and also thoroughly cooked. A little strained spinach mixed with the ground beef does not appear to affront the average cat; that a cat will eat it would indicate, incidentally, that cats really are color blind or else that they believe beef now and then turns green. Strained string beans also may be used; there is too much starch in the more edible puréed peas.

Generally preferable to vegetables, to our minds, and considerably easier to handle are some of the cereal foods prepared for dogs—the one our cats eat a good deal of, and seem moderately to enjoy, is called Milkbone Tiny Bits. This may be mixed with beef; the cats will, naturally enough, eat the beef first, but frequently come around to the Tiny Bits later. If put to it, they will even eat the cereal without the beef, and they are, again naturally enough, the more prone to do this if they can be led to believe they are getting away with something. When they were city cats, and had been put away for the night in the kitchen, they once managed to knock off a full box of the cereal, spreading the bits—the name adequately, if rather coyly, describes the texture—on the floor. By the time the human investigator arrived, all three cats were grazing excitedly, racing against time, one another and the expected intervention.

Cats, who chew almost nothing, will crunch Tiny Bits—and no doubt other similar foods—and this may be good for their teeth, about which cat owners worry a good deal and cats not at all. Cats, of course, normally tear their food into pieces which are merely not too large to swallow; this is one of the reasons for feeding ground beef. They are not equipped for much grinding and have never found it necessary to chew their food thoroughly.

The association of the cat and the pan of milk is so traditional that it has become almost hallowed in the human, as distinct from the feline, mind. Most writers of cat manuals, although by no means all veterinarians, insist that cats must have milk and even the best of them grow a little querulous at the average grown cat's profound indifference to the substance. (Kittens start on milk, as babies do; kittens may wish to continue on it for a time, in which case diluted canned milk or goat's milk—easy to obtain if one keeps a goat or two, as well as cats—are generally recommended.) Most of the adult cats we have known drank milk sparingly and were only mildly interested in cream, and this never worried either us or them, or, indeed, their doctor. Martini, Gin and Sherry, greater water drinkers, will have no truck with milk, although from it they would get nicotinic acid and, simultaneously, a laxative. Since we attend their preferences whenever it is convenient to do so and does them no harm, we do not insist, which probably would do us very little good. (Miss Bryant tells the story of one ingenious woman whose cat was a water drinker and who was, in the end, fooled into mistaking milk for water. This was done by adding milk to the water, one drop the first day, two the second and so on, until the cat gave in. It does not seem to us that a procedure so protracted would add to the fun of having cats.)

Some cats appear not to drink anything, even water; Pete never did, so far as we could see, except now and again a languid lap or two from a flower vase. We nevertheless always provided water and, presumably, he sometimes took a swig, since he must have got water somehow, and it is hard to believe that a meat diet would have provided enough. Our present three, on the other hand, are hard water drinkers, among them emptying a good-sized container a day and, when out of doors, lapping at most of the puddles they encounter. The average is somewhere between, no doubt, but all cats expect water to be available and reasonably clean.

A few of the things cats expect they should not have; most of our cats, for example, have been fond of bacon, which is no food for cats; all of them will eat pork if they can get it, and none of them should; Pete had a great fondness for chili con carne which is, among other things, too highly spiced for cats. And all cats will eat grass if they can find it.

The universality of this last appetite has confused many humans into the belief that cats should be provided with grass, even if the owner has to go to the trouble of raising it. Early writers on cats were of one mind on this; John Jennings, one of the first to discuss cats from a quasi-scientific viewpoint, was certain that grass was essential; as recently as 1946, John Hosford Hickey and Priscilla Beach, in an otherwise acceptable cat manual, expressed the conviction that grass was a substance the cat's "system" demanded, and advocated planting it indoors in pots for the apartment house cat. That this is a good idea presumably is proved by the fact that cats will approve the arrangement and eagerly eat the grass provided. Afterward, they will very probably throw it up.

When cats fell into this grass-eating habit, and why, are matters of conjecture. They probably started on it, as a race, some millions of years ago and may have eaten it as an emetic, which facilitated the vomiting of such parts of their food as they found indigestible— fur, for example, and feathers. For the feral cat, living on what he can catch, it may still have that value, although cats vomit so readily when it seems like a good idea that it is hard to see why they should go to so much trouble. (Grass is hard for a cat to bite through; he lacks appropriate shearing teeth.) For the cat who lives with people, grass is merely an irritant which they would be better off without.

They do not digest it. If they do not throw it up, which they usually do if they eat it on an empty stomach, it passes through their digestive canal unchanged, except that now and then it clogs the rectum and is often difficult to evacuate. It has no more contact with their "systems" than so much string would have, and they will also eat string. (One of our cats swallowed a rather long piece of string which had been around a rolled rib roast and this alarmed us —and him—although everything came out all right in the end.) Cats will also swallow thread, frequently with needles attached; they will eat very indigestible insects, cloth and, on occasion, even steel wool. They have an almost infantile tendency to put things into their mouths and swallow, and not a great deal more judgment than the average baby. If they had, they would not eat grass which, when found out of doors, is usually dirty and may carry parasites which will get into a cat's system, even if grass doesn't.

We have explained these things to a good many cats, quoting Dr. Louis J. Camuti and other authorities, but nothing has come of it. As far as cats are concerned, Mr. Jennings had the last word in the last century. Any cat who goes out of doors will find grass there, and will eat it and, if he certainly will not be the better for it, will probably be not much the worse. But city cats generally live longer than country cats, and their grass-free diet may be a minor factor in this. Major factors include the accident incidence among outdoor cats, which is high. Apartment house cats less often die violently unless, as happens with some frequency, they fall out windows.

But one cannot give a cat everything, and immortality is among the gifts not available. One can only try to meet his expectations— that he will be housed and properly fed, provided with a warm and if possible a sunny place in which to doze; that he will feel also the warmth of human fondness and enjoy the gentle touch of human hands; one can only give him these things, which he expects, and hope for the best. That, and keep an eye on him.

This last is something which all people who live with cats, live with them in companionship and affection, learn to do almost unconsciously. When first meeting a cat in the morning, while greeting him and responding to his greetings, one comes to note those physical things about him which give information as to his health that day. He may have been well yesterday; he may have been well for weeks or months or even years. But there is no assurance that he will be well today, for cats often sicken suddenly, within hours, sometimes—it seems—within minutes. And the first indications of illness may be very slight—an almost imperceptible dullness in the eyes, a roughness in the coat hardly to be detected, a just-discernible lessening of alacrity. These things may mean nothing, or you may imagine them. One cannot tell at once, but one can keep on watching.

Probably it is nothing. The cat may only be sleepy; he may have been kept up by a late mouse. The roughness of coat may be due to a chillness in the room too slight for you to notice. In half an hour, the cat is likely to be himself again. You have lost nothing; you would have watched him anyway, since that is one of the reasons you maintain him.

But if he is, as is said, "coming down" with something you may detect this coming down in time to do something about it. Cats not only sicken quickly; sometimes they die with frightening speed.

Less than two hours after our Pammy first moaned slightly, she
was dead on a veterinarian's operating table. She had been fine the
day before. Probably she was poisoned, and nothing could have
been done. Yet always there is that little doubt. Had we been
more alert that morning, discovered sooner that something had
gone wrong, might we have saved her? We were very fond of her.

14

The Cat's One Life

WHEN ONE OF us was a child there was an attic filled with attic things—things which once were treasures, once were not quite valueless enough to be thrown away, once were objects of no perceptible worth at all, escaping destruction for no reason. The attic was the terminal moraine of lives which had been lived in the house, and to the child it was, for years, of infinite fascination. Unbelievably hot in summer, as cold as all outdoors in winter, reached by narrow, cluttered stairs, it was a place in which anything might be found, and in which some things were to be found over and over again.

One of these often-discovered treasures was a family medical book, published probably toward the middle of the Nineteenth Century, now nameless in memory although once it must have had a name. In it all the diseases known to the physician-author—or corps of physicians, or anonymous toilers in Grub Street—were described and their remedies given; no ailment, so far as the memory of the man who was the child discloses, was without its cure, for what family would purchase a doctor book which did not promise health? With it in one hand, and enough sight left to read, a human could be reasonably certain what he was dying of, and could also nurture the hope that he might recover. A physician present in the flesh can often offer little more.

It was not hypochondriasis, then a condition still to be achieved, but adolescent preoccupations which drove the child again and again to the medical book, each attic trip being made, of course, on the pretext of some more acceptable errand. Certain human functions were mentioned in the book, the tone being one of embarrassed delicacy and the information conveyed to the enquiring mind negligible. Yet at a certain age, even double-talk is better than no talk at all if only it concerns those matters healthily uppermost in the mind.

The book did the child no harm, and probably it was many years since it had done anybody harm. If it had been in use, it would not have been in the attic; to the child's family, the book was only a forgotten curiosity and when the child was ill the doctor called. But once people puzzled over such books, sorting out symptoms, administering remedies, hoping for the best, and even now self-medication from encyclopedias of disease is not unheard-of. However accurately written, however well-intentioned, such books are likely to do more harm than good; fortunately, not too many people rely upon them.

Calling a doctor for a sick cat or dog was, in the days when the child frequented the attic, unheard-of in the social group in which he was growing up, and probably it was not a very common action anywhere. Cats grew sick mysteriously and died suddenly and were mourned and buried under rosebushes; dogs the boy had were similarly perishable. Everyone was sorry when this happened, but nobody did anything about it—not even what the book said. There were books then—there had been since the 1880's at least—but they lacked wide circulation; they did not, at any rate, reach Kansas City, Missouri, so there was no way of telling what the animals had died of. It was the lot of pets to die as, lamentably, it still is.

Nowadays, however, there are many books about cats and dogs, the ailments of both are exhaustively described, and anyone who can read can discover, conceivably before it is altogether too late, what ails this small, warm creature who was so bright and gay yesterday, is today so listless and forlorn. In many instances these books are accurate and in all, we are sure, they are well-intentioned; one of them, to our mind the most useful, has been checked—one is greatly tempted to say "vetted"—by the cat specialist most cat owners in the New York area are willing to contend is the best in the profession. Such books may supplement veterinarian care; they can never be a substitute for it. Reading them, the one of us whose attic was so crammed with oddments is unfairly reminded of the medical book.

If one of our cats is sick, or we think she is sick, we use the telephone, not the cat manual. She may have nothing more serious than a cold; she may have a stomachache, through either of which minor indispositions we presumably could help her. She may be coming down with enteritis, in which case she has about a chance in a hundred of living without the most expert care and is a very sick cat even with it. We are laymen, and no amount of book reading is going to make us anything else. If we try to guess and turn out wrong, we and the cat are out of luck. A cat can die of enteritis in a few hours—a few hours, that is, from the first discernible symptom. Our cats have been inoculated against this disease, which is known by a variety of names, including "cat distemper," and so are presumably to some degree immune. We still decline to take chances with other people's lives.

The services of a good cat veterinarian cost money, just as ground beef costs money and the replacement of slip covers costs money. We would be financially better off if we did not keep cats—or would be if, with no feline responsibilities at home, we did not spend the saving to go more often to more distant places. But the keeping of cats is not compulsory. It is a responsibility voluntarily assumed by those who do not employ working cats in barns or stores—and even such cats, one supposes, are entitled to some sort of workmen's compensation. Those who keep cats for fun must expect to pay for their fun, and doctors' bills are likely to be a considerable part of the payment.

This is rather truer for cat people than for dog people, since more veterinarians are experienced with dogs, the competition is keener and, possibly as a result of this, the fees are likely to be lower. A good many expert dog veterinarians are not particularly good with cats, and some of the best of them would prefer not to treat cats at all—partly because cats are tricky creatures to handle, being prone to bite and scratch and so disapproved of by hospital attendants; partly because they are also tricky to treat, being inclined to die while the doctor is discovering what is wrong with them;

partly because the disease most often fatal to the domestic cat is extremely infectious, so that one cat ill with enteritis in a dog and cat hospital is very likely to be the death of any other feline patients then under treatment and to make the place untenable by cats for a matter of months.

Cats owners living in the country, particularly if it is not kennel country, are likely to find the selection of a good cat doctor particularly difficult, although veterinarians are numerous in the country. They are in country practice, however, largely because the country is reasonably full of cows and horses, which need a great deal of human assistance in keeping alive. All these veterinarians, for anything we know to the contrary, may be wonderful with cows, but a cat resembles a cow only in having four legs and in nursing its young. The cat's ailments are its own; the methods of handling it are also singular, as we and a big-animal veterinarian discovered once when we tried to tie Pete down to an operating table so that an infected wound could be sterilized. One does not, everyone discovered in fifteen minutes or so, tie a cat to anything. If operations are to be performed upon a cat not under general anaesthetic, a couple of people hold the cat while the third operates. Band-aids and iodine are then used, not on the cat.

The ideal cat doctor is a man who is basically fond of cats, and yet willing to carry on activities which will lead him to be hated enthusiastically by every cat who meets him. He must be extraordinarily deft with his hands, since almost everything done to a cat's small, furry body has to be done with the fingertips. (Abdominal operations on a cat, for example, must be performed largely by touch, through incisions which will admit a couple of human fingers and an instrument.) But the hands must also be strong enough to hold a struggling cat and, by preference, covered with especially tough skin. The doctor must be a man who expects no cooperation from his patient, since few cats, unlike many dogs, ever believe that indignities are being performed on them for their own good. He must also expect to find many of his patients under beds and be prepared, if it proves necessary, to go in after them.

Our own cat doctor, for whom our admiration is great, has all these attributes and in addition he calls on the cats, instead of having the cats taken to him. This, for those who can find a veterinarian who will so go about his profession, is best for all concerned —except possibly the veterinarian himself. It is far the best for the cats, few of whom like to be lugged around in boxes even when they are feeling well; almost all of whom are easily frightened in strange places and all of whom would rather be handled by friends than strangers, possibly because they already know how their friends taste.

Each of our cats has, to be sure, made a visit to the doctor's offices, each to be spayed. Martini went first and alone; the other two went later and together. Each time, cat or cats were taken to the office in the morning and collected in the afternoon, at which time they were still unconscious. (Sherry, who proved to have an inexplicable resistance to the anaesthetic, was only partially unconscious; the doctor was never certain she had been entirely out even when he was operating. An hour after she was home she was up staggering around; Gin was still under twelve hours later.) The cats were then nursed at home, by us—which means they were watched, kept warm, and worried about. When anything requiring greater skill was necessary, the doctor came and did it. All three recovered rapidly; much more rapidly than they would have done in a hospital. For us, it was a little nerve-wracking, but on the whole interesting.

A cat who has just begun to come out from under a general anaesthetic is very interesting to watch, at once pathetic and, in an odd way, funny. When they partially regain consciousness, they get up and walk around. And when they walk around they walk exactly like drunken men of a certain sort. They do not precisely stagger; they are not falling-down drunks. Instead they progress, very slowly, precisely as do those intoxicated humans who believe that, if attention lapses even momentarily, they will fall flat, and so move with a ridiculous, painfully careful, utterly rigid, dignity, walking in a dense fog along an imaginary crack. It is funny to see a cat walk so; it is also rather touching.

We could wish no cat owner a more accomplished physician than ours, and we hope for the sake of cats that there are many like him—and that cat owners go to the trouble of finding them. It is a search which anyone taking a cat under care should begin at the moment of the cat's arrival, if for no other reason than to have the cat inoculated against enteritis. There will, however, be other reasons, sooner or later. All cats eventually get something or other and many of them get a good many things. A few of these things— not many—a cat owner may himself cope with, if he is reasonably sure what the trouble is. The rest he should be able to recognize quickly, if not as specific ailments, then as ailments beyond his treatment.

A cat's eyes and a cat's coat, as we have mentioned, tell a good deal about his general condition and, of course, tell more to those who know cats well than to those on mere ear-scratching terms with them. Dull eyes indicate that the cat isn't feeling well; running eyes may indicate that he has caught cold; bloodshot eyes may indicate an infection, which may be serious or may not. It is unwise to wait too long to find out. Roughness of the coat, naturally easier to detect in short-haired cats than in Persians, and lack of gloss, indicate that the cat is out of condition, perhaps only because he is constipated. Generally sluggishness may indicate constipation; it may be the beginning of something more serious. Vomiting may indicate a great deal, or nothing at all; diarrhea may indicate that the cat has been drinking too much milk, eating too much chicken or liver, or that he is coming down with enteritis or other serious gastric upset. Urinary irregularity is generally serious and requires the attention of a doctor, yet Gin, when much younger, had several brief spells of a kind of compulsory urination, got over each of them before a doctor could arrive, and has had no trouble since.

Vomiting is of several kinds, the most common being of grass, with or without food most recently eaten. This does not mean the cat is ill; it means merely that he has no more sense about what is good for cats than have some of the humans who write about him. It is better, however, if he eats food first and grass afterward, if that can be arranged; he then probably will retain both. All the cats we have ever known, or heard of, every so often threw up the food they had eaten a few minutes before—up to half an hour before, as a usual thing. They do this if they have eaten too rapidly, as they will sometimes of food they particularly like; if the food has been too cold and, in the absence of either of these incentives, for reasons known only to the cat's interior. Meat so vomited emerges in almost exactly the condition it entered, except that it has been reshaped by the cat's insides. Such throwings-up mean nothing about the health of the cat or, indeed, the quality of the food. They mean merely that the cat misses a meal, a fact which, as time approaches for another, he probably will call angrily to your attention.

But vomiting some hours after eating and of partially digested food is not natural and probably indicates that the cat is sick. If the vomit has an offensive odor, one can be almost certain the cat is sick and entirely certain that only a veterinarian can be sure. Gin, muscularly the strongest of our cats, seems at the same time the most susceptible to ailments and she, in the middle of a morning which had started out fine for her and with a hearty breakfast, once vomited the food suddenly and without warning. (Cats generally make unhappy sounds before they throw up seriously, and lick their lips.) The odor was extremely unpleasant—and within half an hour, Gin was obviously an extremely sick cat.

She proved this by lying around listlessly in the hottest places she could find and by the appearance of her bad eye—each of the young cats has a weak right eye, presumably because of some hereditary kink; both of them also are cross-eyed, Sherry's vision being further complicated by the fact that one of her eyes tracks not only in but up, so that she goes around constantly with her head on one side. Her inability to focus makes her a bad judge of distance, and she frequently leaps from improbable heights, presumably because she gauges incorrectly. In both the cats, the condition of the right eye is an easily read indication of general health.

On this day, Gin's right eye was running and was almost closed and she was too listless even to paw at it. When the doctor came, he found she had a considerable temperature, diagnosed a gastric infection and began to inject penicillin, also ordering a starvation diet. If the penicillin did not work after a week of injections, he would, he told us, go to sulfa.

As it happened, the penicillin worked almost at once; Gin was much better the next day and by the following day was, as far as she could tell, not only perfectly well but starving to death. And the bad eye was, rather miraculously, a bad eye no longer. Her temperature was normal by that time, and on the third day she was allowed to eat again, which she did furiously. We could not have diagnosed her condition, nor administered the penicillin which, so far as we know, saved her life. We could only with the greatest difficulty have taken her temperature and would have been poor judges of its normality, since cats vary from the norm, as people sometimes do. Quite possibly, one of the cats buried under a back-yard rosebush died of what Gin had and might have been saved, although not, to be sure, by penicillin, then unknown.

There are, indeed, no ailments a lay cat owner can safely treat except mild sniffles—which may mean a cold or a cat's version of hay fever, in which latter event the cat sneezes a good deal—and constipation. Sniffles are treated by feeding the cat lightly, keeping him indoors and in a warm place and, if it seems a good idea, bathing his eyes with a boric acid solution. Constipation is treated by diet, as suggested earlier; by lubricants such as mineral oil and sub-stances commercially known as Petromalt and Laxomel, which are particularly useful in preventing accumulations of hair inside the cat; by milk of magnesia or magnesia in tablet form, and—in an emergency—by the use of suppositories.

Cats are supposed to like the flavor of Laxomel and Petromalt, but neither is really a favorite food of cats and all the cats we have tried it on could take Laxomel or leave it alone and preferred the latter course. It can be administered merely by putting it on the cat, who will then lick it off—together, of course, with additional hair. It can be crammed into the sides of the cat's mouth, which is a messy business. It should not be mixed with food, and neither should mineral oil, although we have mixed mineral oil with meat, achieving the result desired and nobody apparently the worse.

Of the more expeditious laxatives, milk of magnesia is the safest and the most widely used; no laxative pill intended for human consumption should be tried out on the cat, whom it may kill. Liquid milk of magnesia is administered by spoon, not too much at a time, and with whatever grip seems to work best. Magnesia tablets, and other pills which may from time to time be necessary, are supposed to be easy to administer. One person can give a cat a pill, the cat books say. Perhaps the cat will lie on a human lap, upside down and with his mouth open, and the pill need only be dropped. Perhaps one can put the pill in the cat's mouth, hold the mouth shut and gently stroke the cat's throat, in which case the cat will swallow pill. We have never had luck with either method. No cat of ours could be persuaded to lie on his back on either of our laps, and open his mouth for medicine. Cats whose mouths were held closed and whose throats were stroked did not swallow pills. They merely waited until we had completed that nonsense and then spit pills out. Neither of us has ever been able, unaided, to give a cat a pill in any fashion, so that of late we always work two people to the cat.

In this procedure, one is the cat holder and the other the pill poker. The cat holder stands against a table, puts the cat in front of him on the table, and tries to hold both fore- and rear paws, two in each hand. The other, the pill poker, takes a firm hold of the cat's head, forces him—this must be done gently, since the jaw bones are delicate—to open his mouth, puts the pill as far back on the cat's tongue as possible and pokes with a finger. (The handle of a spoon can be used, if one is particular about fingers.) With luck, in this operation, the pill suddenly disappears into the cat, who can then be released and will indignantly hide under something. Without luck, a variety of things can happen, none of them leading to the presence of pill in cat and most of them to the presence of cat teeth in finger. In the event of failure there is no recourse but to recapture the cat and try again; sooner or later, we have always succeeded and once, when Martini needed pills night and morning, we grew fairly adept at it. But it is never child's play.

Putting something—a suppository or a thermometer—into the other end of the cat is also a two-human task and one best left to one owner and a veterinarian. Laymen can, however, give suppositories, with care and a little luck and an infant's size suppository which has been kept in the icebox. (They are made of glycerin and soften at room temperature and when they bend readily they are, of course, useless.) The procedure here is for one human to hold the cat upside down on lap, rear end outermost, front legs secured. The other human holds hind legs, lifts the cat a little and, with luck, does what is necessary. Both gentleness and firmness are required, and the cat will scream bloody murder—and all the other cats will come excitedly and talk about it and help the sufferer worry.

(Dr. Camuti, who takes a dim view of the human's knowledge of physiology—he once was called anxiously by a cat owner who had been told to take and report on the cat's temperature with the information that, after two hours of effort, the cat simply could not be persuaded to keep the thermometer in his mouth—warned us early that, in the case of a female cat, alternative suppository orifices are available. When we indicated that we had already noticed this, he said we would be surprised at the mistakes people can make and, in his experience, have.)

The suppository is, of course, an emergency device, and should only be used when the need is great. A cat who gets enough exercise, occasional cereal food and even a few vegetables, probably will be only mildly constipated. (Very few cats, in our experience, have the stipulated one bowel movement a day.) About country cats it is hard to tell, of course; some veterinarians recommend a magnesium pill once a week or so, just to be on the safe side. A meat-fed cat allowed to become badly constipated may get in a condition so toxic that he partially or wholly loses the use of his hind legs; Pete got in that condition in late middle life, when we had been gone for some time and friends were caring for him, and almost died of it. At that stage, of course, the condition has passed beyond lay competence.

Mild sniffles, ordinary constipation—these are within the ministering powers of the average lay cat owner. Fleas, if a cat gets them, can be combatted if a flea powder prepared especially for cats is used—a powder which, among other properties, is free of DDT., which kills cats. Under instruction of a veterinarian, a lay owner may administer remedies for the various skin diseases cats sometimes get; without such instruction the cat owner probably will treat the cat for the wrong ailment, with the wrong medicines. Inside and out, many things can go wrong with a cat. It is the doctor's business to know what has gone wrong; the owner's merely to notice that something has.

Fortunately, these diseases of the cat are not transmittable to the human, nor the human's to the cats. A human will not give a cat a cold, or catch one from him. Fleas a human can catch from a cat, although cat fleas prefer cats. Ringworm, on the other hand, plays no favorites; would as soon make miserable a human as a cat, and can readily be transmitted from one to the other. A cat with ringworm is, therefore, to be handled gingerly until the veterinarian has cured him. The condition is curable in feline as in human; in feline it is harder to detect. A cat owner's first intimation that his cat has ringworm may be that he has it himself.

Cats scratch a good deal, as people do, when there is nothing in particular wrong except a minor itch and there is no way of indicating what excessive scratching is—it depends on the cat, some of whom itch more than others. Fleas can be seen on examination; so can most other serious skin ailments. Cats also lick themselves, and friendly cats—and some of them people—frequently, and so ingest a good deal of hair. Cats shed more at certain times than others but the difference in the case of indoor cats, living in fairly equable temperature throughout the year, is hardly perceptible; there is never a time in a cat's life when he cannot find excess fur to lick off when he washes up. Hairballs in the digestive tract are a possible result of this, but in our experience not a frequent one. (None of our cats has ever been perceptibly troubled by an accumulation of hair.) All cats should be brushed now and then, or often, by their owners, and long-haired cats have to be—and combed, too, and sometimes washed.

Washing a cat, which one of us sometimes did as a child, is quite a trick; few cats like water in quantity, although all can swim and some do for the fun of it and others for the fish they can catch. There is also danger that a freshly washed cat will get pneumonia. But white long-hairs, especially, cannot keep themselves snowy and all long-hairs require considerable human aid in grooming. Most cats get some hair in the throat from time to time, and try to cough it up, producing a rather alarming wheezing sound. This does not seem to bother them particularly.

Cats can, of course, transmit human germ diseases from one person to another, as can dogs, carpets and articles of clothing. This fact has worried worrying people from time to time; Edward Howe Forbush, whose life was one long worry about cats, accused them of transmitting from person to person almost all diseases known, including smallpox and bubonic plague. Another expert, writing many years ago, was almost equally alarmed, feeling certain that cats transmitted, among other dire ailments, yellow fever—subsequently found to be transmitted by mosquitoes—and cholera.

The element of validity in this concern is obvious; cats, like people, are not surgically sterile. The human animal might avoid many bacterial infections by living in entirely aseptic surroundings, thus assuring himself of death from a degenerative disease or, possibly, boredom. A cat is as clean as he can keep himself in his environment. The human usually provides the environment.

A rabid cat can, of course, transmit rabies by biting a person, as can almost any animal, and a great many animals, from dogs to squirrels, get rabies occasionally. The disease is rather rare in cats, the incidence apparently being lower than in dogs and, of course, a cat who cannot be bitten by a rabid animal cannot contract rabies —an apartment house cat living alone, or with other confined cats, runs no risk of rabies and hence his owner does not, at least from the cat. He does run, of course, that minor risk of infection that all run who associate with sharp instruments, whether or not attached to a cat. A scratch from a cat's claw may infect, as may a scratch from a pin or a can-opener; the risk is about the same, although the cat's claws probably are cleaner. Iodine is the natural, and almost universally employed, precaution. But there is in life no absolute guarantee against septicemia, even for people who do not harbor cats. A cat's bite is a little more likely to cause infection than his scratch because it is likely to be deeper; our own physician takes a dim view of bites by cats or dogs and an even dimmer view of bites by people. Tetanus from a cat's scratch or bite is always possible if the cat lives out of doors part of the time and digs holes in tetanus-infected earth. But people who live in tetanus areas and want to be safe should be inoculated against it whether they keep cats or not.

If the cat gives you anything you would rather not have it will be because he has thus acted as a mechanical agent of transmission, occupying a position analogous to that of an icepick, a hammer, an unsterilized blanket from a sick room or the thorn on a rose. He will not give you what he has, even when he is dying of it. You may readily give him one of his ailments by acting as an innocent, mechanical agent of transmission from cat to cat. The carton in which your groceries arrive from the store—a carton which your cat will certainly examine closely and will, once it is emptied, un-doubtedly get into—may give him enteritis, since many grocery store cats die of the disease. And the pleasure one derives from stroking a strange cat on the street may be the death of one's own cat.

If a cat, with his owner's aid, escapes the diseases which threaten this tenuously held single life of his, and if he is not—as so many free-roaming cats are—the victim of an accident, he may live to be twenty or more. He is not likely to, and if he does he will almost surely show the symptoms of senility which one may see in most very aged humans. No one knows why some cats live so long; presumably, as in the case of humans, heredity and luck enter into it—those things and, on not particularly tenable evidence, a diet including raw potatoes. Many cats do live to be twelve or thirteen, and somewhere in that vicinity is perhaps the "average" optimum age of the cat. At that age, and certainly at nine or ten, a healthy cat may show no appreciable signs of ageing, will eat as he always has and play as has been his custom. Our Pete, who died at about the age of ten of the urinary stoppage which seems to be rather more common in neutered males than in other cats, was a vigorous player until his last illness.

He was the first cat of our joint ownership and things happened to him which now, we hope, are less likely to happen to cats of ours. If we had noticed symptoms of listlessness in him, if we had even assiduously checked his toilet pan, we might have prevented the toxic condition which almost cost him his life and from which, in all probability, he never fully recovered. If we had remembered to secure a cabin door, it would not have blown shut on his tail, cutting off something like two inches of it and leaving a wound which was long to heal. Cats lick their hurts and this, while it may lessen the risk of infection somewhat, also prevents the healing of any major wound. A bandage a cat cannot get off is too tight for the wound; anything more than a scratch should be treated by a veterinarian and one who knows about cats. The first work done on Pete's tail by one veterinarian had to be undone and done over by another, and all this did Pete no good. And we were more casual than we are now about leaving Pete alone, arranging, of course, that he be fed, but allowing him to roam more or less at will. During one such absence he got bitten through the face, possibly by a rat, perhaps by a weasel, and the wound became infected, and that did him no good either.

One lives with cats and learns about them; the early cats, on the other hand, do not always live. No cat does, not even the most carefully cared for. Their furry bodies are frequent on our highways; the necessity of dodging them, particularly at night, is a common experience of all motorists, and some motorists do not, one supposes, go to the trouble. (We once watched a driver try, very deliberately, to run over Pete and a cat with whom Pete was having a brawl, and this in Pete's own New York block. The driver got away before we could run over him, which we would have been glad to do. Fortunately, he missed both cats, being as inexpert as he was humanly objectionable.) Since there is a lapse between the word in typescript and the word in print, the cats who now romp about us may be finally quiet by the time these words are read and we, for all our efforts, may have cause to blame ourselves as we regret their absence.

But we will have other cats, and have them quickly. That much, at any rate, we have learned. After Pammy died, we waited longer catless than we shall again; waited until we were sure that no other cat could ever replace her in our affections, none other ever be the same.

And that, of course, was true. There has not, will never be, another cat "like Pammy." Martini, so flagrantly, so arrogantly herself since the first day she trotted across a cabin floor, owning the place and everything in it, is not like gentle Pammy; she is fire and fury, her loves are violent and her periods of irritation equally extreme. She knows only two humans who are not, at best, to be merely tolerated, and sometimes she finds it difficult to tolerate even them; she takes a prankish, and often very annoying, pleasure in getting under a car just as it is about to be driven out of a garage, so immobilizing it. She is absurdly timorous when there is nothing to be afraid of, and dangerously full of courage when there is. There will never be another cat like Martini—nor another who purrs so loudly as Gin does, nor floats so effortlessly over a plaything as does blue-point Sherry, known variously as The Oyster, for obvious reasons; as The Limpet, because of the way she clings to a lap, and as Blondie.

But the world is full of cats who are not like other cats. There are black cats and red cats and lovely silver tabbies; there are gay cats and serious cats, and some who are bright and some who are not. It is inconceivable now to imagine a house which does not contain, by a narrow margin, our three blue-eyed Siamese, but one day we may have to live with other cats. We will postpone that day for so long a time as our care and the attentions of the doctor make possible, and there is really no assurance they will not outlive us, since neither of us has nine lives either. But it is not possible that we will not have cats while we live.

15

Plain and Fancy Cats

THERE ARE GAY cats in the world and cats who are lachrymose, cats bursting with enthusiasm and cats who prefer never to turn a paw, bright cats and cats barely able to keep up with a mouse. No race, including the human, is more various in personality—in that complex of tastes and appetites, preferences and attitudes, by which, in the end, we tell one individual from another. But no race, also including the human, shows fewer significant physical variations, all cats looking like cats and regarding one another as cats, without discrimination of any kind. Domestic cats vary in weight and size about as people do. A cat may weigh six pounds or, rarely, twenty —about as large a cat as we have ever met weighed twenty-three pounds and was correspondingly lethargic. Humans in reasonable health may weigh ninety pounds or, rarely, more than three times as much, which is about the same scale of variation.

Humans come in several colors, from the "white," which Chesterton so wisely noted should be called "pinkish," to the "black," which is almost never that and is often no more than a slightly deeper pink. Humans are variously shaped, being in some instances chunky and in others long and narrow; having heads which may be round and may be approximately oblong and noses which may turn up or down. In the absence of social pressure to behave otherwise, most people no doubt would take these physical variations in the human as matter-of-factly as cats take similar feline variations, and in basic human animal relationships they frequently do. But some people—Hitlers and Dixiecrats—make a great fuss about these human differences, and a great many people make a considerable point of similar variations in cats.

Cats, like humans, may be affected, adversely or favorably, by such superficial things as color and shape; having long hair or short may be, for a kitten, the factor which determines the whole of life, including its duration—may determine whether the individual's twelve years or so are to be spent in luxury or in a search of garbage cans or whether they are to be lived at all. Hundreds of thousands of cats die annually in gas chambers or, struggling feebly, in the meshes of submerged burlap bags. Few of these unfortunates are long-hairs of the type commonly called Persian, or Siamese; none, one may guess, is a Burmese or an Abyssinian, since for all these special cats people will pay money, and sometimes a good deal of it.

The cats who die young through human intention, or who live precariously or by hard work, are commonly of the colors, conformations and length of coat which classify them as "domestic short-hairs" or "alley cats"; they are, that is, individuals of the group most people think of when they think of cats. Some of them are very beautiful; one of the most exquisite cats either of us has ever seen is a domestic short-hair named Chinnie, who happens to be a silver tabby and who lives with Miss Hettie Gray Baker in what is perhaps best described as a cat heaven. Some of these common cats are black and some are white and some are both; many of them are striped or blotched, and hence tabbies; some are of the color called "blue" by cat fanciers and "maltese" by most other people; a few are of other solid colors, red or cream; now and then one is of black, orange and cream and is a tortoise-shell and almost certainly a female. Their eyes may be green, yellow, copper, orange or—if the cat is white—blue.

In health, and of good inheritance, they are broad-chested cats; the males may be especially powerful in chest and shoulders; they are compact, put together to stay; they have tails rather short than long and tapering toward the end; they have small ears, usually somewhat rounded at the tops, and a broad stretch of forehead between them; they are rather full faced and their coats are short and smooth, soft to the touch.

By no means all of them have these characteristics, often because they do not get enough to eat and sometimes because they get too much. Since they get around constantly, and meet all sorts of cats, they do not often come out in the colors recommended; many of them are black and white in odd places and not a few, whose ancestors met long-hairs and with them sang the cat's wild song of love, have fur too long for their station in life, while it remains too short for any other station. One does not see many of them in cat shows, although they are eligible and do appear—and even win—and they are usually given away, or find homes, if at all, by their own ingenuity and charm, as our Pete did. They are the easiest cats to get; some people have found it almost impossible not to get them. And they are among the easiest cats to love, since all that any cat has, they have, of intelligence and character, of impishness and affection and variety. These qualities do not vary, so far as we know, from breed to breed, and if they do at all—as some people believe—then the domestic short-hair may have them in better balance than the more special cats, since the short-hair is the cosmopolitan who has been everywhere and met everybody, acquiring in his wanderings both knowledge and a variety of genes, which lead to self-sufficiency and adaptability.

He is a quieter cat than some we could name—and shall. He speaks softly, being in general soprano, regardless of his sex. He is apt, indeed, to speak very seldom to humans, except when he wants his dinner, and to be loud voiced only with other cats. He is, perhaps, essentially a healthier animal than are the cats to which men have set special monetary value and hence nurtured carefully and inbred considerably. (Cats have no objection whatever to incest, in any degree.) The average healthy domestic short-hair can go out in all weathers and, if necessary, does, and is none the worse for it; he can go into rough country and become only moderately covered with burrs, which would be almost inextricably entangled in a long-hair's fur, and he often seems able to get along on a diet which would turn a Siamese's stomach, although he should, of course, never be asked to.

Of this basic cat, presumably the offspring of the Egyptian cat and the European wildcat, with admixtures of almost all the other small cats there have ever been, there are more in the world than of any other kind.* In crossbreeding with more specialized cats, of which he is very fond, the domestic short-hair is dominant. The kittens will be basic cats and resemble basic cats, the special cats being represented by wistful traces—perhaps an extra length of body and tail, if the domestic has met a Siamese; perhaps a somewhat longer coat, if a straying Persian was encountered. (Inbred, some of these kittens will revert to their special characteristics, in obedience to Mendel's ruling in these matters.) Pam and Jerry were the children of such a meeting of cats who had crossed the railroad tracks, their mother a wandering Siamese, their father a traveling man. Jerry was a deep gray all over, and very handsome; his tail was, perhaps, a little longer than his father's had been and his face slightly more pointed; Pam was gray and white, rather long bodied. Both were, in all that mattered, basic cats. Pammy, at least, was also quite wonderful.

Reading *Cats,* which is a magazine about them, one would never suspect that most cats in the world are of this basic breed—the plain cats who catch our mice, guard our grocery stores, patrol our wharves. One would assume that the cat world was divided, a little unevenly, between long-hairs—which even this authoritative, if often amusing, publication frequently calls Persians—and Siamese, with now and then a Manx, Abyssinian, Burmese or, even more rarely, a Russian Blue to add even greater tone. One would assume from visiting the average cat show that there are about four long-hairs to every Siamese, one domestic to fifteen of the other two combined and now and then an outsider known merely as Household Pet. At a recent show in New York, 181 long-hairs were entered in all the classes and colors; forty-four Siamese, one each of Burmese and Manx, seventeen domestic short-hairs and fourteen household pets, of which three represented a breeder's earnest, if slightly bewildered, effort to add pink-point Siamese cats to the world.

It would thus appear that most cats who are not basic cats are long-haired cats, who used to be called Angoras or Persians, between the two subvarieties earlier fanciers finding a difference

---

* Nobody knows how many cats there are in the world. It has been estimated that there are 21,000,000 in the United States.

which, as it became less and less apparent to anyone, including the cats, was finally no longer insisted upon. Neither name is now used in cat shows, where cats with long hair have become long-hairs, an appropriate if not greatly imaginative term. Persians did not, in all probability, come from Persia; Angoras were named after Angora, Turkey. Both, in so far as they were not essentially the same, may have derived from Pallas' cat, Felis manul, and may, quite as easily, not. Long hair is very possibly a mutation in the feline, as it is in cattle; it may have occurred anywhere or, for that matter, almost everywhere. It is a fixed characteristic; long-hair bred to long-hair produces long-hair.

These cats, who are often as beautiful as any animal has a right to be, come in a number of accepted colors, as do the short-hairs; since they are more often than not bred under human control, they are less often mixed in color than is the basic cat. They may be white, in which case they must be all white to have a chance in a cat show—and hence to be monetary considerations—or black, but it is not allowed them to be that engaging mixture of both which is frequently so attractive in short-hairs and results in so many impertinent feline faces. They may be "blue" or red or cream; they may be silver or shaded silver; smokes or silver-tabbies or masked silver; they may be striped or blotched, in which case they are all tabbies and may be red, brown, tortoise-shell or blue-cream. If they are solid-color cats, they may not have tabby markings; only if they are white may they have blue eyes, or odd-colored eyes. It is very difficult to be a proper long-hair, and all it gets you is a cage with ribbons on it—that and constant grooming, good food and your picture in the papers. Except for the food, it is hard to believe that these things seem important to cats and it may be here, in the cat show where they seem closest together, that cats and people are in actuality farthest apart.

A proper long-hair must, in addition to meeting these exacting color standards and having, in general, orange or copper eyes, except that silvers must have green eyes, conform to a number of humanly established rules as to shape. For the benefit of any long-hair owner who would like to compare his cat with the ideal, we quote from the regulations of one of the cat organizations—in this case the Cat Fanciers' Federation:

"Long Haired Standard: Type: The perfect cat should be of cobby type, that is to say, low on the legs, deep in the chest, massive across the shoulders and rump with a short well-rounded middle piece. In size, the cat should be large or medium, but there should be no sacrifice of quality for the sake of mere size.

"Head: The head should be round and massive, with great breadth of skull, and be well set on a neck not too long. Ears: Neat, round tipped, set wide apart and not unduly open at the base. Nose: Short, snub and broad. Cheeks: Full. Jaws: Broad and powerful. Eyes: Large, round, full, set wide apart and brilliant, giving a sweet expression to the face.

"Tail: Short, carried without a curve and at an angle lower than the back, but not trailed when walking. Back: Level. Legs: Thick and strong; forelegs, perfectly straight. Paws: Large, round and firm; toes, carried close, five in front and four behind.

"Coat: Long hair. The coat should show, primarily, perfect physical condition. It should be of fine texture, soft, glossy, full of life and should stand off from the body. It should be long all over the body, including the shoulders. The ruff should be immense and continue in a deep frill between the front legs. Ear tufts, long and curved; toe tufts, long; brush, very full.

"It is particularly desirable to eliminate rangy, flat-sized (*sic*), narrow chested, long, spindle-legged, long tailed cats, with long noses, large ears, pointed and upright, eyes set bias or close together, receding chins, light bone and a generally 'foxy' face."

Those who possess cats complying with these standards, and properly colored, have money on four legs, as most such owners already know. For more than two hundred years, such cats have been bought and sold, beginning in England; the market in cats did not, as Nelson Antrim Crawford once noted, break in the 1929 depression, when so many things were broken, including faiths and necks. In 1933, Mr. Crawford found, stud cats who had won championships and otherwise proved their ability, were worth from four to six hundred dollars on the paw, which was about their former value. (The price has advanced since, as have most prices.) Mr. Crawford felt that, in those uneasy days, people were turning from dogs to cats. "I cannot help feeling," Mr. Crawford commented, "that, unconsciously at least, they wanted an animal that would not remind them of bond salesmen, investment counselors and other adornments of the gold-plated era. There is no animal less salesmanlike than a cat."

A long-hair may, in a special group, have a "Peke face," which means that he should, in countenance, resemble a Pekingese dog as closely as possible. These cats are not very good-looking.

Most other long-hairs are, although one long accustomed to short-haired cats may find them a little showy. It is also contended by short-hair addicts, particularly those used to the activity of the Siamese, that long-hairs somewhat lack animation, being at their loveliest in repose, preferably on a cushion in the sun, and knowing it perfectly well. But all cats appear to know when they are well displayed and to enjoy the human admiration which results and a cat in perfect sable, looking out at the world through great copper-colored eyes and seeing it look back at him with admiration, can hardly be blamed for making the most of what life offers.

We have, as it happens, been closely acquainted with few of these luxurious creatures. We know to speak to, a gayly scampering red, sociable and full of spirit, and she is as lively as a cat can be, and as brightly inventive. If she feels that long hair gives her dignity, she does not stand on it; she appears to be sweet tempered and without arrogance. One of us knew, many years ago, a white—were his eyes blue or orange? was he cobby and did he have a massive head and a well-rounded middle piece or was he long-tailed and spindle-legged? Memory does not serve too well; it may be assumed he was no champion, since he was given to a boy. He was beautiful when he was clean, which was not often; his name was Pat (for Patrician) and in the darkness of Sunday mornings, when papers were to be delivered along frosty streets, he used to get up too, and drink coffee with the boy. He was very fond of coffee, with enough cream in it. He did not take sugar.

But he does not seem, for a cat, to have made much impression on the boy—hardly more, indeed, than did most of the humans the boy went to school with and years afterward embarrassedly met and could not for the life of him remember. Pat used to sit at a kitchen door and look out into a backyard and now and then seem to curl his lip at ordinary cats on the other side of the screen, and it was by so behaving that he got his name. But it is hard to remember that he played much, or invented many things, and the feeling persists that he was often languid. It may be that he was not in the best of health and certainly he did not live long; his diet was table scraps and liver, which could be bought in large, unpleasant chunks for five cents from the nearest butcher, and the disagreeable nature of this now-valued food seems to be more persistent in memory than anything Pat did. He had his picture taken often with the boy and, as is usually the case when cats and people are photographed together, was much the better looking of the two. He was bathed often—too often, probably—in a washtub in the basement, and then he was anything but languid, being more than a match for the boy and the boy's father. As soon as he could manage, after a bath, he went into the coal bin.

We really do not know as much as we would like about long-hairs, but we have no reason to believe that they differ inwardly from other cats, since in none of the cats we have known well was character keyed to race, or intelligence or charm either. Under all that lovely fur, the long-hair is still a cat, if a somewhat smaller cat than he at first appears. He expects the same things, and is rather more likely than most cats to get them; he will catch mice for people if people will let him out.

About the "Royal and Sacred Cat of Siam," we know a great deal more—enough, indeed, to look with as much scepticism on this designation as we do with favor on the cat himself. Neither the regality nor the divinity of this quick, slim creature is half so certain as his engaging qualities—his alertness, which sometimes does seem to exceed that of other cats; his tendency to give trust and great affection to one or two people at a time; his habit of following behind such a favorite human, which is not a universal trait in cats and, of course, the oddity of his appearance. It is a little pleasant to have people stop now and then to stare; to say, doubtfully, "Are those *cats?*" and remain a little unbelieving in the face of reassurance. But Sheila Kaye-Smith, who writes with great charm about both cats and kitchens, lost a much-loved Siamese because a farmer saw "something strange" in his field and, since it was alien and he was human, shot it, and that is a risk one presumably always runs.

The legend of the Siamese is familiar, and—like so many legends —commonly stated as a fact. He was a palace cat, jealously guarded there, not to be owned by groundlings. He was an associate of kings; he was also half god—no novelty for any cat—and half watch-dog. In the latter, and less usual, capacity it was his wont to leap on the shoulders of intruders, digging claws in and yelling for the corporal of the guard. All of these things happened in Siam, which to most of us is far away. They must also have happened long ago.

The first Siamese cats to see the western world, legend continues, reached England in the late seventies of the last century, and were the gifts of Siamese royalty to deserving nobility of Britain. It was not until twenty years or so later that the first of them reached the United States, and it is only in very recent years that they have become reasonably common. (There is a certain vogue for them as this is written; they seem to be coming into style.) But not even the most assiduous cat fanciers are much inclined to give names and precise dates for these events; it is thought that the first Siamese cat to come to America went to Chicago where, even then, the need for watch-cats may have been considerable. And there can be little doubt he did leap on shoulders there; almost all Siamese have this trick, and it is offered as confirmation of their ancient Siamese training. Unfortunately, however, all the Siamese we have known leaped on the shoulders of friends, or close acquaintances, instead of upon those of intruders. If our three made any protest when a sneak thief rifled our New York apartment, making off with a typewriter, there was nothing to show it. Apparently they followed him into the bedroom and were agreeable to being locked up there.

If once the blue-eyed cat who wears a mask was cloistered and a friend of kings in Siam, he is certainly so no longer. There are many cats in Siam now; not many of them, as Miss Hettie Gray Baker recently discovered through correspondence with Mr. Floyd A. Wilson, who lives in Bangkok and is an official of the Y.M.C.A. and hence obviously a man to be trusted, are, in the special sense, Siamese. "Cats are as varied and mixed here as anywhere," Mr. Wilson assured Miss Baker, who already knows more about cats than almost anyone, but is always willing to learn more.

She had written Mr. Wilson, enclosing a pamphlet illustrating the proper points of Siamese cats and asked, in effect, how things went with the cats of Siam. "Siamese cats are difficult to find in Bangkok," Mr. Wilson said in the course of his letter of reply. They could be found now and then in small towns.

"As to the legend that cats are jealously guarded in temples and palaces, some people express the idea that any Siamese cat is jealously guarded," Mr. Wilson continued. "It is difficult to keep the cats from running around promiscuously. However, some people laughed when asked about this legend and commented that most of them keep cats to catch the rats. I don't believe cats are considered any more sacred than any other animal. It is against the Buddhist religion to kill any animal and cats are included. From the number of dogs running around loose and stray, one would think that dogs are sacred. There are many stray cats and nearly all have some indications of Siamese cat blood or Korat cat blood. . . . Regarding the blue eyes, Siamese cats do have blue eyes, as do the Korat cats. Even one of our rabbits has blue eyes, while the others have pink eyes. As yet, I have been unable to get a good snapshot of a Siamese cat which will be typically Siamese."

It was not for want of trying, either. The mayor of Bangkok was interested by the pamphlet setting forth standards; out of this interest there grew one of the first—possibly the first—Siamese cat shows Siam had ever known. It was not entirely a success. An "authority," not otherwise identified in newspaper clippings sent to Miss Baker, complained that the quality of the cats was not very good. It was decided to establish a stud and breed for points, the points being supplied by the late Louise Frith, a breeder whose cattery was in Maine. If the people, and the cats, of Bangkok are diligent, the Siamese cat may yet be established in the home of his birth.

Presumably it was the home of his birth; presumably, also, he has a different inheritance from the domestic short-hair and from the long-hair. This ancestry does not, as some have thought, include the rabbit, which is a food and not a mate of cats, nor the monkey. It does not, either, include the dog, although Siamese are now and then, for reasons entirely obscure, called "doglike." It is conceivable that the Siamese is a partially albino mutation of some Asiatic cat. Nobody really knows. There are a great many things about the derivation of Felis domestica about which people are uncertain. (Including his taxonomic identification; Ida M. Mellen tirelessly assures the readers of *Cats* that he is Felis catus.)

The Siamese, whatever else he may be, is all cat, and invariably behaves like a cat. He climbs more than most cats; he speaks more often, and in a harsher voice. Carl Van Vechten, a long-hair man himself, asserts flatly that "Siamese and Russian short-haired cats have an odor," echoing, one is sure unconsciously, the statement made by C. H. Lane in 1903 that "a friend of mine who has had some experience with the variety [Siamese] says they are much in their habits like other cats, but that strangers notice a peculiar wild animal odor about them like I have observed with Russian Blue short-haired cats." We have smelled our own Siamese carefully, and seldom meet any others without smelling them, and have yet to detect any odor other than that of warm fur, which is the rather pleasant way cats smell when they have not been eating fish.

The Siamese is not, in our experience, especially delicate, in the sense of being prone to illness. (He is delicately built, and delicate in his movements.) It was once thought, and is still said in authoritative publications—the *Encyclopaedia Britannica,* for example—that he can exist only in warm climates and is hence unsuited to much of the United States. Certainly, even more than most cats, he likes warmth. But ours have without misadventure survived Aprils and

Novembers in New York's Putnam County, where both are often cold, and today Gin and Sherry went out in this winter's first considerable snow. They did not enjoy it, nor stay long; they did much indignant shaking of feet. But there is nothing to indicate they caught cold, or were much more put out at the weather than any proper cat is when it is cold or, most particularly, damp. Gin swears furiously on rainy days, and swears specifically at us, knowing that we could do something to improve matters if we only would. Martini is more philosophic. Once she establishes in the morning that the weather is unfavorable, she catches up on her sleep. If it clears up in the middle of the day this makes no difference to her; once she has written a day off, she does not try to write it in again. She waits until tomorrow.

This much is true of Siamese: They are either all Siamese, and hence to strangers look very much alike, or they are not properly to be called Siamese at all, and are not likely to look much like Siamese. This does not, of course, mean that they must all be perfect on points, able to win prizes wherever they go. None of our cats is within many, many points of perfection; even if they were not spayed, which eliminates a cat from active show life, it would have been absurd to enter them in competitions. They are, none the less, "pure-bred" Siamese, and show it unmistakably—as unmistakably as Pam and Jerry, who were half-Siamese, showed themselves as domestic short-hairs. "The Siamese pattern," as Doris Bryant notes, "never breaks up." It is there, or it isn't.

Siamese cats come in two, and only two, color combinations, and they are always blue-eyed. They are, as described by another cat association—the Cat Fanciers' Association, Inc.—of "even pale fawn or cream, shading gradually into lighter color on belly and chest" or "bluish," which is to say blue-grayish, white. In the first case they are seal points, and are the more common; in the second they are blue points, rather rare—the blue genes are recessive—and, some think, not quite so vigorous as their darker companions. In either case they have "points," of deep seal-brown or a gray-blue deeper than the body color, depending on their group.

These "points" are what make the Siamese so distinctive in appearance. They have dark faces and, ideally, this darkness forms a well-defined mask, leaving much of the forehead lighter, although crossed by darker tracing lines to the ears. Their ears, which should be large, wide at the base and pointed, are of the same color; so are their lower legs and their tails. They are small to medium in size, the females often very small, and they are—or should be—long slim cats, ending in long, slim tails. They have slender legs, and the hind legs are longer than the fore, so that they seem a little to be walking downhill; their fur is extremely fine and lies close to the body and they have eyes which slant downward toward the nose. (This is very noticeable when they half close their eyes; if their eyes are round—a bad show point and one of Martini's greatest beauties—this slanting is barely perceptible except when they are blinking at you.) Their eyes should be, and usually are, deep blue; if they are not, it is stretching a point to call the cat a Siamese. And their faces are pointed, "wedge-shaped."

(Recently some breeders, seeking to assure this last characteristic, have succeeded in overdoing it, as humans will when left to their own devices. Now and then one encounters Siamese with faces exaggeratedly pointed, more like cones than wedges. Such a face is not becoming to a cat and with it goes—or appears to go in those we have seen—a narrowing of the head and hence of the area available for brains. It will be lamentable if breeders succeed in doing to Siamese cats what breeders have already done to collie dogs; one can only hope that cats, who have resisted so many things in so many millions of years, will resist this also. It is not good that cats should have faces like rats.)

As is the case with other cats, and even with humans, not all individuals attain the standard laid down for the race. Martini is too cobby by far and her tail is not long enough; both the younger cats are crosseyed and that, while once considered no great defect—the breed is much prone to it—has now been bred out of the bloodlines which lead to championships. None has a kinked tail, also once not greatly objected to, and now a defect; Martini has a darkish area on her belly, which is not as it should be, and Sherry has faint, but perceptible, tabby markings on her legs—a color defect not uncommon, and supposed to disappear as a blue reaches about two years of age, but which in her case has not as yet. Sherry is also oddly put together; there is an insecurity about her articulation which is, until one watches her run and leap, faintly disturbing.

Siamese show none of their special characteristics when they are small kittens, except the blue eyes—which, in kittens, are a general feline rule. They are all white at first; they color slowly, like meerschaum pipes, and this slow deepening in color may continue all their lives, so that in late maturity a seal point may be largely a brown cat and a blue point a deep maltese one. (There are in any case considerable variations in the depth of body color; some prize-winning cats are fairly dark and others much lighter. The show preference nowadays seems for the lighter Siamese, but this is only human whim.)

The Burmese cat is in most respects like the Siamese; even so recently as 1949, Doris Bryant wrote that "very dark Siamese are sometimes called chocolate Siamese and sometimes they are called Burmese" and the show rules and classifications supplied us as the most recent by the Cat Fanciers' Association do not recognize the Burmese at all. One of the rival fanciers' groups, the Cat Fanciers' Federation, has, however, recently established new standards for this kind of fancy cat. It is provided that the cat shall wear very dark seal-brown, which shades to slightly lighter on chest and belly and that the ears, mask and tail points shall be only slightly darker than the body. The Burmese should be of the same build as the Siamese —"svelte," a favorite word among "the fancy"; the face wedge-shaped and the eyes the shape of almonds and slanting "towards the nose in true oriental fashion." But the eyes should not be blue; Burmese cats have yellow eyes. (It is conceivable, and sometimes argued, that Siamese are a partially albinic variation; if so, they may have varied from the group now called Burmese.) So anyone's very dark Siamese with yellow eyes is now a Burmese cat, may be shown as such—if without white spots or tabby markings—in CFF shows. Burmese are not very common.

Abyssinian cats are also brown cats, but their fur is "ticked"—has, that is, bands of dark brown or black on each hair, and the more bands there are the better for the cat, or, at any rate, for the cat's owner. They have long pointed heads and sharp ears; should not be barred but are apt to be—almost all cats are apt to be; the tiger has difficulty in changing his stripes—and are slender cats with long and tapering tails. We have not known personally any Abyssinian cats, but they sound fine. They have green, yellow or hazel eyes and black feet, with the blackness extending up the back of the legs.

Manx cats, as everyone knows, are tailless—"cats from the Isle of Man, they have no tails; all other cats, cats from England, Ireland, Wales, have nice l-o-n-g tails; it seems like a rank injustice," this to be sung to a guitar, after a reasonable number of drinks. They also have long hind legs and round rumps—"as round as an orange being the ideal" the CFF writer advises. They have double coats, like rabbits, and move like rabbits and if they have any tails at all they are merely funny-looking cats, suitable only to be loved. To win prizes, they must have a hollow where other cats have tails and their backs should be very short; they can come in any of the colors considered appropriate for long- or short-haired cats, and in addition may be "ticked" tabbies, and no one cares greatly what color eyes they have. The absence of a tail presumably does not bother a Manx cat, since cats have no real use for a tail, which is often stepped on and sometimes caught in doors. (It has been argued that the tail is used as a rudder by a cat who, dropped upside down, wants to land on his feet, but Miss Mellen and some friends dropped a number of Manx cats and all of them turned over contentedly.)

There are also Russian Blue cats, very rare in the United States; Maine cats, which are long-hairs and come in all colors and combinations of colors, are considered by their owners to be without equal in all that makes for delightful cats and are not countenanced in shows; and there were once Mexican hairless cats, which became extinct, possibly by volition after seeing themselves in mirrors. (Not all cats, incidentally, seem able to see themselves in mirrors; some of them do but without identifying the image; Martini used to get very excited when she was young by the cat she saw in a mirrored coffee table, would dance on the table in an effort to touch the other cat and would go under the table in search of it. But she gave this up early, although whether she solved the mystery or merely dismissed it we could never tell. Sherry used to try to reach the cat in a mantel mirror by attempting to get behind it; Gin never gave indication of seeing anything whatever in any mirror.) Long-haired Siamese cats have been experimentally bred, although both long hair and Siamese patterns are recessives; the cats are very handsome, but are not yet acknowledged by cat show organizers.

People who are fond of cats are apt to have, overlying this basic affection, a special regard for a certain kind of cat; to feel, even if they are reluctant to say, that there is no cat quite like a long-hair red or a "coon cat" from Maine or a Siamese or a domestic short-hair. Other cats, they think inwardly, are all very well, having the essential quality of being cats. But none is quite so beautiful, so affectionate and intelligent, so altogether all that a cat should be as this special breed of their favor. These are minor disagreements, and all in the family; among other cat people one may uphold his favorite almost to the point of derogating the lesser cats, but this may not be done, of course, in the presence of outsiders who do not like any cats. Even the Mexican hairless, unattractive as they appear from photographs to have been, were after all cats, and so may not be let down.

We, as has all along been evident, are to a considerable degree Siamese cat addicts; when we find a Nelson Antrim Crawford saying that they are "perhaps the most affectionate and intelligent" of cats, we nod our agreement and read the praise aloud to Martini and Sherry, and to Gin also, if she does not at the moment happen to be out or wanting to get there. And we think of stories which seem to us to prove the point. Only the other day, for example, a pretty little domestic short-hair, hardly out of kittenhood, came calling; the other night it was, and a cold and snowy night, and she cried anxiously to be let in.

The problem presented—while not the point of the anecdote— was a considerable one. We were fully stocked with cats; it is not wise for home cats to associate with wanderers, although inevitably they will; cat fights may result from sudden introductions. Nevertheless, one may not leave a cat to cry outside the warmth on a cold wet night. So, while our own three sat on a staircase which commands the best view of the front door, we coaxed her in, providing cream and soothing words. She drank the cream and did not appear much to listen to the words; we saw that she was well-cared-for and decided—which we subsequently more or less established —that she was a cat with a home she had merely elected not to stay in.

After the cream, she was phlegmatic for a cat—at any rate, and this is the point of the anecdote, by comparison. She sat on the floor and wrapped her tail around her and now and then made that small, high sound which we had almost forgotten cats made, since ours speak so differently. She looked at the other cats with interest, but with little excitement. Our own tense creatures, whose least emotional response is of tornadic intensity, were momentarily puzzled at this quiescence. Then Gin jumped the newcomer in fury, gave up in mid-attack, yelled, and rushed off almost literally in all directions. The visiting cat withdrew under a sofa while this went on and emerged when the storm had passed. Sherry suddenly spoke in anguish, dashed across the room, and leaped into a chimney aperture which houses a charcoal grill, fortunately not then in use. She yelled up the flue.

Martini, of course, took matters into her own paws. No hasty starter of tasks fated to incompletion, no retreater into apertures when only the four-footed offer peril, she began a slow and bristling advance, every hair on end, ears laid back, a growl of menace uninterrupted. Since we have been told by her veterinarian, who knows many cats, that Martini is by instinct a killer, we decided it was time for the young visitor to go home, and put her out again. The Siamese then ran excitedly from door to door, making faces at her through the glass and lashing their tails, and saying what they would do to her if she ever dared come in again.

Now we do not consider that their behavior was ideal, or even that it was—by those human standards all so freely applied to cats —defensible. They should, as some cats will under similar circumstances, have recognized one of their own kind in need and offered sympathy, and even to share the food. It is not a good thing to spit at guests, and afterward we told them this.

But we told each other, too, where they could not hear us, that we would not have cats without fire in them, without the incredible alertness to all that goes on, the instant responsiveness, which we have come to associate with this quick, bright, blue-eyed breed. It is all very well for a cat to be amiable and to take things as they come; such cats are easy to live with. They may even not climb curtains, nor flare as suddenly into rage as into loud-purred love. Pete, although less phlegmatic than our visitor, was not as our present cats are made up of fire; we have not known other cats so constituted except those with fawn-colored bodies and brown ears (or the colors Sherry is) and with blue eyes slanting downward toward the nose. But all such cats we have known had that intensity of spirit, although one or two, being elder cats, did not display it quite so extravagantly. This quality we like in cats and this quality we have, as this is written, certainly got.

Whether Siamese are more intelligent nobody can say without prejudice, since no one has ever tried to find out. The cats subjected to intelligence tests have been domestic short-hairs. Martini is very bright; Sherry, although her mind is evasive, probably equally so; Gin is a darling, but she will never write a great book or propound a mathematical theory of monumental importance. Her I.Q. is probably not much above the even hundred which represents normality.

Whether Siamese grow fonder of people than do other cats is equally a matter of guesswork. Many people have guessed they do, largely because they often act as if they did. But this acting-out of love for humans may be an aspect of their general responsiveness, and of their loquacity, and may so represent a depth of affection essentially no greater than that other cats have. Martini is, as we have said, tempestuous in her love, highly selective in bestowing it, and enraged by any action which she interprets as a human failure to respond. Compared to hers, Pammy's love was a steady glow. Gin, although not a lap-sitting cat, is rather like her mother in her occasional demonstrativeness, although she has an essentially sweeter

nature—as, we suspect, have most cats and even a great many people. Sherry wishes much petting, but prefers it brief; when she sits on a lap, it is to sleep there, and it may be that she does not love anyone unduly.

Except for Pammy, who was after all half-Siamese, we have not known cats of other kinds so adept at showing love for humans as Martini and Gin can be, and often are. Pete was fond of us in a tolerant fashion; the long-haired Pat did not, so far as memory serves, show much affection for anyone. But is it delight in our return which brings three cats to a door, their noses pressing against it, when they hear the proper car, which Martini, at any rate, instantly recognizes? Or when, in the old days, they heard familiar footsteps on the stairs? Or is it primarily that alertness, that restless curiosity, which they all possess? Pete used not to meet us. Yet he was fond of us, and had many human friends, and was widely regarded as a most amiable and affectionate cat.

People vary similarly in demonstrativeness, of course, and those outwardly phlegmatic have assured their fellows that still waters run deep, an assertion not backed by overwhelming evidence. Most of us, nevertheless, prefer a reasonable measure of responsiveness in those we love, and from whom we hope for love, providing that it does not degenerate into effusiveness and a resulting loss of that moderate dignity which is to be desired in all living things. One would not wish a dog's effusiveness from a cat and one certainly never gets it. But it is nice to be told now and then that one is thought well of, and this Siamese cats do tell their humans when the mood is on them. Perhaps they do it more frequently than do most other cats. From our experience, it seems almost certain that they do it more selectively.

No "one-man dog" ever made sharper distinctions among humans than Martini does; she is a two-person cat and bitterly so. Gin is almost equally determined although she will, after she has known them for a few months, permit alien humans to touch her and may even pause a moment while the touch is given. Sherry is interested in most humans, and less convinced that they will do her ill, yet of the two laps available in her family center she sits almost exclusively on one and this, since it has been true all her life, can hardly be one of those curious habit-preferences which all cats have, so that for a week or so only one place is worthy to be sat upon and is then superseded by another, which for perhaps another ten days has to the feline mind unique advantages. Sherry's preference is partial one-personishness.

Siamese cats are rather widely known for this habit of cleaving to one or two humans and being uninterested in, or even antagonistic to, others. We have heard of one, clearly a psychopathic cat, who not only preferred his mistress to other people, but tried to kill all other people he encountered; tried, quite literally, to kill them; was wont to sit in a screened window of his home and try to break through to destroy any passing alien human. When this cat was in need of doctoring, his mistress had to feed him sleeping pills before the veterinarian was due, since otherwise the veterinarian, a man who respects cats, would decline to call. Obviously, a cat who carries things to such extremes is in need of a psychiatrist, but the tendency is in the breed.

And a human is apt to find it a pleasant thing about the breed, and one of its charms. We flatter easily, we humans; we can take a good deal of special treatment, although some prefer it to stop short of fawning. It may be that, to the two of us, Siamese cats seem so perfect as pets because they compromise a little, insisting less than some—under certain conditions—on the fabled aloofness of the feline. It is pleasant, after all, to be met at the door by three expectant cats, their large, sharp ears pricked to our coming.

But most of all, Siamese cats seem to us especially gay and especially beautiful. There is a clarity about them, both in the shape of their bodies and the pattern in their fur, which is a delight in a blurring world, where so few things are any longer as clear as things should be. When you see a Siamese cat you seem to see him all, delicate bone and long muscle; you see him plain, with no fluff between you and cat. And when his mood is gay, he is the gayest thing on earth.

16

Cat People, Plain and Fancy

THE CAT OF THE YEAR for 1949, the All-American Cat, the winner of the beauty contest, was Grand Champion Dixi-Land's Felice of Nor-Mont, a blue long-hair female, owned by Mrs. Merald C. Hoag of Arlington, Virginia, if the typographical errors to which *Cats Magazine* is a little prone have not crept into the listing. The Best Opposite Sex Cat of the Year was Champion Dixi-Land's White Historian II, a white long-hair with orange eyes. Felice is a very pretty little cat, from her picture, taken when she was sitting—as any cat likes to sit—in a hat box.

Felice, if one may speak so familiarly of so grand a cat, did not earn her honors by sitting in a hat box. She earned them by sitting in cages, with other cats to right of her and to left of her, and across the aisle from her, in cat shows in Chicago and Miami, in Milwaukee and Denver and, no doubt, points between. She sat in these cages and people looked at her and someone—perhaps Mrs. Hoag herself—sat near her on a stool and frowned upon people who, seeing so much long-haired beauty, could hardly forbear to touch it. Now and then Felice was taken out and combed and brushed and to this grooming one who does not know her personally can only guess her response. Now and then even grand champions try to get away from it all. When they do there is a general shout, "Close the doors!" and many people move rapidly in many directions, seeking a cat who has gone under something.

At intervals during these cagings, each of which lasted a couple of days, Felice was removed from her home cage and placed in a portable cage and carried to a table, where her cage was placed in a row of cages occupied by other grand champions of her color.

People sat in rows of chairs on one side of the table and on the other side was another person, probably a woman, who looked at all the grand champion cats one after another. Felice was looked down upon and looked up at; she was tempted to turn her head to bring her eyes in better view and to move to display the contours of her body and the arrangement of her glossily brushed coat. She was lifted from the cage and carried to a smaller table and there examined with both eyes and hands—eyes which had looked at, hands which had felt, many long-haired cats. Each of the other cats competing was so examined, and in the end the judge dropped a winner's ribbon on the top of Felice's cage. Perhaps sometimes it dangled through, and Felice played with it. She looks in her pictures like a cat who would like to play, business permitting.

Having been thus established as best in color, Felice went on to new competition. In this contest, she met "the best male and best female cats of each color, both long and short hair," and then the chips really were down, for out of such contests come Best in Show. Seven times in 1949 the best was Grand Champion Dixi-Land's Felice of Nor-Mont, and the lady rolled up points. During the year, she accumulated a total of nearly four hundred and fifty points. Points are awarded by formula rather too intricate for these pages; ten points constitute a cat a champion; best champions in a show earn points toward grand championship, one point for every three champions in competition, and become grand champions on acquiring fifteen such points.

The Best Opposite Sex Cat of the year, White Historian II, went through similar experiences, no doubt being best in show often and perhaps sometimes "best opposite sex" if he came up against Felice. He was All Southern Cat in 1948 and 1949, so meeting, in the end—although possibly not in person—cats from other areas, from the West and the East, the Northwest and the Southwest. Hundreds of other cats lived many weeks of the fall and winter in cages, and traveled many miles, and ribbons festooned the cages of most of them, although none—during that year—won so many as did Felice and White Historian II—who must have a "call name," since it is improbable that his owner summons him to dinner by saying "Come here, Dixi-Land's White Historian II." Perhaps sometimes he is called "Histy," in the privacy of the cattery—if there is privacy in his cattery.

In at least six of the shows in which she appeared, Felice's ribbons bore the letters "C.F.A." in addition to the words designating what she had won. These were the shows sponsored in Chicago by the North Shore Cat Club, by the Milwaukee Cat Club, Inc., by the Cleveland Persian Society, the Miami Florida Cat Fanciers, by the Buffalo Cat Club and, in Denver, by the Colorado Cat Fanciers, all of which are members of the Cat Fanciers' Association, Inc. She won also in a show sponsored by the St. Petersburg Cat Club, which is a member of the American Cat Association. That she competed also in shows sponsored by the Cat Fanciers' Federation and the United Cat Federation, Inc., does not appear from the article in *Cats Magazine* to which we are indebted for the news of Felice's triumphs.

Many people live long with cats, and watch them with pleasure and grow fond of them without encountering this other world of cat people—this world of The Fancy, usually so capitalized. Most cats have never heard of it and many would be provoked to learn that Felice, lovely as she is, is better cat than they. Martini would be furious, not believe a word of it for a moment, and we have not told her. She will never know how this other half—this other fraction—of cats live. She has never, except unknowingly when she visited the cattery of a New York psychologist who breeds cats in her spare time, met a member of The Fancy.

In general, the term is applied not simply to those who fancy cats but to those who breed and show them. One may, to be sure, belong to a cat club on an amateur basis; the American Cat Association, in an advertisement, invites the formation of member clubs by those who are "lovers of cats, whether as owners of pets or breeders and exhibitors" and perhaps membership in such a club constitutes a person a true member of the American Cat Fancy. But the term seems commonly less wide in usage; it does not seem to us, addicts that we are, that we are in any proper sense Fanciers, although, as the owners of Martini, we were, for a time, technically breeders, since the "breeder" is the owner of the dam. At this world, we look, as it were, between the pickets of a fence, and much that we see is strange and fascinating.

We detect, for example, a considerable degree of jealousy existing among the various associations and this results in something which Mr. Charles A. Kenny, editor of *Cats,* is wont to refer to gloomily as "politics." (He is even more gloomy in noting that members of The Fancy do not advertise enough in cat magazines, and never have.) "Do you know," a recent editorial article in *Cats* demands sternly, "that one cat club has placed a ban on its members from showing their cats at exhibitions sanctioned by another registry association under penalty of being expelled from the club? Is this the American way? Is this the American Cat Fancy?"

Apparently the answer to the magazine's questions is "Yes." At any rate, there appear at the present time to be four associations with which one can register a cat and whose rules govern the shows held throughout the country. In the fall of 1949 and the winter and early spring of 1950, forty cat shows were scheduled, and each of these was conducted under the regulations laid down either by the Cat Fanciers' Association, Inc., the American Cat Association, the Cat Fanciers' Federation, or the United Cat Federation, Inc. Of these, the American Cat Association advertises itself as the first to be incorporated and the CFA as the largest. Fifty-eight clubs were affiliated with the CFA at the beginning of 1950 and Mrs. James S. Carpenter, the recorder, writes us with natural pride that her organization, although "not the oldest of the registering bodies, is larger than all the rest combined, and growing so rapidly that I sometimes think cats are breeding like pigs, not felines. Over 40,000 cats are registered with us; their owners write from Alaska and Hawaii, from Peru and Nassau. Also from Podunk and New York." Of the forty shows in 1949-1950, the CFA sponsored twenty-four.

The ACA, whose advertisement in *Cats* lists thirty-four member clubs, sponsored eight of the shows during that period; the CFF, which names seventeen clubs in a similar advertisement—Mr. Kenny is perhaps unduly morose about the amount of advertising in his magazine, but most publishers are—sponsored six of the shows and the UCF, which does not list its member clubs, provided the rules and regulations for two. "Personally," Mr. Kenny writes, "*Cats* is of the strongest opinion that the Cat Fancy should be composed of one registry association, national in scope with officers represented from every section of North America and with terms of office not exceeding three years. Until such action is taken, the American Cat Fancy will continue in its confused state."

Mr. Kenny prints the words "one registry association" in capital letters to emphasize his feeling, and his irritation with the wrong-headedness of people is an emotion easy to share. Not even fondness for cats will, it appears, bring people into unity; even The Fancy, precisely as if it were the population of the world, is split into rival groups and, resultingly, in a confused state. Cats would know better, obviously. Cats' feuds are individual, not those of association, and they seldom show indications of confusion. If people who live with cats, and to some degree by them, cannot learn rationality from them, there may be little hope for non-feline-minded humanity.

Professional members of The Fancy do, to varying degrees, live by cats. The value of a cat, and of the cat's bloodlines, is enhanced by winning ribbons, by championships, by grand championships. As with other animals so bred for certain qualities, the registry associations provide reference material and to some degree what might be termed title guarantee. One may, for example, by consulting the ACA Stud Book, Volume 42 (21000-21099) discover that Morrison's Ling Tang, Seal Point Siamese Male, Reg. No. 21004, has blue eyes, was born September 10, 1948; that his breeder was Mrs. Richard Johnston of Minneapolis and his owner is Mrs. B. E. Morrison of the same city; that his sire was Archie Blue Boy, 20362, and his dam Olson's Tinker, 19015. One may also learn that Pearl Harbor Radiant Durdana, 21072, born May 20, 1948, is the son of Champion Pearl Harbor Duke O'Courageous and Pearl Harbor Bonny Maid. Radiant Durdana is a white long-hair and has blue eyes.

Since Duke O'Courageous was (one hopes is) a champion, and so qualified and certified by the American Cat Association, his son, other things being equal, is of greater monetary value than the next cat one may meet on the sidewalk, since he is more likely to win championships in his turn. As among race horses, and dogs, certain bloodlines commonly produce animals of superior speed or other attribute—of more absurdly undershot jaw or narrower head among dogs, of silkier hair and cobbier bodies among Persian cats—and these things are of value to the owners of the animals. Progeny of such lines sell for more money; stud fees can be set higher. The cattery may even pay its running costs.

Our Martini was bred to a cat of famous Siamese bloodline, and his mother and father, his four grandparents, his eight great-grandparents and his sixteen great-great-grandparents were CFA registered cats. His pedigree, as well as his seed, came back to us with Martini; there was even a notation at the bottom of his registration form which read, "Bred to Mrs. Lockridge's seal point" and gave a date. This was Martini's only brush with the real aristocracy of the cat world and it cost us twenty-five dollars. Had we been breeders, had she had a similar registered pedigree, had her children been of show standard, this attested record would have been of value. We could have proved good bloodlines on either side, had Martini's equalled her husband's, who was a champion or perhaps a grand champion. We have lost the record, now.

Martini, had we sought to establish a line of cats, could, however, have been registered without a pedigree in the "foundation record" of one or more of the registering associations. It would have been enough if one or the other of us had signed, before a notary, an affidavit reading in effect: "I hereby state that to the best of my knowledge and belief the cat named Martini is pure-bred Siamese," as to the best of our knowledge and belief she is. We would have been required to give one or two alternate names, in case there is already a registered Martini. The fee would have been one dollar.

And if we had chosen, we could have shown her—and anyone can show any cat he owns, even though adopted from the street, if the cat fits into any of the recognized color and breed groups—without having registered her with any of the associations. The associations are tolerant. "Any cat of sound health is eligible for exhibition at shows held under the rules of this Federation, and may compete and be entitled to win in any class," reads Section 1 of the article on eligibility of the CFF. Some cats, including domestic short-hairs, entered under this section, possessing not a known ancestor to their names, have won prizes. (It may be this relaxed attitude on the part of The Fancy which led a writer in the Boston *Sunday Globe* recently to assure his readers, some of whom must have been surprised, that for cats "there is no registration similar to that used by most kennel clubs." Owners of silvers, shaded silvers and silver tabbies must have been further surprised to read that cats with green eyes seldom win in shows, since silvers do not win without them.) All one needs to participate in a cat show is a cat and twenty-five cents to give the show manager.

But in modern cat shows, most of the prizes are carried off by such cats as Dixi-Land's Felice of Nor-Mont—Dixi-Land being the cattery of her origin and Nor-Mont that of her present residence. Most champions and grand champions have registered ancestors for several generations; among Siamese some lines are reputed to go back to the land of origin. Siamese, and to a lesser extent Persians, are likely to be to some degree inbred, much as if they were members of a royal family. The purity of the breed is so maintained; so are certain undesirable recessive characteristics, like crosseyes, which Siamese breeders have sternly tried to eliminate for some years. Martini's eyes glare their defiance, glow their love, straight ahead and so, no doubt, did her mate's. It is very difficult to tell whether either of her kittens is looking at one, or whether she sees one if she is. Possibly Martini and the male she met so briefly were, in spite of his majesty and her un-recorded past, distant cousins, both bearing the gene which results in the defect of crosseyes. And she, since she "threw" a blue point, must have also had blue point genes, that coloration being a recessive characteristic, so that it would not have been enough for the male to be, as he was, a thorough-going blue point.

The Fancy has flourished in the United States for a little over fifty years and, in its special form, seems largely an importation from England, where cats had been bred for points for a considerable period and have had pound and shilling value—as pets and show animals, rather than as mousers—for many cat generations. The first formal cat show in this country was held in Madison Square Garden in 1895. But there had been informal shows, relaxed and jolly affairs one imagines, long before that. Shows of a kind were held in New England, and chiefly in Maine, in the 1860's and the cats—in the opinion of Mr. Kenny, who is, with difficulty, compiling a history of the American Cat Fancy—were mostly Maine cats, who thus become the first feline aristocrats of the United States. They reigned briefly; by the turn of the century they were no longer recognized exhibition cats, and have never been since.

Cats from England, Persians for the most part, took over, dragging their pedigrees behind them; showing cats became a serious business; breeders sat tense with anxiety while judges considered. Now relaxation in feline competition can be found only where a few cats are gathered together, most often in the arms of children, at pet shows such as the Greenwich Village Humane Society now and then promotes. It must have been jollier, for cats and people both, in 1891 when, Mr. Kenny reports, prizes at a Boston cat show were given in the following categories: Largest cat, smallest cat, handsomest cat, homeliest cat, finest angora cat, finest coon cat, largest family of kittens, cat with the largest family, blackest cat, whitest cat, oldest cat, best trick cat and most curious freak cat. (The headline of the article which, in *Cats,* follows the installment of Mr. Kenny's history from which these facts are taken reads: "English Judges Will Officiate at New York Show.")

But by 1901, The Fancy had so far progressed as to have a magazine of its own, *The Cat Journal,* and since then there have always been magazines devoted to cats and intended for The Fancy. In 1908, there were five such magazines in competition, none of them doing very well. The ranks have thinned perceptibly since, although the cat business moderately booms. Only last year, *Our Cats* merged with *Cats Magazine;* there had been two, then there was one. In the early days, cat magazines were devoted to discussions of Persians almost exclusively; it was not until 1909 that the first Siamese cat club was founded, and at that time the CFA had only two

Siamese listed in its stud book. All of the early Siamese were English imports, or descended from them; some nowadays have ancestors who came through France, but such are a little suspect, since French breeders are thought to be somewhat casual. A member of The Fancy is not casual about cats.

Now and then, to be sure, members of cat clubs go on picnics and, presumably, leave their cats at home. This we discover through the peephole Mr. Kenny's magazine provides into this other, this special, world of the cat. One presumes that they talk about cats at picnics and that they also, like golfers home from the green, describe their triumphs and their narrow misses. Show judges come in for considerable consideration at such picnics, one suspects; the play by play of recent benchings must be gone over, not lightly, not perhaps without acrimony. But sometimes, one hopes, they talk about cats as cats, since surely no one would embark on the risky business of breeding who was not a lover of cats. There are, surely, easier ways of making a living, and less chancy ones. It is improbable that anyone makes a fortune out of cats.

Twenty-five dollars, or more or less, may be picked up now and then as a stud fee. Kittens may be sold and there prices vary widely. *Cats Magazine* will not permit the specific announcement in an advertisement of any stud fee less than ten dollars, or any kitten going at less than fifteen. Most of the pedigreed kittens offered begin at twenty-five dollars; many catteries do not sell for so little; for a really good prospective show kitten the price may be several times as much. One can pay hundreds of dollars for a cat; it may be possible to spend thousands. To the average person who likes cats and wants them around, and knows that they are very likely to come around in any case, this means of acquiring a cat may seem a little ridiculous.

Yet, this side monumental extravagance, the purchase of a kitten from a good cattery is quite probably the wisest way to acquire a cat, unless one is particularly addicted to the domestic short-hair, who is a fine cat but no finer than another. The pedigree may not matter one way or another; one may want, as most people do want, a cat to have around the house, not a cat to put in a cage. But from a good cattery, one is almost certain to get a healthy cat and a cat of healthy parentage. Catteries do not keep, nor do the good ones sell to individuals, cats which are not pretty good cats; it has been charged that some of them sell their less vigorous cats to pet shops. A cattery kitten may not know much about home life, may be more accustomed to other cats than to people. That is a deficiency in training easily corrected.

What is more important is that such a kitten will be physically sound, will have been kept with his mother for a sufficient length of time, will be free from ailment when purchased and will, almost certainly, have been inoculated against enteritis. If he is a Persian, he will—again almost certainly—have fur of one of the approved colors, and cats with such coats are, generally speaking, the best looking cats. If he is a Siamese, he will have, although perhaps this side grand-championship, the shape of body and the markings which make the breed so distinctive and so delightful. We would not trade Martini for anybody's grand champion, but she would be a better looking cat if she had a longer, more slender body and there is no particular reason to suppose that she would not be the same cat otherwise. With a cat's personality, one of course takes a chance, wherever the cat comes from.

From a cattery one can also order in advance, which may some-times be an advantage. One cattery which advertises in *Cats* was, when the advertisement was printed, "taking orders for spring kittens" and another had excellent type seal points "ready in April." One would not, of course, like merely to send an order for "one spring kitten, seal point," and take one's chances; any cat person would prefer to shop for his cats, choosing one to suit his taste. A good deal about a cat's future propensities can be told from his behavior in a litter; usually one cat is a leader, another follows close, somebody brings up the rear. The leader may turn out to be a holy terror; we are convinced that Martini bossed not only her brothers and sisters in infancy, but probably their mother as well. The slowest cat may be less bright than the others, or less well. Some cat people advise taking the one behind the leader, and this may be safest. We, however, would pick the boss any time, looking to a relationship which might be arduous, but could never be dull.

Short of theft, we have now come into the ownership of cats in most of the accepted ways—by adoption from the sidewalk, by gift, by purchase, by breeding. Since we have liked all our cats, it follows that we have found all these methods satisfactory enough, although growing your own kittens is certainly the most arduous. Our next cat will, however, be a purchased cat because—but what is that sound? Not The Waif back again, surely? When she went this morning, after Gin hissed at her so angrily, it looked as if she were gone for good. One can never tell about cats; it is absurd to predict concerning them.

Only a few days ago, not many thousand words ago, The Waif was anonymous, was merely "kitty, here kitty." She was a cat who came mewing at a terrace door on a bad night and was let in and solaced, was enquired about, was established—we let ourselves believe—as a cat who lived across the road. A pretty little thing, in her heavy-ish, non-Siamese fashion; white-chested, short-bodied, tabby-marked and green-eyed; a cat into whom almost all color combinations had entered, including ticked-tabby; a cat to be used in an anecdote.

But she turned out not to live across the road, where among felines only a widely traveled tomcat lives. Across the road they had only just got rid, by giving, of the last but the tom of the summer's eight cats. They would take our small mewing visitor, of course, if we were determined to turn her out into the winter. Anyone would. But——

It was unquestionably our door she had picked, and we who had let her in. It was possible the Siamese and she might learn to get along. We could feed her separately for a time; lock her in a guest room overnight, and hope she was used to torn-up paper in a toilet pan. We could feed her and watch her ravenous eating; lift her—while Martini swore and Gin hissed and Sherry cried in disapproval—and discover how frail she was under her rather shaggy coat. (Discover also, as well as lay fingers could, that she did not seem particularly pregnant.) And she would sit on, could hardly be pried from, the lap of the gentle old man who had come to live with us and who was hurt, and un-understanding, that none of the shy blue-eyed ones would let him more than touch her.

Two nights, now, she has spent in the guest room, and she is housebroken. She has lived with people all her short life, except for perhaps two weeks. The two weeks have made her shy, but the shyness will not last. She knows as well as any cat the sound of an opening refrigerator door and last night she tried to join the others at their dinner. There was not quite a cat fight, but she had to be withdrawn, and then for a long time the Siamese would not eat, but would only crouch outside the guest-room door. She is not a very lively cat, certainly; she is pretty, but not beautiful. If we keep her, and it is not too late, we will need to have her spayed and inoculated. Martini is very nervous because she has been here, and is now crying to return; last night Martini hissed at one of us, briefly, and when Gin came on her innocently from behind, Gin was snarled at and cuffed before Martini got control of her nerves. . . . If the part-tabby, part-everything, decides to stay, we will have to think of a better name for her than The Waif. . . . A plague on the so-and-sos who deserted her on the road we live on, or who desert cats on any road.

But the next cat after this one, if we are not to be let off this one—and do we now really want to be?—will surely be a purchased cat. There are Siamese catteries within motoring distance, so we will have no need to take pot luck. We can pick from two- or three-month-olds; it may, now that we live in the country and our female cats are spayed, be interesting to try a male.

But we will not breed cats, even as amateurs, and we will never show them. Of those things we are almost certain. The world of The Fancy is interesting and strange, but it is not ours. We, who belong to few clubs and visit those infrequently, do not plan to join a cat club. They may be fun, but they seem somehow a little anomalous. Cats never join clubs, and cat lovers, plain as opposed to Fancy, are not often of the strongly gregarious type.

But perhaps even that statement is too sweeping. It is almost as risky to generalize about cat people as it is about cats themselves;

there is almost as much variety among them as among the purring (or snarling) objects of their affection, although people do not come in so many pretty colors. Warriors seldom like cats, one postulates—and remembers Mahomet, who was warrior as well as prophet, and reputedly a great lover of a cat. Writers often are fond of cats, although a few have hated them; it is not even necessarily true that good writers are aelurophiles and bad ones not, since there are too many obvious exceptions on all sides. (Shakespeare appears to have had little use for cats.) Many actors are fond of cats and, since actors are for the most part a physically attractive crew, can take the risk of being photographed with cats, a comparison risk most humans should avoid. Many more women than men are cat addicts, but the best known, and most articulate, from Mahomet to Carl Van Vechten, have been males.

Cats fit into many and varied lives, being in themselves so varied as animals and so adaptable. They are content enough in a city apartment, and may be left there through a working day and be none the worse, and leave the apartment none the worse. A furnished room will house a human and a cat, if nothing better offers and the landlady is lenient; a lonely person of either sex, living so, will be less lonely with a cat on lap. Dogs, except very old dogs, demand considerable vitality in their humans; they should be played with heartily, and must be walked. But it is not hard to satisfy a cat, if he likes you, if he is a generous-hearted cat. He can doze by the fire with you and only dream of mice—you can tell his dreams by the twitching of his muscles; sometimes he is almost running in his sleeping hunt. He is cozy by the fire, as few creatures are. There is a restlessness in him which would have more, but if restlessness has, with years, ebbed slowly in his human, he will make do with what remains. If need be, a cat will share a cloister.

But he is big enough, too, for all outdoors; the biggest house and the widest fields are not too big for a cat, once he is accustomed to them. He will search the outdoors by himself, finding in it all manner of fascinating things, and also great dangers; he may not live so long as in a room, but he will live more excitingly, come home with brighter eyes and sleeker coat—albeit full of burrs—to tell of his conquests. He may, and many cats do, take walks with his human, sometimes trotting quietly enough behind; more often dashing furiously ahead to investigate a thicket, and lingering afterward on the scent of a mouse until one grows certain he is lost and stops to call him.

Or, if it comes to that, he may be content enough with a barn, given food and a human leg to rub against when the notion takes him. Two or three cats of our acquaintance work in a barn outside Ridgefield, taking care of things while the truck farmer who owns the barn is busy in his greenhouse and his wife is helping us. They are happy enough cats, if business-like, and seem not to notice the fat dog who lives there too, and gets in the house more often than they do. They are good cats, we are told; since they came, no rats, no mice, barn *or* house. (But enough was enough; the gardener's wife did not want to take on The Waif.)

One may like a cat for any reason and find justification in the cat's behavior. If you need a mousetrap, no activity pleases a cat more than catching mice; if an ornament is required, almost any cat supplies it and if cats go badly with upholstery, they more than compensate as decorations; if you are alone and wish around you something which is alive, warm to the touch, confiding to your hand, a cat likes nothing better than to purr for you. If you would be entertained, almost any cat will provide engaging activities with little encouragement, or none; one has only to play with a cat or give him playthings to turn the relaxed dozer by the fire into a gymnast, turning cartwheels. For any of these rewards—mouselessness, decoration, companionship and entertainment—people may keep cats, and do. Anyone who has a cat around can count on them.

And now and then one may find, or almost find, more in a cat than the best of these simple things. For all our ability to destroy one another, our aptitude in carnage, we are regimented animals; tamely and in herds we are guided, we guide ourselves, to destruction. Looking at a cat, being looked at by a cat, one may glimpse dimly that other, unherded, way of living which cats more than any other animal adhere to and exemplify.

Martini sits and looks at one of us, and although she is with us, although she surely loves us, Martini sits alone; although she and her daughters may sleep in a pile on chilly nights, they sleep alone, as they walk alone and hunt alone and know alone the horrid fear of death which makes them spring for height when the dog is tough and then lie trembling along a branch. This wild aloneness is not the simple thing romantics make it, nor the obvious one. A cat is as "tame" as a dog, and remarkably less noisy about it; he is as far from the jungle as humans are, returning to it, as humans do, to kill its residents.

But yet we detect in him a creature essentially, and perhaps significantly, different from ourselves; there is a strangeness there and it may be because of it that so many people cannot be quite matter-of-fact about the cat, as all but their breeders are about dogs, however much they may love them. The cat is the individualist, the aberrant; he is the creature who has never run in packs nor fought in herds nor thought in congregations. He has the dignity of the self-contained and the confidence of the self-sufficient. If, looking at a cat, one knows for the instant some envious admiration of the unhumanly free, this is no more than momentary nostalgia, and nostalgia for a dream. It should not be blamed upon the cat.

BIBLIOGRAPHY

Aberconway, Christabel: *A Dictionary of Cat Lovers;* Michael Joseph, London, 1949.

Adams, Donald Keith: *Experimental Studies of Adaptive Behavior in Cats* (Comparative Psychology Monographs); Johns Hopkins Press, Baltimore, 1929.

Animal Protection, Magazine of the American Society for the Prevention of Cruelty to Animals; Vol. 3, No. 1, Spring, 1949.

Baikie, James: *A History of Egypt;* The Macmillan Company, New York, 1929.

Barton, Frank Townsend: *The Cat: Its Points and Management in Health and Disease;* Everett & Co., London, 1908.

Bryant, Doris: *Care and Handling of Cats;* Ives Washburn, New York, 1929.

Buchanan, Lt. Col. A., M. D.: "Cats as Plague Preventers," *British Medical Journal,* May 30, 1908; October 24, 1908.

Burroughs, John: "Do Animals Think?", *Harper's Monthly Magazine,* February, 1905.

Champfleury (pseudonym of Jules Fleury-Husson): *The Cat, Past and Present;* translated by Mrs. Cashel Hoey; George Bell & Sons, London, 1885.

Colbert, Edwin H.: "Triumph of the Mammals," Am. Museum of Nat. Hist., 1942; "Descent of the Cat," *Natural History,* 1940; "The Native Cats of North America," School Nature League *Bulletin,* Series 13, No. 5, January, 1943; "The Origin of the Dog," Am. Museum of Nat. Hist., 1946; "The Tiger in the Parlor," *Frontiers,* 1939.

Conway, William Martin: *Dawn of Art in the Ancient World;* London, 1891.

Crawford, Nelson Antrim: "Cats," *American Mercury,* July, 1933.

Darwin, Charles: *On the Origin of Species;* John Murray, London.

Day, Clarence: *This Simian World;* Alfred A. Knopf, 1936.

Devoe, Alan: "Our Enemy, the Cat," *American Mercury*, December, 1937.

Eliot, T. S.: *Old Possum's Book of Practical Cats;* Harcourt, Brace & Co., 1939.

Elliot, Daniel Giraud: *A Monograph of the Felidae,* 1883.

Errington, Paul L.: "Notes on the Food Habits of Sou. Wisc. House Cats," *Journal of Mammology,* February 14, 1936.

Fairchild, Dr. L. H. and Helen F.: *Cats and All About Them;* Judd Pub. Co., New York, 1942.

"Food of Feral House Cats in Oklahoma," *Journal of Mammology,* May, 1941.

Forbush, Edward Howe: Economic Biology Bulletin 1-2, 1915; Massachusetts Agricultural Board.

Frazer, Sir James George: *The Golden Bough, A Study in Magic and Religion;* The Macmillan Company, New York, 1927.

Gates, Dr. Georgina Ida Stickland: *The Modern Cat;* The Macmillan Company, New York, 1928.

Gay, Margaret Cooper: *How to Live with a Cat;* Simon and Schuster, New York, 1947.

Gudger, E. W.: "Cats as Fishermen," *Natural History.*

Hall, G. Stanley, and Browne, C. E.: "The Cat and the Child," *Pedagogical Seminary,* March, 1904-1905.

Herrick, Frances H.: "Homing Powers of the Cat," *Scientific Monthly.*

Hickey, John Hosford, and Beach, Priscilla: *Know Your Cat;* Harper & Bros., New York, 1946.

Hobhouse, L. T.: *Mind in Evolution;* The Macmillan Company, New York, 1901.

Hopkins, Ralph C.: "Status of the Domestic Cat in Wisconsin," *Wisconsin Conservation Bulletin,* May, 1940.

Howey, M. Oldfield: *The Cat in the Mysteries of Religion and Magic;* Rider & Co., London, 1931.

Hudson, W. H.: "Do Cats Think?", *Cornhill Magazine,* 1926.

Huidekoper, Rush Shippen: *The Cat;* D. Appleton and Co., New York, 1895.

Ingersoll, Ernest: *The Life of Animals: The Mammals;* The Macmillan Company, New York, 1906.
———: "The Domestic Cat," *Encyclopedia Americana.*

Jennings, John: *Domestic and Fancy Cats;* V. Upcott Still, London, 1883.
Joseph, Michael: *Charles, The Story of a Friendship;* Michael Joseph, Ltd., London, 1943.
———: "The Intelligence of Cats," *The Spectator,* 1936.

Kaye-Smith, Sheila: *Kitchen Fugue;* Harper & Bros., New York, 1945.

Lane, C. H.: *Rabbits, Cats and Cavies;* I. M. Dent & Co., London, 1903.
Langton, N. and B.: *The Cat in Ancient Egypt;* Cambridge University Press, 1940.

Mellen, Ida M.: *The Science and Mystery of the Cat;* Scribners' Sons, New York, 1946.
Mills, Wesley: *The Nature and Development of Animal Intelligence;* The Macmillan Company, New York, 1898.
Mivart, St. George: *The Cat, An Introduction to the Study of Back-boned Animals, especially Mammals;* John Murray, London, 1881.
"Minor Menace," *The New Yorker* (Talk of the Town), August 27, 1949.

Neill, W. N.: "Witch Cats in Scotland," *Occult Review,* 1924.
New York Herald Tribune, March 10, 1949.
New York Times, April 13, 1949; August 30, 1949.

Pitt, Frances: *Animal Mind;* Allen & Unwin, London, 1927.

Repplier, Agnes: *The Cat: Being a Record of the Endearments and Invectives Lavished upon an Animal Much Loved and Much Abhorred;* Sturgis & Walton, New York, 1912.
Romanes, George J.: *Animal Intelligence;* London, 1883.

Shaler, Nathaniel Southgate: *Domesticated Animals,* Scribners' Sons, New York, 1895.

Shuey, Audrey M.: *The Limits of Learning Ability in Kittens,* (Genetic Psychology Monograph), Clark University Press, Worcester (Mass.), 1931.

Simpson, George Gaylord: *The Principles of Classification and a Classification of Mammals;* Am. Museum of Nat. Hist., New York, 1945.

Stables, Gordon: *The Domestic Cat;* London, 1876.

Thorndike, Edward Lee: *Animal Intelligence;* The Macmillan Company, New York, 1911.

Van Vechten, Carl: *The Tiger in the House;* Alfred A. Knopf, New York, 1920.

Warner, Charles Dudley: "Calvin, A Study in Character," from *My Summer in a Garden;* Houghton, Mifflin, Boston, 1898.

INDEX

KODANSHA GLOBE

International in scope, this series offers distinguished books that explore the lives, customs, and mindsets of peoples and cultures around the world.

ON FAMILIAR TERMS
To Japan and Back,
  A Lifetime Across
  Cultures
Donald Keene
1-56836-129-7

KNOTTED TONGUES
Stuttering in History
  and the Quest for a
  Cure
Benson Bobrick
1-56836-121-1

LIVING IN, LIVING OUT
African American
  Domestics and the
  Great Migration
Elizabeth Clark-Lewis
1-56836-124-6

ECHOES OF DISTANT
  THUNDER
Life in the United
  States, 1914–1918
Edward Robb Ellis
New Preface by the Author
1-56836-149-1

GRINGA LATINA
A Woman of Two Worlds
Gabriella De Ferrari
1-56836-145-9

LOOKING FOR THE LOST
Journeys Through a
  Vanishing Japan
Alan Booth
1-56836-148-3

IN GOOD HANDS
The Keeping of a
  Family Farm
Charles Fish
1-56836-147-5

YANOAMA
The Narrative of a
  Young Girl
  Kidnapped by
  Amazonian Indians
Ettore Biocca
Translated by Dennis
  Rhodes
New Introduction by
  Jacques Lizot
1-56836-108-4

JOURNEY TO KHIVA
A Writer's Search for
  Central Asia
Philip Glazebrook
1-56836-074-6

A BORROWED PLACE
The History of Hong
  Kong
Frank Welsh
1-56836-134-3

SINGER AND THE SEWING
  MACHINE
A Capitalist Romance
Ruth Brandon
1-56836-146-7

MY LIFE AS AN EXPLORER
The Great Adventurer's
  Classic Memoir
Sven Hedin
Translated by Alfild
  Huebsch
New Introduction by
  Peter Hopkirk
Illustrated by the Author
1-56836-142-4

To order, contact your local bookseller or call 1-800-788-6262 (mention code G1). For a complete listing of titles, please contact the Kodansha Editorial Department at Kodansha America, Inc., 114 Fifth Avenue, New York, NY 10011.